KU-300-961

WITHDRAWN

EDINBURGH NAPIER UNIVERSITY LIBRARY

*Brand Risk*

*To Rosalind*

# *Brand Risk*

Adding Risk Literacy to Brand Management

DAVID ABRAHAMS

GOWER

GRL 658.827 ABR
7dy

© David Abrahams 2008

All rights reserved. No part of this publication may be reproduced, stored in a retrieval system or transmitted in any form or by any means, electronic, mechanical, photocopying, recording or otherwise without the prior permission of the publisher.

Published by
Gower Publishing Limited
Gower House
Croft Road
Aldershot
Hampshire
GU11 3HR
England

Gower Publishing Company
Suite 420
101 Cherry Street
Burlington
VT 05401-4405
USA

David Abrahams has asserted his moral right under the Copyright, Designs and Patents Act, 1988, to be identified as the author of this work.

**British Library Cataloguing in Publication Data**
Abrahams, David
 Brand risk : adding risk literacy to brand management
 1. Brand name products - Management 2. Risk assessment
 I. Title
 658.8'27

 ISBN-13: 9780566087240

**Library of Congress Cataloging-in-Publication Data**
Abrahams, David, 1953–
 Brand risk : adding risk literacy to brand management / by David Abrahams.
     p. cm.
 Includes bibliographical references and index.
 ISBN 978-0-566-08724-0
 1. Branding (Marketing) 2. Marketing--Risk management. I. Title.

 HF5415.1255.A27 2008
 658.8'27--dc22

                                                              2007041403

BRANDZ™ is a trademark of Millward Brown.
Crystal Ball® is a registered trademark of Oracle Corporation.
Microsoft® and Excel® are registered trademarks of Microsoft Corporation.
Mindjet® and MindManager® are registered trademarks of Mindjet LLC.
OptionFinder® is a registered trademark of Option Technologies Interactive LLC.
Palisade® and PrecisionTree® are registered trademarks of Palisade Corporation.
RISK™ is a trademark of Parker Brothers, Division of Tonka Corporation and is used by Palisade Corporation under licence.
reputation@risk® is a registered trademark of Marsh Ltd.
Six Thinking Hats® is a registered trademark.
TreeAge Pro™ is a trademark of TreeAge Software, Inc.

Printed and bound in Great Britain by TJ International Ltd, Padstow, Cornwall.

# Contents

# List of Figures

# Acknowledgements

It would not have been possible to produce this book without advice, assistance and inspiration from many people, to whom I would like to express my gratitude: David Bateman, Robert Chase, Man Cheung, Jonathan Day, Anita Edmonds, Phil Elwell, Craig Ferri, Mary-Ellen Field, Maura Finigan, David Gamble, Nikhil Gharekhan, Allan Gifford, Stephen Gilbert, Seamus Gillen, Duncan Green, David Haigh, Graham Hales, Ken Hall, Ove Haxthausen, Randy Heffernan, Tim Hoad, Matthew Hogg, Garry Honey, Tim Hopkirk, John Hurrell, Felicity Jones, Peggy Kelley, Nicola Males, Giulia Ajmone Marsan, Eddie McLaughlin, Ruth McNeil, Dan Mitzner, Yvonne Morris, Scott Nicholl, Consuelo Remmert, Karina Robinson, Alan Rundle, Joel Sartori, Robert Shaw, Dawn Southgate, Jeff Stripp, Hilary Sutcliffe, Hobart Swan, Frances Tangye, Louise Tingström, Brian Toft, Melinda Venable, Richard Waterer, David Wethey, Robin Wilkinson, Stewart Wilson and John Woodcock.

My particular thanks to Frances Tangye for signposting developments in the ever-evolving field of corporate governance and statutory reporting discussed in Chapter 1. Nikhil Gharekhan, Stephen Gilbert, and Ove Haxthausen kindly gave of their time to review the brand valuation section in Chapter 2. Brian Toft was similarly generous in reviewing the material on organizational learning in Chapter 3, which draws substantially on his own work in this field of behavioural science. My thanks go equally to Eddie McLaughlin for his review of substantial parts of Chapter 4 and Chapter 6. Their advice has been invaluable; any shortcomings that remain are mine. Robin Wilkinson first revealed to me the powerful features and benefits of dependency modelling. She has invested much of her time and expertise in our collaboration, transforming an earlier marketing tool of mine into a respectable model of dependencies that fully reflects the qualities of her approach. It is superficially represented in Chapter 6 of this book.

I am most grateful to Marsh Ltd for allowing me to draw freely on copyright material written by me under their auspices: 'Social and Ethical Risk' (The Marsh Topic Letter – Number V, 2001) and 'Brand Risk' (The Marsh Topic Letter – Number IX, 2002). Pearson Education Ltd gave permission to reproduce Exhibit 4.11 'The Cultural Web' from page 202 of Johnson, Scholes and Whittington (2006), *Exploring Corporate Strategy: 7th edition*. Elsevier B.V. gave permission to reproduce an extract from Table 2 'EVI as a percentage of the maximum loss $L$, (EVI/$L$) x 100' from page 386 of Lacava, G. and Tull, D. (1982), 'Determining the Expected Value of Information for New Product Introduction', *Omega – The International Journal of Management Science*, Volume 10 (Number 4), pp. 383–389.

TreeAge Software, Inc. kindly gave permission to reproduce output from their decision analysis tool TreeAge Pro™. Thanks also to Palisade Corporation for their kind permission to reproduce copyright materials from their risk analysis software @RISK. Oracle Corporation granted their kind permission to reproduce copyright materials from their risk analysis software Crystal Ball®. I would particularly like to record my gratitude to Mindjet® Corporation for their generous agreement to my using original output from their mapping and visualization software MindManager® for many of the diagrams in the book.

Jonathan Norman, Fiona Martin and Gillian Steadman at Gower have been ever helpful and reassuring during the process of bringing one small volume into the world. Helen Parry lent her experience and professional eye to copy-editing the manuscript.

Above all, to my wife Rosalind, untold gratitude for her encouragement throughout the project and for her inexhaustible charity during the many unsocial hours of authorship.

David Abrahams

david.abrahams@brandmediation.com

# Introduction

This book is about a meeting of professional minds. Whilst the importance of brands and the relevance of risk have been widely acknowledged, it is debatable whether the marketing and risk management communities have yet perfected their collaboration. This may be a wasted opportunity. After all, risk-taking is what marketers do.

Nearly a decade ago, a short feature in the financial press described how an industrial company's actuaries, the masters of probability and statistics traditionally concerned with pension fund adequacy, were now offering their services to colleagues in the marketing departments who might want to model uncertain demand for the company's new products. Since that time, we have moved into another era of accelerated change and market opportunity, laced with risk and uncertainties. There is an unfinished global revolution in mass communications. There are new markets, new corporate accountabilities and new competitors. The pressure on marketers remains: to produce the same for less or more for the same.

Authoritative observers have remarked how often marketers appear ill-equipped to argue convincingly in support of their plans when the inevitable challenges come. This book proposes that risk literacy can help marketers to make better decisions and to make their professional case more effectively. There is no magic bullet, no prescription and no attempt to sterilize the marketing imagination. There is just the practical idea, based on my own experience as marketer, product developer and corporate adviser, that there is value in a familiarity with risk thinking and some of its methods for opportunity assessment and decision analysis. These recognized approaches are available to help marketers structure their evaluation of issues and opportunities, whether formally or informally. They will support them in their thinking and in their dialogue with those who invest in it. Business risk is best taken (and better tolerated) if it is done with a degree of self-awareness, some insights into what risk means and some assessment of the probabilities. In this sense, risk literacy is the third necessary competence for marketers, alongside their strategic insight and financial understanding.

Meanwhile, numerous management studies have described the contribution of brands and reputations to the prosperity and viability of business, in ways not limited to earning customer preference. There has been a corresponding diffusion of brand-related responsibility to other parts of the firm, so that marketing departments are no longer sole custodians of the brand. For their part, risk management professionals have not always found it easy to support this wider accountability for brand stewardship. Brands need to be understood as more than trademarks and 'reputations', if they are to be fully represented on the firm's risk management agenda.

This practical book is principally intended for marketing professionals and those in brand planning functions. It will also be of value to risk management professionals and other senior managers who would like to develop their understanding of brand function and brand risk. Much of the marketing literature is implicitly concerned with risk. However, the blend of approaches to brand risk thinking and decision-making you will find in this book is not usually presented as a whole: some qualitative, some quantitative, some intended to guide intuition, some designed to support more rigorous evaluation.

Chapter 1 ('The Case for Risk Literacy') is introductory, establishing the book's key themes with a brief history of risk reporting and risk management in the wider corporate context. It reviews the role of resolving uncertainty in creating organizational influence and suggests how this might have relevance to the marketing function. It also defines and advocates risk literacy in practical terms. If you are a seasoned risk manager, you may want to skip the first part of the chapter ('Corporate context'), but read the final two sections ('Marketing and risk' and 'Risk literacy').

Chapter 2 ('Defining Brand Risk') introduces an enhanced model for brand risk thinking, supported by a detailed rationale for each of its elements. There is discussion of a four-part framework and aide-mémoire for the management of brand exposures. The chapter ends with a review of brand valuation and its meaning for risk management.

Chapter 3 ('Learning to Take Risk') begins the progression towards classical risk literacy with an exploration of the psychology of risk-taking and related perceptual issues. This chapter aims to furnish the risk-literate mind with an appreciation of the alternative thinking styles in risk-taking and a greater self-awareness. It concludes with an important discussion of hindsight ('Learning from failure'), presenting a simple, authoritative technique for looking back and learning from experience.

Chapter 4 ('The Language of Risk') builds on the foundations of risk awareness developed in Chapter 3. It describes and demonstrates in outline each of the important concepts used in risk and probability estimations. Simply acquiring this means of expression extends the reach of risk thinking. It is also an important chapter to read before moving on to Chapters 5 and 6, which assume that you have done so or that you are already familiar with the concepts reviewed.

Chapter 5 ('Identifying and Managing Risk') equips the risk-literate marketer with the tools and techniques necessary to create a complete risk management plan. It describes four markedly different approaches to the identification of risk, which are nonetheless entirely complementary. They represent a progression from 'hunch' to due diligence, in terms directly relevant to marketers. With acknowledgement to their creators, I have deliberately strayed from the conventional path to present two powerful alternatives that simultaneously prompt risk identification and development of a recipe for success. There is also much talk of cause and effect in risk management. The chapter includes a general framework for the evaluation of cause and effect, together with brief sections on predicting stakeholder behaviour. The chapter concludes with a section describing the elements of a risk management plan and two techniques for assessing the value of risk management efforts.

Chapter 6 ('Modelling Risks') introduces the most powerful techniques relevant to risk thinking: decision trees, dependency modelling and stochastic modelling (or risk simulation). These are the techniques to consider – possibly with expert support – when intuition or a simple spreadsheet model are not enough. There is also a special use for decision trees in helping to decide the value of market research ('Expected value of information').

Chapter 7 ('Making Progress') is the concluding chapter. It takes stock of the body of knowledge presented in the book, suggesting ways in which the techniques described can be usefully combined for specific purposes. It also highlights some of the cultural issues in adopting risk thinking in an organizational context.

The book contains four single-page advisories ('Snakes and Ladders') on topical subjects: managing customer service complaints, pitfalls in market research, crisis management and the licensing of brands.

Finally, to assist the reader in navigating and recalling all of the material presented, the Appendix precedes the Bibliography. It provides a diagrammatic summary of each chapter, based on the headings and subheadings in the text.

Whatever your purpose, whatever your interest, I hope that this book will help you to chart an appropriate course.

# 1 *The Case for Risk Literacy*

Organizations of any kind face two fundamental challenges: problems of co-operation and problems of predictability.[1] The burden of management would not amount to much at all, if everything turned out the way we had predicted and if everyone involved in achieving our business plan, including dutiful customers, co-operated to perfection. In this sense, risk management lies at the heart of brand management.

In this first chapter we will:

- define risk literacy and suggest its value to marketers
- consider how corporate risk reporting creates an opportunity for the marketing function to make its case
- set the agenda for the chapters to come.

'Risk literacy' is not about reading (or writing) books on risk. Risk literacy is concerned with the adequacy of a manager's 'underpinning knowledge' of risk and uncertainty conceptually, familiarity with suitable risk assessment approaches and an ability to deal appropriately with the risk issues identified.[2] Brand risk literacy applies this underpinning knowledge to marketing problems and to other brand-related issues that are faced by marketers and non-marketers alike. It sits alongside strategic insight and financial understanding as the third required competence for people who manage brands.

## Corporate context

### RISK AND REGULATION

It was the corporate scandals of the 1980s that moved investors and regulators to promote risk management as a discipline and as a matter of explicit board accountability in the decade that followed. The existing risk management approaches were judged insufficiently transparent for institutional investors, who demanded the reassurance of a structured assessment of a company's risks in pursuit of its objectives. Investors and expert commentators not only required these new risk management processes to withstand administrative scrutiny, they also wanted to ensure that the new emphasis on risk management would positively affect the behaviour of both organizations and their individual employees. After all, many of the share shocks of the 1980s had arisen from fatally bad judgement by companies or fraudulent dealings by individual managers.

The United Kingdom Turnbull Report (1999) reviewed and consolidated the various codes of corporate governance that had preceded it, obliging listed companies to consider the effectiveness of their systems of internal control and risk management. Since sudden collapse of public confidence had been the cause of several outright corporate failures, the report recommended that the boards of listed companies should consider reputation as a significant risk in its own right.[3]

In 2002 the United States legislature also responded urgently to a number of corporate scandals, among them those that had led to the separate collapse of two leading US corporations, Enron and WorldCom.[4] The resulting Sarbanes-Oxley Act (SOx) of that year established new accountabilities for company officers, accountants and auditors. These supplemented their existing obligations to report on 'risk factors' in the annual Form 20-F submissions to the United States Securities and Exchange Commission (SEC), to comment broadly on the company's systems of internal control and risk management. Companies are now required to undertake risk assessments of critical financial processes and ensure that controls are effective.

By 2003, with ever more visible disparity of wealth between rich and poor in the global economy, the degree of commercial freedom accorded to the managements of large businesses was being questioned. In particular, the social and environmental impacts of large-scale operations were being attacked by activists and single-issue lobby groups. This wider activist concern meant that many firms could now expect to be called to public account for their conduct in pursuit of profit, even though they were abiding by the law. There had been damaging and disruptive media exposés involving famous-name companies in energy, pharmaceuticals, foods and consumer goods.[5] Leading investors came to realize that a higher quality of earnings might be achieved through 'sustainable' business practices. These would consider the longer-term consequences of corporate decisions, not just the opportunities for short-term gain. This conscious balance was especially important to the managers of pension funds and insurance capital, generally amongst the largest institutional investors. These institutions are obliged to take a prudent long-term view, usually investing their funds in the globally active companies with greatest exposure to the new demands and the new uncertainties.

In the United Kingdom, standards and expectations in corporate governance are principally set down through legislation in the Companies Act 2006 and through the requirements applicable to listed companies in the Combined Code. In response both to EU requirements and to pressure from non-governmental organizations favouring fuller disclosure of business impact on the environment and communities, there is now an obligation on all but the smallest of companies to include a narrative Business Review in their directors' reports to shareholders. This review supplements financial reporting with information intended to help the shareholders judge the extent to which the directors have performed their legally enshrined duty 'to promote the success of the organisation'.[6] Whilst United Kingdom legislation is evolving and is almost certain to place the greatest demands on the largest companies, directors' attention is evidently drawn to risk issues of direct concern to marketers:

- strategic and commercial exposures
- competitive benchmarking
- adequacy of key performance indicators and other vital information
- reputation risk
- quality of relationships with key stakeholders (such as communities, customers and suppliers)
- forward-looking risks and opportunities.[7]

## Comparing the UK and USA

Sarbanes-Oxley in the United States is prescriptive. It emphasizes transparency in financial dealings, commitment to a stated code of ethics by senior financial officers, protection for whistleblowers and the elimination of conflicts of interest that might affect the independence of auditors. In the United Kingdom the regime is not as prescriptive, but is based on the view that regulatory *principles* are more difficult to evade than absolute rules and tend to remain robust in changing circumstances. Called upon to 'comply or explain', the obligation on United Kingdom directors is to interpret the given principles, with the interests of shareholders and other stakeholders in mind. As to whistleblowers, the United Kingdom's Public Interest Disclosure Act 1998 provides certain protections for employees who disclose corporate malpractice in good faith.

## RISK MANAGEMENT

A number of functions have long been accustomed to the disciplines of formal risk assessments of one kind or another: finance, insurance procurement, legal, health and safety and others. Over the last decade, as a result of the new obligations placed on firms, risk management has evolved substantially both in theory and practice. An international study conducted by the Economist Intelligence Unit for Lloyd's of London (2005) reported that the amount of time company boards spent on risk management had risen fourfold in the preceding three years.[8]

Nowadays, ongoing responsibility for the establishment of appropriate risk disciplines throughout the firm often lies with a risk management professional: the risk manager, director of risk management or chief risk officer. In smaller companies and leaner corporate headquarters, the role is frequently taken by the company secretary. Internal auditors, whose function is mandatory under Sarbanes-Oxley in the USA, may also have an important role to play in awareness-raising and coaching. However, the internal auditors' role in assurance requires that they remain independent of the actual business risk evaluations. Ultimate accountability for effective risk management remains with the directors and officers of the company, commonly through a nominated subcommittee that convenes on a more regular basis than the main board.

A reasonable test for the effectiveness of risk management is whether it appears to support sustainable business growth by promoting a culture of acceptable risk and by improving the quality of decision-making:

> *For most organisations, the shift in mindset will need to be accompanied by a development in the range of risk management activities applied to decision-making ... This means bringing a range of quantitative and qualitative risk management techniques to bear upon the way in which strategy is set, from value-at-risk and scenario planning to extending and improving the qualitative process of risk identification and analysis to include opportunity analysis as well as the analysis of potential threats.*[9]

Behavioural studies in risk assessment appear to support the hypothesis that an organization engaging in proactive risk management can make worthwhile improvements in both human and financial performance. At its best, the process for risk assessment gives people an opportunity to re-examine the internal and external environment in which the company is operating, to test hitherto unchallenged assumptions and to think constructively about the likely determinants of success and failure, either strategic or operational. The risk assessment process creates a stimulus for reviewing the lessons of the past, contributing to a culture of continuous improvement. The development and rehearsal of business continuity and crisis management plans in simulated incidents not only produces a better organizational response on the fateful day. As an absorbing exercise in teamwork, it highlights the interdependence of different functions and promotes better collaboration between them.

A major focus of corporate governance should be how a company communicates to its employees on risk matters: how it is made clear what is expected of them; how the board defines the scope of their freedom to assume risk on behalf of the firm and when to alert company officers to escalating issues. In this connection, Hillson and Murray-Webster (2005) expressed concern that there was still no natural home in many organizations for understanding and managing the *risk attitudes* of individuals, teams and entire organizations. In their view, this can often explain why a risk management project fails to deliver on its promises.[10] Consistent with this view, Toft and Reynolds (1997) found analysis of disasters arising from operational failure revealed that their underlying mechanisms invariably had organizational and social dimensions.[11] Technical causes were sometimes, but not always, present. This is perhaps obvious with hindsight. But its implications are profound. Good risk management is as much a state of mind as it is a state of the art.

## RISK AND THE BRAND

Since it is the duty of directors to promote the success of the company, risks to the brand (or 'reputation') must always be high on the agenda. If the brand is a fundamental source of competitive advantage, it needs to be understood. Yet it can sometimes be challenging for non-marketers to take complete account of the brand in risk analysis and decision-making. The absence of a framework for brand thinking may mean that important risk issues are not fully considered or adequately managed. Meanwhile, brand issues may arise across the organization, often exceeding the capacity of brand managers to contribute effectively if organizations are 'marketing-lite' in resource, brand understanding and board-level representation:

> When mid-level marketers were asked, in the course of our research, what they considered to be the single largest impediment to better marketing performance, we received a wide variety of answers ... The most frequent response, in large companies, was the difficulty in gaining cross-functional support. Lack of conceptual understanding of marketing, and brand equity in particular, was part of that.[12]

It is conceivable that the regulatory interest in risk and reputation has created one opportunity for marketers inside another: the opportunity to add *risk* literacy to *brand* management, in order to add *brand* literacy to *risk* management. Perhaps the language of risk can be the basis for a meeting of minds.


# Marketing and risk

## PERCEPTIONS

As a professional community, marketers are not universally perceived as performing effectively by those who need to invest in their judgement. The public and private debate about the marketing function polarizes. The financial right wing frankly accuses marketers of chronic self-indulgence: an overemphasis on intangibles; insufficient attention to mundane distribution effects as the real drivers of increases in revenue and market share. Meanwhile, the advocates of creativity and innovative risk-taking disparage the 'arithmocracy'[13] for their conservatism and their apparent dismissal of anything that cannot be measured.

Perhaps there is some truth in the caricature both ways. It is challenging to put a precise money value on the long-term brand effects of a specific marketing investment. On the other hand, in a profit-seeking enterprise there can be no argument that marketing performance must ultimately be seen to translate into financial gain. In fact, good marketing requires both competences: strategic imagination and financial rigour.

Unfortunately, too many senior executives are said to have expressed their lack of confidence in the business maturity of the marketing function, in the following terms:

- *Lack of financial accountability.* Marketing is largely perceived to be financially unaccountable, especially for the payback on its marketing expenditures.[14] This perceived lack of financial responsibility makes it harder for marketers to secure adequate funding. In some companies marketing budgets are released to marketers piecemeal, on a project-by-project basis, so that someone else has an eye on the money.

- *Strategic myopia.* Marketers are accused of missing the bigger business picture because they 'think small (i.e. at the individual product or brand level)',[15] when they should be thinking in terms that connect their activities more directly with the creation of shareholder value.

- *Change for its own sake.* There is also a view that marketers have a tendency to justify their existences by gratuitous and unnecessary changes to the marketing mix. At best this wastes money; at worst the resulting inconsistencies may undermine the very foundations of the brand.

- *Operational indiscipline.* Marketers, finally, are said to indulge themselves with opportunities to demonstrate creativity, at the expense of proper attention to profitability and operational effectiveness.

Whenever these unfortunate perceptions arise in high places (not in all companies, not of every marketer), they compound the professional challenges that marketers face.

## CHALLENGES

Marketers are, among other things, judged by their ability to predict demand and shape customer behaviour. This means that they deal with risks and uncertainties continuously, even in mature markets if there is a corporate ambition to achieve substantial top-line growth. At the same time, the firm's focus on near-term financial results is sometimes at odds with the longer view that marketers ought legitimately to be taking. This divergence of perspective has a number of practical consequences:

- *Budget raids.* Under pressure to deliver on investors' immediate expectations, it is not surprising that managements should pay greater attention to colleagues who control short-term outcomes in areas such as finance, operations and sales. There is accordingly less interest in discussion of longer-term brand effects and a probability that the marketing budget will be one of the first places management will look for money to plug an earnings shortfall. The 'nice-to-haves' in a weakly defended brand investment plan are likely to be summarily removed.

- *Absence of brand performance measures.* A common by-product of a short-term financial focus has been that annual reviews of progress at board level have tended to be predominantly financial too, with no 'brand dashboard' representing the brand's vital functions. Not only does the absence of brand-related measures obscure any emerging weakness in the brand – and therefore future earnings risk – it also prevents management from seeing any progress attributable to marketing efforts that is not yet reflected in financial results.[16] Making out a reasonable case for the *financial* return on an investment in market *information* can be challenging to marketers, unless they are familiar with techniques known to statisticians and their risk-literate colleagues elsewhere.

- *Demand for certainty of outcome.* The importance of short-term financial accountability means that companies cannot tolerate adverse drift from a declared short-term earnings objective. In order to ensure that targets are met, personal goals and compensation are typically tied to annual budget commitments, based on fixed forecasts of revenue, costs or a combination of the two (i.e. profit).[17] Such a system is ill-suited to entire fulfilment of the marketing mission, which needs to remain alive to changes in demand and respond accordingly. Assuming that the marketing budget is not simply an imposed 'balancing item',[18] a rigid budget approach encourages marketers to proceed in one of two unfortunate ways. At one extreme, they feel compelled to budget ultra-conservatively at the top line, with the consequence that they can 'afford' to ignore emerging opportunities. At the other extreme, they are driven to open a Dutch auction for resources, in which unjustifiable investments are pitched in expectation of the inevitable cuts. Unfortunately, neither of these approaches does marketing people any credit. A dialogue based on a common acknowledgement of the uncertainties – and their implications – would be preferable.

## UNCERTAINTY AND INFLUENCE

In 1985 Nigel Piercy took stock of marketing's status.[19] He presented a rare and comprehensive review of organizational power and politics as it affected marketing. Drawing on a wide range of studies, Piercy related organizational power to the capacity of a given function to process information and (as it happens) address uncertainties. After March and Simon (1958)[20], he described the value created in this way as 'uncertainty absorption'. Any function in an organization that deals effectively and appropriately with critical uncertainties earns influence. The collective power of marketing and marketing research had arisen from their indispensability in gathering and interpreting market-based information. The uncertainties addressed by the various marketing functions had allowed 'the organisation's core to make decisions and plan under conditions of "pseudo-certainty"'.[21]

Meanwhile, the possibility that marketing activities might progressively become reduced to mere routine, cut off from strategic planning, had already been predicted by Campbell and Kennedy in 1971.[22] To judge by this heartfelt observation some 30 years later, they were right:

> *The tendency of many marketing departments to experience a deterioration in empowerment has transformed many of them from brand managers to administrators deprived of power, responsibility and strategic input ... This is hardly the way to channel talent.*[23]

Paradoxically, as firms have become more sensitive to the need for a meaningful market orientation and as brands have become more important to their success, there appears to have been a foreseeable decline in the influence of the marketing function. Piercy provides alternative explanations for this:

> [The] marketing department may not exist, or may be low in organisational power if: (a) boundary-spanning functions [interpretations of the external environment] are provided by others, whether top management or another functional department; (b) market uncertainties are not critical; (c) others cope more effectively with those uncertainties that are critical.[24]

On one view, the evidence appears to confirm the hypothesis:

- *Wider information access.* Information technology (IT) has transformed the speed and ease with which real-time market knowledge is distributed beyond the marketing department. Knowledge is no longer, in itself, a sustainable source of advantage, internally or externally.[25] Whereas IT decentralizes the availability of knowledge and information, ultimate control of its presentation may sit outside the marketing department, with the IT or knowledge management specialists.

- *Reduced influence of marketing researchers.* In principle, the marketing research function should be (and usually is) a valuable ally, supporting the development and external validation of marketing plans. Unfortunately, some observers have noted the waning of marketing researchers' direct influence at board level. In his study of marketing metrics, *Marketing and the Bottom Line*, Ambler (2003) attributed this unfortunate diminution of persuasion power, among other things, to cost-consciousness.[26] Financial focus sacrificed longer-term business partnerships with research agencies in favour of competitive tendering on a project-by-project basis. Ambler argued equally that interest in marketing research at board level was governed by the extent of the board's direct identification with the issues that were being researched. For this reason, corporate reputation research or a brand valuation exercise is sometimes said to hold more interest at board level than a piece of research commissioned by the marketers on customer brand equity:

  > More likely is that the Exec listens to those [researchers] they commission to address the problems they define and those problems are rarely seen by the Exec as marketing, or market, issues.[27]

- *Growth of services.* The growth of the service economy and the services that support products has increased the responsibility borne by operations colleagues for providing a satisfactory 'branded customer experience'. Higher levels of end-customer contact gives front-line operations colleagues improved opportunities to interpret evidence-based market signals on behalf of the firm.

- *Growth of risks to reputation.* The emphasis given to corporate responsibility and risk reporting has given greater prominence to risks to reputation at board level. These strategic and operational exposures are matters of corporate governance, beyond the remit of the marketing function, even though they may have far-reaching effects on strategic choices and the tactical options available to the brand. Alternative functions have arisen to support the corporate brand, none of whom seem to call themselves marketers.

## OPPORTUNITY

On another view, new uncertainties may have reversed the process that Piercy characterized. The pressure to respond to foreseeable change has never been greater. Sull (2006) describes a 'kaleidoscopic shifting of numerous volatile variables, such as regulation, technology, competition, macroeconomics and consumer preferences'.[28] Change in the structure of demand creates risk. Speed of response in new products and service offerings creates more risk. We are now likely to be faced with greater complexity and more uncertainty in the development of marketing strategies and in assessing the returns each alternative plan might offer.

In tandem with adjustments in social values and habits of consumption, there is also the considerable impact of change in channels of audience communication, for example the convergence of web-based content, broadcast television and telephony. The continuing fragmentation and concentration of audiences according to their interests is expected to have profound implications for the ways in which organizations interact with individuals and the business models that connect them. The interactive nature of new communication channels, including social media such as MySpace, means that marketers and managements must grow more accustomed to marketing as 'a smarter conversation' with individuals, rather than as a broadcast to a captive audience.[29] Word of mouth is increasingly recognized as a legitimate measure of brand performance,[30] with strategies to match.[31] Marketing people can no longer look to a single agency to fulfil traditional communication objectives and support them as the 'brain of the brand'. A greater proportion of the responsibility for overseeing the coherence of new strategies and their co-ordinated execution across multiple channels has come home to the marketing department. Given the turnover of marketing people in their assignments, this means that they must also ensure continuity of learning from experience in-house. All of this amounts to an unfinished revolution. To judge by Piercy (1985), these uncertainties may also be creating professional opportunity for marketers.[32]

Without killing creativity or compromising innovation, there is new scope for marketers to support the board's increasing need to communicate effectively with external audiences about market-based risk. The language of risk can become a common currency of communication and understanding between the marketing function and the board of management that invests in its judgement. The tools and techniques of risk thinking are designed to support cross-functional decision-making of this kind.

A risk-literate presentation of marketing recommendations can help a non-specialist audience understand how risks and uncertainties have been addressed in development of a marketing plan, building their confidence in the recommendations. It prepares all concerned for any likelihood of departure from the plan, so that the firm is better prepared to accommodate the possible consequences and act appropriately if the 'unexpected' should occur.

As 'masters of uncertainty',[33] risk-literate marketers will be no less energetic in pursuit of profitable opportunity than their reckless counterparts. It is clear that *not* to take a business risk may lead to an adverse outcome. Failure to keep up with competitors can render your product or service obsolete, bit by bit or suddenly. There is a need to experiment wisely and scale up with confidence. On the other hand, shareholders are entitled to expect that the project delivers a return that is in excess of their next best investment alternative, assuming an equivalent risk profile.

# Risk literacy

For as much as risk literacy is a state of mind, it needs to be underpinned by a range of tools and techniques that support strategic thinking, decision-making and performance management:

*Winning brand managers simulate future opportunities to anticipate the potential fields-of-play. They use models that reveal the range of possible outcomes instead of the allure of a single big idea, and align resources and investments to scenarios with the highest likelihood of making an impact. Estimation, probabilities, risk – these are new additions to the branding lexicon and a challenge for those content to play it all from the hip. Having foresight helps companies make informed choices about their brand and frees leaders up to make bold moves with full knowledge of the implications – essential to thriving in a competitive environment.*[34]

## STRATEGIC THINKING

Risk analysis should clearly not overwhelm a firm's principal purpose, which is to create wealth by taking risks to add value. Nevertheless, a brand strategy should be presented in terms of reward *and* risk, with due attention to each. The question is not whether a risk exists, but whether or not it is acceptable, given (for example) equivalent choices made by competitors.[35] With this in mind, risk-literate marketers will be clear about their appetite or scope for risk-taking.

Risk-literate marketing people will also be aware of the common behavioural biases that arise in risk thinking. In practice, this helps them to determine when it is best to check intuitions or challenge conventional wisdom.

Among the concepts and techniques we will review to support strategic thinking are these:

*   the brand risk model (Chapter 2)
*   brand valuation (Chapter 2)
*   attitudes to risk (Chapter 3)
*   learning from failure (Chapter 3)
*   setting risk tolerance thresholds (Chapter 4)
*   scenario planning (Chapter 5)
*   anticipating stakeholder behaviour (Chapter 5).

## DECISION-MAKING

When it is appropriate, risk-literate marketers will use formal or informal techniques to evaluate alternative risky courses of action. In this sense, they are conscious or 'calculating' risk-takers, who make such considerations explicit. On occasion, this means modelling decisions with tools expressly developed for the purpose of risk analysis, supported by specialist colleagues. The input of assumptions about risk and uncertainty enables a transparent review of cause and effect, given the declared state of knowledge. It is then easier for all concerned to judge:

*   whether the plan is realistic
*   what the consequences of changes or chance events might be
*   the extent to which contingent resources for 'the unexpected' (good and bad) might need to be built into the base plan (and ring-fenced).

One of the practical benefits of risk literacy is that it offers to decision-makers and their collaborating colleagues a consistent and transparent platform for addressing such questions of risk and uncertainty. In principle, those properly engaged in the process should be more comfortable with the conclusions drawn and the commitments made.

Among the concepts and techniques we will review to support decision-making are these:

- probability and 'expected value' (Chapter 4)
- risk-adjusted decision-making (Chapters 3 and 6)
- 'Marketing Due Diligence'[36] (Chapter 5)
- calculating the value of new information (Chapter 6)
- Monte Carlo simulation (Chapter 6).

## PERFORMANCE MANAGEMENT

As a discipline, risk management balances risk and opportunity. It sets out consciously to improve the likelihood that a given strategic or tactical objective will be attained, and that the adverse impact of controllable, uncontrollable or unknowable events can be minimized:

> *The essence of risk management lies in maximizing the areas where we have some control over the outcome while minimizing the areas where we have absolutely no control over the outcome and the linkage between effect and cause is hidden from us.*[37]

Risk-literate marketers will therefore take steps to manage the risks in marketing operations. These might include issues relevant to effective brand stewardship, target attainment, project management or the assurance of productive relationships between the company and its agencies. In practice, this means that they systematically identify and prioritize operational risks, estimating the cost-benefit of their risk management activities relative to the exposure.

Among the techniques we will review to support performance management are these:

- Six Thinking Hats* (Chapter 5)[38]
- risk mapping (Chapter 5)
- cause-and-controls assessment (Chapter 5)
- cause and effect analysis (Chapter 5)
- defining risk management alternatives (Chapter 5)
- dependency modelling (Chapter 6).

# Summary

We have established the rationale for risk literacy and a framework for its exploration:

- We have identified the growing importance of corporate risk thinking and reporting about the brand.
- We have highlighted new uncertainties as a particular opportunity for marketers to demonstrate their unique worth and contribution.
- We have suggested that a risk-literate component in marketing thinking will be well received and worthwhile.

Let us start by defining brand risk.

---

\*    Six Thinking Hats® is a registered trademark.

# References

1   Elster, J. (1989), *The Cement of Society: A Study of Social Order*, Cambridge University Press.
2   Petts, J., Wheeley, S., Homan, J. and Niemeyer, S. (2003), *Risk Literacy and the Public – MMR, Air Pollution and Mobile Phones, Final Report For the Department of Health*, January 2003, Centre for Environmental Research & Training, University of Birmingham.
3   Internal Control Working Party of the Institute of Chartered Accountants in England and Wales (1999), *Internal Control: Guidance for Directors on the Combined Code*, Institute of Chartered Accountants in England and Wales.
4   Haig, M. (2003), *Brand Failures: The Truth About The 100 Biggest Branding Mistakes Of All Time*, Kogan Page Ltd.
5   Haig (2003), op.cit.
6   KPMG (2006), *The Directors' Report and the Business Review*, KPMG LLP (UK), p. 5.
7   KPMG (2006), op.cit.
8   Lloyd's in association with the Economist Intelligence Unit (2005), *Taking Risk on Board: How Global Leaders View Risk*, Society of Lloyd's.
9   Green, P. (2005), 'Risk Management in the Balance', *StrategicRISK*, October, pp. 10–12.
10   Hillson, D. and Murray-Webster, R. (2005), *Understanding and Managing Risk Attitude*, Gower Publishing Ltd.
11   Toft, B. and Reynolds, S. (1997), *Learning from Disasters – A Management Approach: Second edition*, Perpetuity Press.
12   Ambler, T. (2003), *Marketing and the Bottom Line*, FT Prentice Hall, p. 253.
13   Tasgal, A. (2003), 'Marketing: Art, Science or Alchemy?', *Market Leader*, Issue Number 21, The Marketing Society, pp. 43–49.
14   Shaw, R. and Merrick, D. (2005), *Marketing Payback – Is Your Marketing Profitable?*, FT Prentice Hall.
15   Lehmann, D.R. (2003), Foreword, in Ambler, op.cit., p. xiii.
16   Ambler (2003), op.cit.
17   Hope, J. and Fraser, R. (2003), *Beyond Budgeting – How Managers Can Break Free from the Annual Performance Trap*, Harvard Business School Press.
18   Shaw and Merrick (2005), op.cit.
19   Piercy, N. (1985), *Marketing Organisation: An Analysis of Information Processing, Power and Politics*, George Allen & Unwin.
20   March, J.G. and Simon, H.A. (1958), *Organizations*, John Wiley and Sons, Inc.
21   Piercy (1985), op.cit., p. 66.
22   Campbell, I. and Kennedy, S. (1971), 'Routinisation in Marketing', *European Journal of Marketing*, Volume 5 (Number 3), pp. 83–92.
23   Tasgal (2003), op.cit., p. 46.
24   Piercy (1985), op.cit., p. 120.
25   Kelly, E. (2006), 'The Tall Order of Taming Change', *FT Mastering Uncertainty Part 1*, supplement to *Financial Times*, 17 March, pp. 4–5.
26   Ambler (2003), op.cit.
27   Ambler (2003), op.cit., p. 259.
28   Sull, D. (2006), 'Difficult Decisions for an Uncertain World', *FT Mastering Uncertainty Part 1*, supplement to *Financial Times*, 17 March, pp. 2–3.
29   Macleod, H. (2004), *Thoughts on 'Smarter Conversations'*, www.gapingvoid.com, http://www.gapingvoid.com/Moveable_Type/archives/000939.html.
30   East, R., Hammond, K. and Wright, M. (2007), 'The Relative Incidence of Positive and Negative Word of Mouth: A Multi-Category Study', *International Journal of Research in Marketing*, Volume 24 (Issue 2), Elsevier, pp. 175–184.
31   Gladwell, M. (2001), *The Tipping Point: How Little Things Can Make a Big Difference*, Abacus.
32   Piercy (1985), op.cit.
33   Kelly (2006), op.cit.
34   Interbrand (2007), *All Brands Are Not Created Equal: Best Global Brands 2007*, Interbrand in association with BusinessWeek, p. 7.
35   Toft and Reynolds (1997), op.cit.
36   McDonald, M., Smith B. and Ward, K. (2006), *Marketing Due Diligence: Reconnecting Strategy to Share Price*, Butterworth-Heinemann.
37   Bernstein, P.L. (1996), *Against the Gods: The Remarkable Story of Risk*, John Wiley & Sons, Inc., p. 197.
38   de Bono, E. (1999), *Six Thinking Hats®*, Penguin Books.

# Snakes and Ladders

## LICENSING BRANDS

### Make Haste Slowly

Premature consideration of a 'standard' licensing agreement may hinder constructive communication between the parties. Do not proceed to the first legal draft of a licence until the respective managements have spent time discussing commercial objectives (hopes and fears) and the general heads of agreement (the matters that need to be formalized). A number of the frameworks and techniques described in this book will help the parties to do this, firstly on their own and then together.

Each party should expect the other to carry out financial due diligence on the other. A prudent licensor will seek references from the licensee's existing customers as to their operating methods and reliability.

Contractual arrangements should take account of any actual, impending or potential regulation likely to hinder or wholly frustrate performance of the contract. These may be known to the licensee, but not to the licensor.

### Discuss the End at the Beginning

One of the significant exposures in the event of contested royalty discrepancies is the unforeseen accumulation of legal and other expert fees. These costs can become disproportionate to the sums in dispute. This exposure should be assessed. Wherever possible, the matter of legal cost control and allocation should be the subject of contingent agreement between the parties in the original contract.

Contractual arrangements should also envisage the practical effects of termination. In product licensing situations there should normally be a provision enabling the licensee to sell off product stocks for a reasonable period, subject to overriding considerations such as public safety or regulatory compliance.

### Create 'Firebreaks' in Global Arrangements

It is generally advisable not to grant single global licences even if you want to license globally. The probability of unsatisfactory performance in one or two isolated territories is better managed by granting a set of single-territory licences to a global licensee.

It is prudent to ensure contractually that a licensee cannot register any trademarks that come out of the collaboration between licensor and licensee anywhere. A licensee may otherwise claim rights in local sub-brands or any agreed local alternative to the licensed brand. A licensee may conceivably discover that the licensed brand has not been protected in a territory and register a confusingly similar mark.

### Prevention is Still Better than Cure

The general risks of non-compliance are best addressed with a provision for regular financial and operational audit, based on the principle of 'little and often'. This maintains frequent dialogue between the parties on performance issues. It also helps to avoid the damaging and potentially explosive consequences of accumulative breach of licence conditions, even if as a result of innocent oversight. Dealing with questions of fact and evidence years later is fertile ground for contention.

Breach of licence often arises from staff turnover within the licensee organization (especially marketing people). Satisfy yourself that there is adequate and continuous communication of contractual terms and conditions to all relevant employees.

Be aware if counterfeiting is likely to overwhelm the licensee's efforts to fulfil commercial conditions and their obligations in brand stewardship. These are usually the licensor's obligation to address.

# 2 Defining Brand Risk

We have considered risk literacy in marketing from an organizational and operational perspective. We now turn to the brand itself.

In this chapter we will:

- specify the nature of brands
- explore the relationship between brand and reputation
- identify how and where brand risk arises
- describe the scope of brand risk management
- consider the role of valuation in brand risk management.

## What is a brand?

It is important to be clear what a brand is, before you can identify and address its risks and uncertainties. A brand is not a trademark or a reputation. Brands are complex intangibles, whose character is a property that emerges from a blend of attributes, some of them seemingly insignificant. It is the sum of all information about a product, a service or a firm that is communicated by its name. This holds true in industrial and professional markets, where brands can create and project emotional and self-expressive benefits just as they do in consumer markets. Every organization with an identity therefore has a brand (or brands) that it must manage and protect in order to survive and prosper. A brand can be embodied in a globally advertised symbol. Alternatively, it can be expressed by the renown of partners in a services firm that bears their names.

Brands stimulate demand for a company's offerings and a consequent desire by others to associate with (or disassociate from) the company. This makes brands focal points not only for the company's customers, but also for other stakeholders and audiences: employees, partners, investors, regulators and communities (Figure 2.1).

In essence, an active and well-managed brand is a three-part intangible asset:

- a legal asset, affording rights
- a relational asset, building affinities
- an economic asset, creating value.

Unlike a firm's capital equipment, which generally depreciates in value through usage and over time, the worth of a brand can rise with increased utilization. Unlike patents, brands have no predetermined expiry. Their ability to create value can outlive many generations of management and substantial market change.

**Figure 2.1    Brand as focal point**
*Source: Author, reproduced by permission of Marsh Ltd*

## IMPORTANCE OF BRANDS

However a brand's identity is projected, its importance to the sustainability of an enterprise has never been greater. Companies with strong brands tend to outperform their relevant stock market indices around the world.[1] Whether positively or negatively, 'brand' unavoidably drives an organization's capacity to create value and sustain it. The performance of the business is at risk if such a vital source of competitive advantage is inadequately nurtured and protected.

Fully functioning brands create value in a number of ways:[2]

- *Mature markets.* In mature markets, brands with strong positions reduce the uncertainty of future demand by maintaining differentiation between offerings, raising barriers against competitive attack and minimizing the impact of price erosion.
- *New markets.* Brands enable more efficient expansion into new markets and new channels. It is less costly to build on existing brand awareness than to start afresh. All other things being equal, the resulting profits accrue sooner and at lower risk.
- *Employees.* Brands attract new employees efficiently, build their commitment and direct their performance. A company with a weak brand is likely to find it harder and more expensive to recruit and retain staff than its stronger competitors.
- *Terms of trade.* The relative strength of an organization's brand(s) affects bargaining power. This includes, for example, the cost of capital, conditions of material supply, leverage in negotiation with distributors and the apportionment of risk in joint ventures.
- *Licence to operate.* Brands enhance or protect an organization's freedom to operate, by projecting and substantiating its response to the expectations of regulators and communities.

- *Disaster recovery.* Well-managed brands support business continuity efforts if disaster strikes, giving customers, employees and investors credible reassurance that full business recovery is a realistic prospect.

## BRAND VULNERABILITY

In 1978, intangibles including brands accounted for about 5 per cent of the market capitalization of the firms comprising the Dow Jones Industrial Average index. By 2007 this proportion had risen to 72 per cent.[3] Appreciation of the importance of intangibles by investors has been matched by their concern to see that all risks to brand performance and reputation are well managed (see Chapter 1). The damage done to a brand owner's business following crisis or catastrophe can substantially outweigh the direct costs. For example, a misjudged customer promotion by the UK subsidiary of a US household products company cost the parent company nearly half of its annual profits. The discounted sale of the entire European subsidiary one year later, following significant falls in market share, all but tripled a cost that was already high.[4]

In tandem with their growing economic importance, the general vulnerability of brands has been increasing for a number of reasons:

- *Growth imperative.* As markets mature, firms are often encouraged to 'stretch' their brands into new categories and environments, beyond their legitimacy and their owners' operating capabilities. The resulting disappointment or outright failure of an overoptimistic plan can undermine the parent brand and confidence in company management.

- *Merger and acquisition.* As corporate consolidations continue, growth through acquisition calls for a deep understanding of the brands acquired. The positive momentum necessary to seize an acquisition opportunity can encourage managements to proceed with insufficient attention to the non-financial risks. For example, there may be customer or employee affinities that rely on the brand's association with its present owner. If acquired brands performed strongly under previous ownership, the acquirer's temptation to 'fix what isn't broken' can be difficult to resist – especially in the marketing department if there has been a wholesale change of personnel. For example, a US food giant aimed to accelerate the transformation of an acquired 'alternative' soft drinks brand into a mainstream brand. The company lost 80 per cent of its purchase price when the strategy failed and the brand was sold. A rapid and radical change of positioning had lost touch with the brand's original franchise.[5]

- *Accountability to customers.* The internet and its burgeoning blogosphere increase a brand's accountability. At one point in 2007 there were said to be over 51 million identified blogs worldwide.[6] Coupled with the relentless scrutiny of professional commentators, companies are exposed to the wide circulation of public comment in online forums. Online search capabilities perpetuate these messages and extend their reach.

- *Service economy.* The growth in services, including the development of diversified service offerings by former monopolies, means that a larger number of firms rely on customer-facing employees to deliver explicit promises made by the brand. People are not machines. The consequences of variability in customer experience have therefore become more significant. The challenge of maintaining proper 'brand manners'[7] amongst employees has been magnified by customers' expectation of swift personalized response to telephone, e-mail and company website enquiries.

- *Reliance on third parties.* The pressure on companies to outsource services for cost saving and to license brands for growth creates corresponding risks and uncertainties that may be new or unfamiliar to the brand's owner. Brand exposures are increased by the challenges of communication and control between separately owned companies with potentially different values, interests and objectives.

- *Corporate conduct.* Globalization of business has been matched by increasing sensitivity to the social consequences of corporate conduct. Heralded by the early protests at the environmental and community impacts of oil exploration in the 1980s and US class actions against the tobacco industry, companies are now subject to regular attack by activists and single-issue lobby groups, whether in their business-building endeavours at home or abroad. Widely reported examples of such issues have included the use of child labour by fashionable apparel brands; directors' (over)compensation; corporate racism; affordable access to life-saving drugs in the developing world; the alleged encouragement of child obesity by branded food and beverage companies.

## COMPLEXITY OF BRAND RISK ISSUES

Whilst an investor's view of risk finally resolves into a buy or sell decision, it is the company's managers who are left to address the full range of identified risks in practical detail.[8] Company executives have consistently ranked brand and reputation risks amongst their most significant exposures. For example, a global survey of 269 risk managers and senior executives conducted by the Economist Intelligence Unit (EIU) reported in 2005 that 'reputational risk emerged as the most significant threat to the business out of a choice of 13 categories of risk'.[9] The report explained that the priority given to reputation risk arose from its potential impact, its ubiquity and its complexity:

- *Impact.* The most serious and widely reported cases of corporate crisis had predominantly drawn attention to issues of reputation and trust. Dramatic loss of confidence in managements had resulted from perceived shortcomings in their conduct, beyond their accountability for financial results. These have included the inadequate supervision of risk-taking employees, unethical behaviour or poor judgement.

- *Ubiquity.* Managers understood that damage to reputation can be the indirect consequence of almost any badly managed incident. This means that many of the operational risks and uncertainties known to a company could potentially escalate into a crisis of reputation in the eyes of one or more stakeholder groups, including investors. Examples of these have included environmental pollution, delayed product recall and maintenance shortfalls.

- *Complexity.* Managers acknowledged the particular challenges of managing reputation risk. The EIU found that 62 per cent of companies believed reputational risk was 'harder to manage than other types of risk'. Three factors accounted for this perceived complexity:

    1. *[C]onfusion over how reputation risk should be categorized.*

    2. *[T]he lack of widely-accepted techniques to quantify such an amorphous risk.*

    3. *[N]o formal ownership of reputational risk, with responsibility spread amongst a wide range of business managers.*[10]

It is not surprising that respondents in this survey should be confused over categorization. In some quarters, 'brand' and 'reputation' are assumed to be synonymous. In other quarters, people see reputation and brand as near-opposites: reputation as a real outcome of corporate performance and brand (or branding) somewhat disparagingly as the output of a firm's propaganda machine.

Reputation has gained some acceptance as the principal expression of a firm's corporate brand. It is a term readily understood at board level, especially in non-consumer companies. It aligns directly with the board's particular concern to respond to the expectations of its external evaluators, such as investors, regulators and local communities. As it happens, reputation is also colloquially close to 'goodwill', the financial balance sheet item under which the economic value created by non-acquired brands usually sits.

Brand or reputation risk is often judged by the amount of media exposure or adverse comment likely to arise in a crisis or at 'moments of truth', such as a product recall or the annual general meeting of a company. Although crisis readiness is unquestionably important in brand management, we do not favour such a limited definition of brand risk. A brand is not a reputation. It follows that reputation risk is an incomplete concept of brand risk. The scope of risk thinking about brands (and reputations) should accommodate all the risks and uncertainties about the sustainability of profitable demand for the brand, together with its continued capacity to create value, influence or commitment amongst each of its key constituencies – not just customers.[11]

## Brand risk model

How can one usefully define brand risk in order to perceive it with clarity and manage it well? As a stimulus to risk thinking, we believe that a useful model of brand risk should:

- promote wider understanding of how a brand works in the absence of crisis
- apply equally to the assessment of risks and opportunities
- help non-marketing colleagues take account of the brand in a way that is accessible and relevant
- create insight into the basic patterns of brand variability and vulnerability (cause and effect)
- support decision-making about brands and their management
- remain compatible with any existing and more detailed measures of brand health.

Our suggested model for brand risk thinking has six interacting components that address the brand's overall structure and condition. It is important to emphasize that we are not defining risk solely in terms of crisis or catastrophe, but as an encapsulation of all the controllable or uncontrollable variability and volatility in a brand's performance. The six interacting components are:

- identity risk
- presence risk
- equity risk
- reputation risk
- status risk
- market risk (see Figure 2.2).

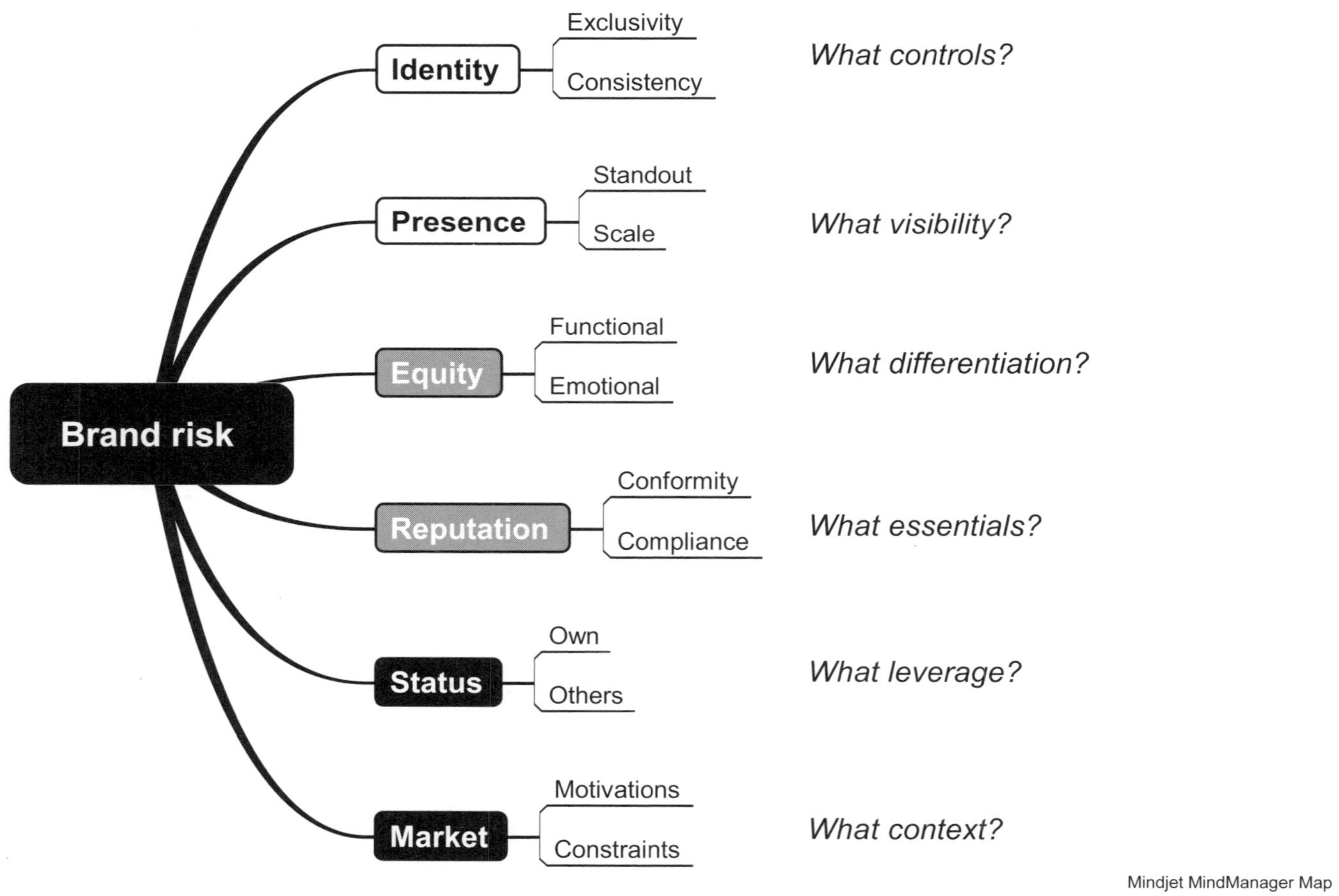

Mindjet MindManager Map

**Figure 2.2    Components of brand risk**

This high-level 'risk anatomy' of the brand is relevant to all organizations operating in any market. You may prefer to think of these components as the six cylinders of a brand's engine, running simultaneously and interdependently. The scope of each component is explained by two contrasting elements that are also shown in Figure 2.2.

## IDENTITY RISK

Identity risk arises in two forms, both related to the way in which the brand is represented: *exclusivity* and *consistency*.

- *Exclusivity*. These are issues associated with the exclusive use of brand identifiers (name, trademarks, logos, web domains). Enforceable rights need to be defined and protected if they are valuable. Exposures arise through inadequate registration of company names or trademarks in the necessary jurisdictions or by shortcomings in safeguards against infringement, counterfeiting and 'look-alikes'. An exclusivity risk may also arise if two *legally* operated brands or identities are easily confused.

- *Consistency*. Consistency is one of the golden rules of marketing. Lack of consistency can undermine perception of a brand's quality and weaken its projection. Accordingly, this identity issue arises from inconsistent, inappropriate or incomplete representation of the brand, whether in look, style, tone or content. This can be a strategic dilemma for some global brands. They need to accommodate the special requirements of local markets, whilst maintaining the highest common denominator in their projection worldwide. Consistency risk may equally be a matter of outright brand contradiction. For example, an office cleaning company with clean vehicles and presentable people positively reinforces its brand, whereas dirty vehicles and dirty work clothes can undermine it. All of these identity risk issues may become more challenging where intermediaries, agents or licensees are involved.

In evaluating the causes and effects of a crisis or controversy affecting the brand, the issues of exclusivity and consistency have somewhat different meanings, but still apply:

- *Exclusivity*: 'Are we the only ones affected?'
- *Consistency*: 'Is the issue the same everywhere?'

## PRESENCE RISK

A brand's qualities are devalued if they are misunderstood or go unnoticed. *Presence risk* describes issues of awareness and attention amongst key constituencies. It is defined by two parameters that determine the visibility of the brand: standout and scale.

*Standout* captures all the qualitative issues of a brand's relative conspicuousness from the perspective of a single respondent. An alternative term for this is 'salience'. In other words, how prominent is our brand (or a brand issue) in the consciousness (or subconsciousness) of customers, investors or opinion formers?

The exact nature of standout depends on context. For example, to what extent is a vital attribute of our brand going unnoticed? Does our advertising have sufficient impact? Are our efforts to shape investor opinion crowded out by other events?

Conspicuousness is not always desirable. Some customer segments respond better to low overall standout from their brands, if the qualities of discretion and understatement are the badges of their own status or aspiration.

Standout can equally describe the significance of a negative issue and the extent of its association with our brand. For example, would activists identify us as the worst offenders in their public attack on an industry?

*Scale* is the quantitative complement to standout. It measures the numbers and locations of people for whom a particular brand (or brand issue) achieves a given level of standout for a given length of time. This is the place to consider how a crisis might escalate through publicity or network effects.

In new product or service introductions, achieving the right standout and scale are central to achievement of the business plan.

## EQUITY RISK

*Brand equity risk* describes issues that affect a brand's ability to maintain its desired differentiation or competitive advantage. However these attributes may be defined or measured, they are the components of a brand's image that have the ability to shift economic demand in favour of the company or its products (or against – brand equity can be negative too). Equity attributes will, for example, demonstrably affect the willingness of a customer to pay a price premium, to transact more frequently – or to transact at all. Brand equity, in particular, underpins the future of the business because 'it stores what marketing has achieved but has not yet reached the profit and loss account'.[12]

The detailed composition of a brand's equity is often not explored beyond marketing circles. It is, for instance, an important characteristic of brand equity that it should reflect both the functional and emotional (or psychological) benefits provided by the brand. An example of a functional benefit is 'speed of service'. An example of an emotional benefit is 'confidence'. The consideration of emotional benefits can be the area of 'fluffy stuff' that non-marketers sometimes find hard to work with. However, there is no doubting its importance in understanding a brand's workings and its resilience. This is true in both consumer and non-consumer markets:

> *In fact, brand equity may be more important in industrial goods markets than in consumer marketing ... [M]any purchase alternatives tend to be toss-ups. The decisive factor then can turn upon what a brand means to a buyer.*[13]

The exact blend of emotional benefits provided by a brand is much harder for another brand to replicate, even where competitors are able to offer customers the same technology or the same service features.

Most people know that the equity they have in their homes is its net value to them, once anyone else's charge on the property has been deducted, typically a mortgage lender's. Brand equity is a related idea: it describes the net beneficial properties of the brand once the qualities common to all other competing brands have been deducted. It is also a 'net' quality because the brand asset may also have liabilities (characteristics that detract from its appeal).[14] For example, it is possible that a brand's promoted associations may project its intended benefits whilst simultaneously creating unintended negative connotations. Aaker (1991) cites the case of a leading potato-chip brand that performed better in taste tests where the identity of the brand was hidden than in taste tests where it was revealed. Reflection on these surprising results led to a conclusion that the branded product's appearance and novel packaging, though positively received in other ways, had inadvertently led to consumer perceptions of 'artificiality' and inferiority of ingredients. This caused consumers to downgrade the branded product on *taste* relative to its more traditional competitors.[15]

A simplified structure of the equity in a hypothetical automotive brand is illustrated in Figure 2.3. It identifies four components:

- *Product/service*. This component of brand equity draws on the particular qualities of the products or services with which the brand is associated.

- *Authority*. This component identifies the other differentiating claims made by the brand for itself.

- *Approval*. This subjective component deals with the brand's appeal to its target respondents based on how they believe they *ought* to behave by reference to external factors. It is 'the internalized influence of people who are important to a respondent', though there is no need for actual feedback from this reference group.[16] Different influences arise in different contexts: parents, social peer group, political peer group, business associates and so on.

- *Identification*. This fourth component captures the feelings and emotions that accrue from brand use.

By no means every discernible element of a brand's image is a driver of its equity. Coupled with the need to identify these crucial equity elements, it is important to bear in mind that whilst customers, investors and communities may be stakeholders in the same brand, they are likely to have different, if overlapping, priorities and perceptions. For example, as a consumer you may know something about the CEO of your mobile phone company, but this is unlikely to have played a part in your brand selection. By contrast, your choice of designer clothing may have been greatly influenced by the public image of its celebrity designer. This makes the designer an equity element of the clothing brand, but leaves the CEO of your phone company as an image element without influence on the brand's customer equity. However, you may also be an investor in the phone company as well as its customer. Your perceptions will be different as an investor. From the investor perspective, the CEO's conduct and image as an effective business leader may easily have become an equity element, one of the criteria upon which you made the investment decision.

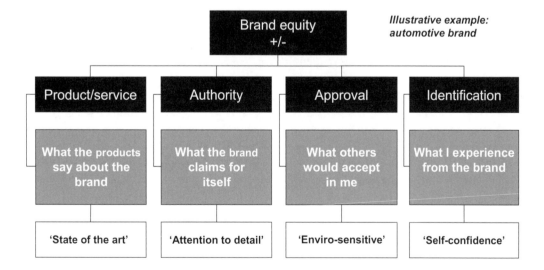

**Figure 2.3    Components of brand equity**

Brand equity analysis such as this – or its equivalent – helps to determine what qualities must be reinforced by the brand's identity and presence, as we have defined them. It also suggests where the brand's equity might be most vulnerable to changes in market factors or company performance. Typically, threatened or inadequate brand equity tends to weaken over time. This makes incipient failure harder to detect and harder to reverse. It is also worth noting that brand equity can be eroded by the conduct of a brand's *customers*. For example, the appeal and value of a tourist destination can be damaged if it becomes associated with the wrong crowd.

Brands differ in their complexity and the extent to which each type of equity element applies. In reality, the process of isolating a brand's equity is not a simple matter of making competitive comparisons, checking off the commonalities and seeing what remains. Just like great dishes from great chefs, a brand's equity can have subtle or complex qualities that emerge from the way in which the common and uncommon ingredients have been combined.

## REPUTATION RISK

Reputation risk groups together those issues that arise from failure to meet expectations of performance that apply to any comparable organization operating in the same field. We need to make a further distinction between compliance and conformity, because some expectations are created by the need to comply with regulation, others by social and moral norms. Ethical risk is an increasingly important issue. Regulation consolidates and mirrors societal expectation, but does not anticipate it. This means that merely abiding by the rules may not be enough.

By our definition, risk to reputation typically applies to factors that are 'brand essentials'. Merely complying with norms of performance in these essentials will not create competitive advantage – unless you include actions to restore reputation that 're-ignite' other strengths in the brand. Reputation elements are therefore the minimum stakes required to stay in the game. By contrast, bad performance or catastrophe in any one of these areas can quickly destroy the confidence that the brand enjoys amongst its customers and other constituencies.

Typical matters of potential reputation exposure include the safety of individuals, fitness for purpose in a product, issues of trust or ethics and the fulfilment of commitments made by the brand or its owners. Culpability plays a role in attribution and the impact of a reputation issue. A brand may fail to conform or comply for reasons understood by forgiving stakeholders to be beyond its control. On the other hand, reputation issues may sometimes arise from conflicting interests within a company.

Unlike a brand's equity, which may be responding in part to unconscious or inadmissible motivations in its customers, reputation elements tend to be clearer-cut matters of public knowledge or public concern. As market expectations, community interests, regulatory and other standards evolve, so the performance necessary to maintain a good reputation can change.

A key characteristic of reputation is that it can only ever refer to past behaviour as an indication of future behaviour.[17] This means that in principle nothing in reputation itself can ever be new about the owner of the reputation. Reputations can be earned, saved, invested and expended, but not minted. Conversely, a new brand equity element may be an entirely novel contribution to a brand's competitive identity, even if shallow-rooted. It is then a matter for assessment whether the new equity element is reinforced or contradicted by the brand's reputation (though it may take time to become established). Reputation can certainly operate to make a new proposition more or less credible. Firms often lend their corporate reputations (and their status) to their variously named customer brands. This adds a new dynamic to the risk position, because there is the possibility of multiple 'disqualification' of a whole brand portfolio in the event of corporate malpractice. Culpable disregard for the essentials of production hygiene in a multi-brand food company would be a case in point.

## Balancing equity and reputation

The distinction between brand equity and reputation (more simply, 'differentiators' and 'essentials') is useful because it helps to determine whether a brand's structure is complete and robust. Understanding the balance between equity and reputation elements can help to determine where the sources of brand risk and opportunity may lie. The disassembly of a brand into its qualitative components is also helpful in goal setting and the allocation of responsibilities. This is because different elements of a brand's equity and reputation may be differently measured and separately managed within the firm.

A brand's reputation acts as a foundation for the equity element that creates competitive advantage. Without the distinctive equity element, adequacy in reputation 'essentials' is insufficient for a brand's sustained success. A brand with a rich blend of equity elements may have greater resilience to competitive attack and to certain reputation failures. Conversely, strong brand equity in one market category may be insufficient for a move into another category, if substantially different reputation criteria apply. Credibility in one competence may be insufficient to presume another. For example, a package holiday company may need to reassure its clients that a 'real airline' is flying the planes in its own-brand charter fleet.

Depending on context and circumstance, it is possible for a reputation element to operate as a basis for differentiation, as if it were an equity element. For example, in competing for public authority contracts, the reputation advantage of one firm over another may influence the outcome. In effect, the firm's reputation-building activities have contributed at two levels, extending its performance in 'essentials' beyond the minimum to create a competitive edge.

## STATUS RISK

*Status risk* describes issues arising from the relative standing of the brand in a hierarchy of brands. Every transaction between parties reflects either their equality or their inequality.[18] Like reputation reinforced or squandered by association, there may be an exchange or flow of status to and from the brand. For example, the flow of status between a brand and a celebrity spokesperson may be unequal, to the possible detriment of one or the other. However, brand status is not the same as its reputation or equity. To take a homely parallel: our much-loved dog has a good reputation because it is well behaved by canine standards. Unfortunately – for all of us – its status remains low. Similarly, a corporation can succeed in setting itself apart from other companies without necessarily affecting its own status or the status of other brands in the current hierarchy (for example, by adopting a compelling new business model).

As Podolny (2005) demonstrates in his sociological study of market competition, perceptions of status can be highly relevant to the behaviour of market actors in the face of uncertainty.[19] This clearly applies to a product's fitness for purpose: if we do not understand a new technology or have a low level of psychological involvement in the purchase, we will rely more heavily on the status of the brand (or its producer) in making our choice.

Status should be considered as a distinct component of brand risk assessment for the following reasons:

- *Unique characteristics*. Status is relative and is always a 'zero sum game'. When one brand's status rises, another's must fall.[20] It follows that the status of our brand can be affected simply by the actions of others. Unlike reputation and brand equity, status is not directly controlled by our own actions.[21] Reputation and brand equity both contribute to status over time. However, the effects of our actions (good or bad) on our own status are not immediate. Meanwhile, status nevertheless exerts an immediate influence on the results we can achieve in the other two dimensions: 'Status ultimately provides the lens through which another signal – like reputation – is viewed.'[22]

- *Status adjusts risk.* Podolny (2005) considered how status can in itself affect the risk of success or failure in product development and introductions. To generalize, higher status is not only rewarded with more immediate and wider market acceptance. It is also reflected in the 'virtuous circle' of fuller co-operation or better terms offered by suppliers and other key constituencies, given the uncertainties that they are being asked to accept.[23] This is evidence of how status operates as a means of transmitting the benefits of achievement in one aspect of performance to another. Brand leaders appear more easily to generate positive word of mouth than others.[24] Unfortunately, such high status also increases reputation risks. This is both for reasons of greater visibility (standout) and an expectation that high-status organizations should lead by example in their response to the social, ethical and environmental issues which they encounter.

- *Status influences risk-taking.* There is a tendency for high- and low-status firms to associate only with their peers in status, whether as partners or suppliers. This may lead a high-status firm to shy away from an emerging market opportunity, because it would be required to associate with lower-status firms in procurement and distribution.[25] The conservatism that arises from higher status has its apparent corollary: that lower-status firms adapt more quickly to radical market change.[26]

## MARKET RISK

*Market risk* describes the brand issues that arise externally from its market or industry context. We are concerned with two parameters: motivations and constraints.

Assessment of *motivations* should embrace all risks and uncertainties associated with changing segment needs and interests, whether positive or negative. These considerations apply equally to all of the brand's constituencies, though in different forms. Just as customers have changing motivations, so do investors and regulators. Changing attitudes to consumption of a particular product (such as tobacco); unresolved issues of cultural fit in new markets; the relegation of a particular industry in the eyes of potential new employees or investors: all such general issues may directly or indirectly affect the positive impact and performance of a brand, globally or selectively by region.

It is quite conceivable that a brand can succeed in strengthening its affinity (equity + reputation + status) within a market segment that is nevertheless declining in volume or in its capacity to pay a premium price. Conversely, a general surge in market demand can mask underlying weakness in the strength of the brand – or lead management to postpone attention to an identified problem.

*Constraints* are issues affecting the brand's 'licence to operate', its strategic freedoms and other market-based limitations. For example, there may be new regulatory imposition in response to the failings of another organization. Political issues may inhibit international acceptance. Social opinion beyond the brand's immediate customer group may affect the brand's freedom to meet latent demand – for example, in promoting certain foods to children. (A social constraint such as this might create a corresponding reputation exposure, if the company were not conducting its business in an acceptable way.) A brand may also be constrained in its access to particular channels of distribution for reasons of market structure.

## APPLYING THE MODEL

Our six-part risk model can be applied to the analysis of most issues or opportunities related to a brand and its performance. For example, in the course of a brand extension project, each determinant of success can be assessed for its particular risks and uncertainties (see Figure 2.4). The model can also be used to compare brands for competitive benchmarking (see Figure 2.5). It can serve as a basis for exploring the compatibility between two brands for co-marketing or merger. In that case, the analysis needs to consider the 'stock and flow' of each element between the two brands. How might the strengths and weaknesses of one brand affect the other? Would the functional equity of Brand A be given additional leverage by the emotional equity of Brand B? In negotiating the contractual details of a co-marketing venture, for example, is Brand A bringing more to the party than Brand B? If so, what? Where do the associated risks and uncertainties lie?

# Addressing brand risks

Brands evolve by default if not by design. Unfortunately, it is not uncommon (especially in non-consumer businesses) for brand strategies and marketing strategies to be implicit and therefore at least partly inaccessible to risk management:

> *For many companies, marketing strategy is developed in a largely unconscious way, building incrementally on to previous strategies with small-scale decisions about allocating resources to certain markets and products. In such cases, the marketing strategy is rarely stated explicitly.*[27]

In practice, responsibility for strategic and tactical marketing may not devolve to a single individual or team in the firm with 'marketing' in their job titles. As a result, there may be gaps in coverage or management understanding, especially about brand health or brand performance, to say nothing of the brand-related aspects of demand management that look beyond the current financial year.

In the absence of a specific project requiring brand risk evaluation, we suggest that organizations should nevertheless build brand impact assessment into their overall process of risk identification. This is because many cases of brand and reputation damage result from other operational failures. A corporate risk management framework without proper insight into the role of the brand is incomplete. The six-part model of brand risk that we have described provides a basis for discussion of the causes and consequences of brand vulnerability (see Figure 2.6 on page 32).

For each of the 12 dimensions of brand performance, the questions to ask are:

- *Causes.* Is this dimension of brand performance vulnerable? Why? How likely are these causes to arise?

- *Consequences.* What would be the likely consequences if this dimension of brand performance were to be affected in the manner described? How probable is it that these consequences will occur and endure?

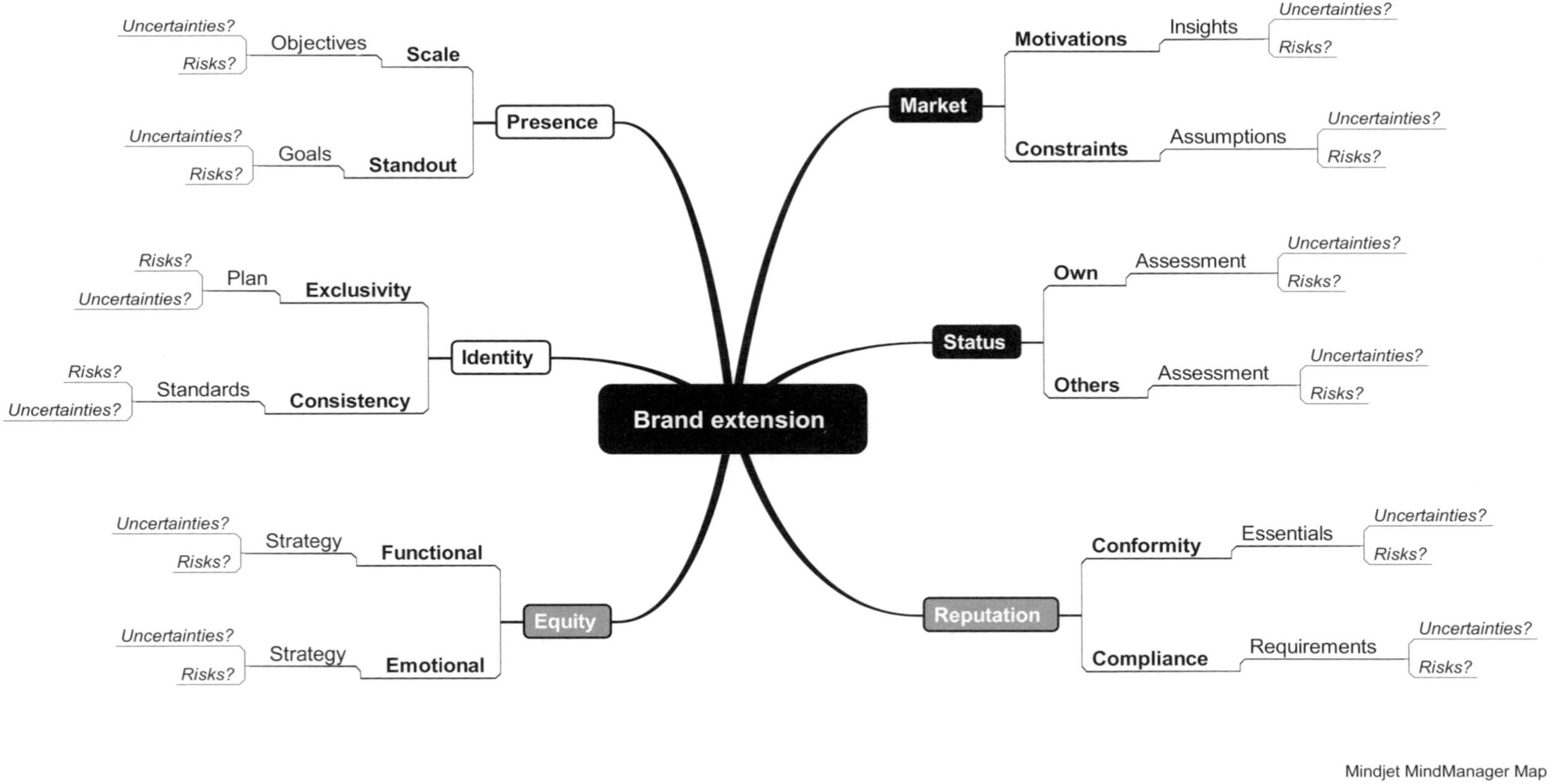

**Figure 2.4**     **Applying the risk model to a brand extension**

Mindjet MindManager Map

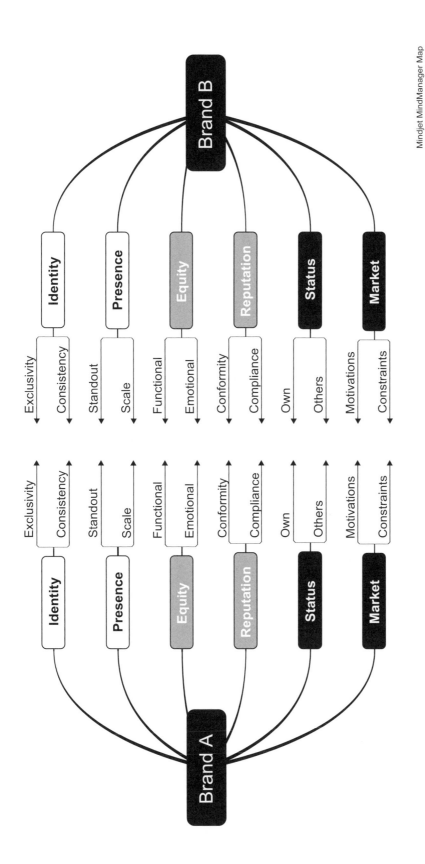

Mindjet MindManager Map

**Figure 2.5**    **Comparing two brands for risk**

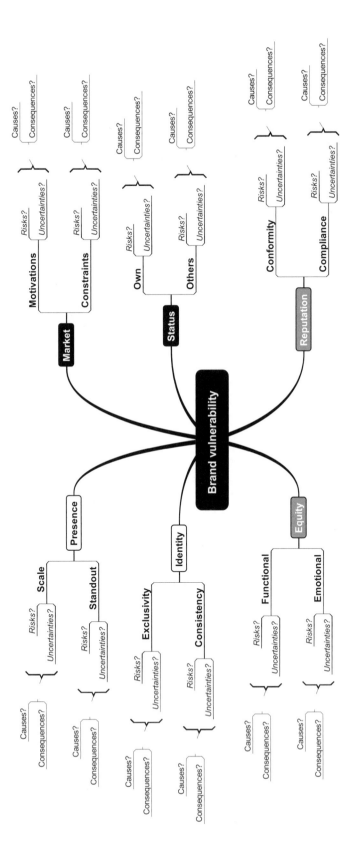

**Figure 2.6    Assessing brand vulnerabilities**

Mindjet MindManager Map

Figure 2.7 provides an alternative operational view of brand risk. In the vertical dimension of the diagram, brand value arises from the brand's response to market conditions (brand strategy). The risk to brand value is represented in the horizontal dimension of the diagram by its two key categories: erosion and catastrophe. A brand can weaken over time or fail suddenly. A combination of the two is the 'creeping catastrophe' we referred to earlier, when causes of erosion reach a tipping point and crisis ensues.

According to this operational view, there are four fields of brand risk and its management:

1. *Delivery* – processes that ensure consistent presentation and fulfilment of the brand and its promise.
2. *Renewal* – processes that align the brand promise with changing demand.
3. *Protection* – strategic actions to build goodwill and reduce potential scale of impact.
4. *Response* – tactical readiness for effective crisis management.

The following discussion provides an initial aid to exploration in these four key areas.

## DELIVERY

Use your understanding of the brand's equity elements and performance standards to check that your operations will deliver consistently on the brand's overall 'promise' to its customers and other stakeholders. For each component of the brand promise, assess the key processes and capabilities that will ensure sustainable fulfilment. Do not forget the special risks posed by outsourcing. In service delivery, identify the 'moments of truth', the occasions that arise during the provision of a service which act to confirm or disconfirm the brand's claims and

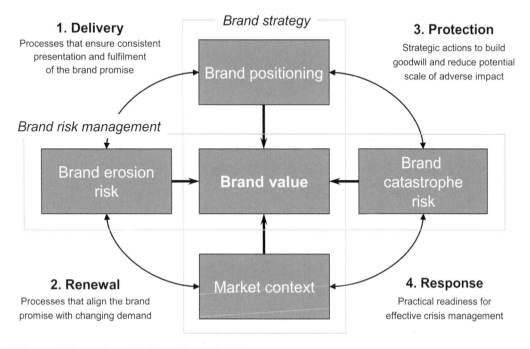

**Figure 2.7    Four fields of brand risk management**
*Source: Author and Paul Hinton, reproduced by permission of Marsh Ltd*

values. The obvious ones include the major steps such as order-taking and final delivery, as well as the handling of customer enquiry or complaint. Where the service is delivered in the presence of the customer, such as in restaurants or hotels, this attention to detail may need to extend to 'defining gestures': the appropriate characteristics of individuals' behaviour and mannerisms (for instance, consistent anticipation of a customer's needs before being asked or a handshake and smile on arrival).[28] Pringle and Gordon (2001)[29] identify the common absence of recruitment criteria that adequately specify applicants' required aptitude for delivery of a particular 'brand experience'.

Expect some key aspects of your brand to describe the experience of dealing with your organization as a business partner or of belonging to it. Remember also that if employees do not know what the brand promise is, they will find it harder to deliver. Company-approved blogs by employees require a transparent and sensitive balancing of interests.

Always supplement financial measures of a brand's recent performance (share of market sales and profits) with non-financial indicators, so that you are able to act on a deeper qualitative problem sooner rather than later. For example, Ambler (2003) has suggested a set of general measures that can be supplemented by further investigation into specific causes and effects as appropriate (Figure 2.8).[30]

## RENEWAL

Stakeholders' needs and expectations will evolve with time. An organization that is not in touch with these changes will find that the power of its brand steadily erodes. Knowing when and how to revitalize your brand is important. Some core equity elements may never need to change, even if the style and tone of their communication needs refreshment. Repositioning work that sets out to 'energize' a brand but does not take full account of this complexity may risk upsetting the balance of elements: 'In general, it is best to build upon existing associations, or even to create new ones, rather than to change or neutralize existing ones.'[31] Aaker (1991)

| | |
|---|---|
| ❑ **Familiarity** | Salience, i.e. familiarity relative to other brands in the consideration set |
| ❑ **Penetration** | Number of customers or the number of active customers as a percentage of the intended market |
| ❑ **What they think about the brand** | Brand preference as a percentage of preference of other brands within the consideration set or intention to buy or brand knowledge |
| ❑ **What they feel about the brand** | Customer satisfaction as a percentage average for the consideration set |
| ❑ **Loyalty** | This may be behavioural (share of category requirements, repeat buying, retention, churn) and/or intermediate (commitment, engagement or bonding) |
| ❑ **Availability** | Distribution, e.g. weighted percentage of retail outlets carrying the brand |

**Figure 2.8    Non-financial brand measures**

*Source: Ambler (2003)*

also warns against the temptation of abandoning an attribute just because it has low ranking in a hierarchy of attributes. If such a low-ranking attribute discriminates (differentiates meaningfully) between the brand and its competitors, the attribute may be worth retaining and promoting: 'There may be something hidden that makes it more influential than it appears it should be.'[32]

Check the effectiveness of your forward-looking processes, change management or innovation capabilities. Are there sufficient resources to meet known renewal objectives? What are the identifiable risks to their achievement? Aaker (2002) warns that even strong brands make the error of over-promising when trying to break the bonds of their current niche.[33] Where necessary, use dependency models to identify critical contributors to brand fulfilment throughout the organization (see Chapter 6).

On the broader front, is your organization's culture sufficiently open that it can acknowledge fundamental threats to your current way of doing business? Ensure that the organization keeps up with changing expectations in reporting on brand performance to shareholders (and other constituencies) or in communicating about the wider social, ethical and environmental impacts of your operations.

## PROTECTION

There are a number of key measures to protect your brand that may improve its immunity to attack or reduce the likelihood of its impairment. Look particularly for gaps between the organization's newly stated aims or claims and its corresponding actions. This is a common cause of reputational exposure.[34]

Invest in an open and ongoing relationship with the local or national media. Ask yourself whether your reputation would survive wide reporting of your activities ('the Press test'). For example, have we unreasonably transferred a cost of our activity to others? Are there substantial risks to others arising from our activity that they are unaware of? What precautions would our customers and other constituencies reasonably expect us take on their behalf? Have we taken them?

It is important to recognize that word of mouth has become much more significant as an influence since the 1970s, because blogs, forums and websites provide such an engaging means of dissemination.[35] There is evidence that reducing negative word of mouth can have a greater positive impact on sales than an equivalent increase in positive word of mouth.[36] Establish a continuous monitor of relevant external developments, including the concerns of special interest groups that may justifiably (or unjustifiably) affect stakeholders' perception of you and your brands.

Risks to your customers and business partners may well be risks to you. Develop a structured insight into their exposures and act to reduce those that have the ability to affect your brand. Transfer risk through insurance where this is available and appropriate, but do not expect conventional insurance to indemnify you against normal business risks.

Take expert advice on the enforceability of your trademarks and internet domain names.

## RESPONSE

Prepare for the worst and the unforeseeable. When brands fail, companies are often taken by surprise. Ensure that your business continuity plan includes a crisis communication programme that continuously manages the flow of news and keeps all those affected fully informed from the outset. Rehearse the plan regularly, especially when internal or external developments may have increased the likelihood or impact of an incident.

Understanding your brand and the nature of brand risk is the first step towards protecting your brand from possible failure – and towards improving its value performance in the process.

# Brand valuation

In common with any productive asset viewed from a financial perspective, the value of a brand depends on its ability to deliver incremental profits at an acceptable level of risk. We need to consider the role that valuation can play in the risk management of brands.

## HISTORY

In 1988, a milestone in the financial history of brands, two major UK corporations, Grand Metropolitan and RHM, first used brand valuations to dispel ill-founded perceptions of financial impairment. Following their large expenditures on brand acquisition, both companies had been obliged by the accounting standards of the day to write off the substantial goodwill elements involved, with consequent distortion of their balance sheets. Valuation of the brands, involving an analysis of their sustainable returns in proper context, successfully demonstrated that the write-offs were misleading.

Since that time, it has become possible in the United Kingdom to recognize acquired brands separately on the balance sheet, at their acquisition cost or less. Current opinion is tending not to favour an extension of this principle to brands that an organization has developed itself or has owned historically. Nevertheless, the regular appearance of proprietary brand valuation surveys has contributed greatly to a wider awareness of the importance of brands in wealth creation. For example, Interbrand has presented its annual league table of global brand values since 1994. Derived from a proprietary analysis of publicly available data and published in association with *BusinessWeek* magazine, the 2007 table identified 100 brands each having a value in excess of $3 billion and ten brands with values exceeding $23 billion (Figure 2.9).[37] In a similar study undertaken by Brand Finance (2006), the consolidated brand value of ten leading banks was estimated at $201 billion.[38]

## METHODOLOGIES

It is generally said that there are four possible approaches to the valuation of a brand:

- cost of creation
- market price
- royalty relief
- economic use.

The first three approaches are commonly regarded as a means of adding perspective to valuations produced by the 'economic use' method, which has found the widest acceptance and in practice offers the most insight into the brand concerned.

| Rank | Brand | Country of origin | Sector | Brand value (MM) |
|------|-------|-------------------|--------|------------------|
| 1 | Coca-Cola | US | Beverages | $65 324 |
| 2 | Microsoft | US | Computer software | $58 709 |
| 3 | IBM | US | Computer services | $57 091 |
| 4 | GE | US | Diversified | $51 569 |
| 5 | Nokia | Finland | Consumer electronics | $33 696 |
| 6 | Toyota | Japan | Automotive | $32 070 |
| 7 | Intel | US | Computer hardware | $30 954 |
| 8 | McDonald's | US | Restaurants | $29 398 |
| 9 | Disney | US | Media | $29 210 |
| 10 | Mercedes | Germany | Automotive | $23 568 |

**Figure 2.9     Values of global brands 2007**

*Source: Interbrand (2007)*

## Cost of creation

The cost of creation approach restates the original costs of launching the brand at current values or estimates the current cost of re-creating the brand. However, the cost of building a brand does not in itself give any indication of the value it creates. In particular, the method is not considered suitable for well-established brands.[39]

## Market price

The market price approach estimates the value of a brand by looking at the prices paid to acquire comparable brands, whether they were purchased in isolation or as part of a larger corporate transaction. This approach tends only to be relied upon as a sense check, because it is often difficult to find equivalent brands as a basis for sound comparison.

## Royalty relief

The royalty relief approach is based on the hypothesis that if the firm did not own its brand (or brands), it would have to pay someone else a royalty to use them. Since the firm actually owns the brand, it is 'relieved' of the burden of paying royalties and this cost avoidance becomes a measure of the brand's value.

The method first takes an estimate of future annual sales and applies a selected royalty rate to these projected revenues. Evaluation of the brand's qualities and performance relative to competition helps to select the most appropriate royalty rate within the relevant category range. The forecasting time-frame used is typically five years, with an added annuity based on the final year's earnings to take account of the brand's survival beyond the forecast period. This first step in the valuation process produces an amount of forecast income theoretically attributable to royalty payments which have (in effect) been 'avoided' by reason of brand ownership. The annual flow of these royalty payments is then discounted at an appropriate rate to calculate a net present value for the brand.

The royalty relief method is able to draw on information in the public or private domain on actual royalty rates negotiated in brand licensing transactions. In the United States there is a legal obligation to register certain details of licensing arrangements as a matter of public record. Where available, these data provide a further objective basis for determining the range of royalty rates that is relevant to a particular category and regional market.

## Economic use

For profit-making businesses, the notional value of the brand is the premium that results from its ability to charge higher prices than comparable competing products or to secure greater market share at price parity. The favoured technique to arrive at this value is known as the 'economic use' approach. This methodology applies discounted cash flow analysis to a multi-year financial forecast, from which all but the brand's incremental contribution to earnings has been removed. A risk-adjusted discount rate is used to arrive at a net present value for the brand's isolated financial contribution over time. It is the more demanding approach of the four acknowledged methods and is also the one more commonly used in combination with other methods to arrive at sensible 'cross-cut' valuations. The process is summarized in Figure 2.10.

As in the case of royalty relief, the process requires an estimate of future branded sales, typically over five to ten years. It also requires estimation of an annuity to represent a period beyond the final year of forecast, on the assumption that the brand will survive well beyond the valuation time-frame.

Having established that the forecast is reasonable, the next step is to isolate the incremental cash flows solely attributable to the brand. Proprietary approaches may differ in their refinements and data sources, but they generally involve a three-stage process. In the first place, all operating costs, charges and a notional return on tangible assets employed

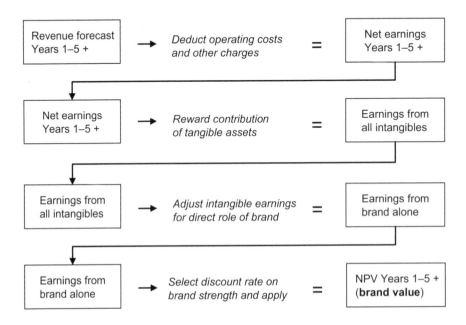

**Figure 2.10    'Economic use' brand valuation**

are deducted from the forecast branded revenues in each year. The subtraction produces an earnings figure representing the contribution of all the intangibles involved, including the brand, but also reflecting the part played by associated patents, licences and commercial or other technical skills.

Once these total intangible earnings have been identified, a 'role of brand' analysis sets out to determine what proportion of these earnings is properly accounted for by the power of the brand alone. The aim is also to exclude other influences or constraints on brand selection in the category. For example, in preparing its annual valuation study of the top 100 global brands, Millward Brown Optimor draws on its established brand equity research database (BRANDZ*)[40] to filter out effects such as market sector commoditization, distortions arising from availability, purely functional advantage or customer switching cost (spurious loyalty).[41] Lindemann (2007) provides some illustrative benchmarks for the role of branding in a number of categories: perfumes (95 per cent), consumer electronics (70 per cent), financial services (40 per cent), hotels (30 per cent) and bulk chemicals (10 per cent).[42]

The third and final step is to discount the resulting forecast of brand-attributable earnings over time, to produce a net present value for the brand. This calls for selection of an appropriate risk-adjusted discount rate, which typically takes four considerations into account:

- the underlying 'risk-free' return rate demanded by investors in the relevant geography (for example, the ten-year government bond yield)
- an additional element for investors' equity risk on the relevant stock market (this being the added return investors demand for the extra risk of not investing in government bonds)
- an adjustment for the category-specific risk applicable in each case (for example, food markets being generally considered more stable and lower-risk than technology markets)
- a final adjustment to the average category discount rate according to the relative strength of the brand within the category (so that the long-term leader might typically be discounted at a lower rate than its recently introduced competitor, even if they had comparable revenue projections).

Figure 2.11 shows the factors used by Interbrand in assessing brand strength.

There has been a growing preference amongst some valuation practitioners to add perspective to the result of an economic use valuation by cross-checking with known royalty rates for licensed brand equivalents (or near-equivalents), as described earlier. This may not always be possible.

## CONSIDERATIONS

### Published surveys

However carefully constructed the model, an income-based or economic use valuation of brands calls for the exercise of judgement, at some point, to which the final outcome will be sensitive. The pursuit of accuracy is all the more challenging when valuations must be developed solely on the basis of the top-line information that a company puts into the public domain. The producers of the published global rankings of brand value acknowledge this challenge. They aim for a consistency of proprietary approach, so that their successive annual

---

*       BRANDZ™ is a trademark of Millward Brown.

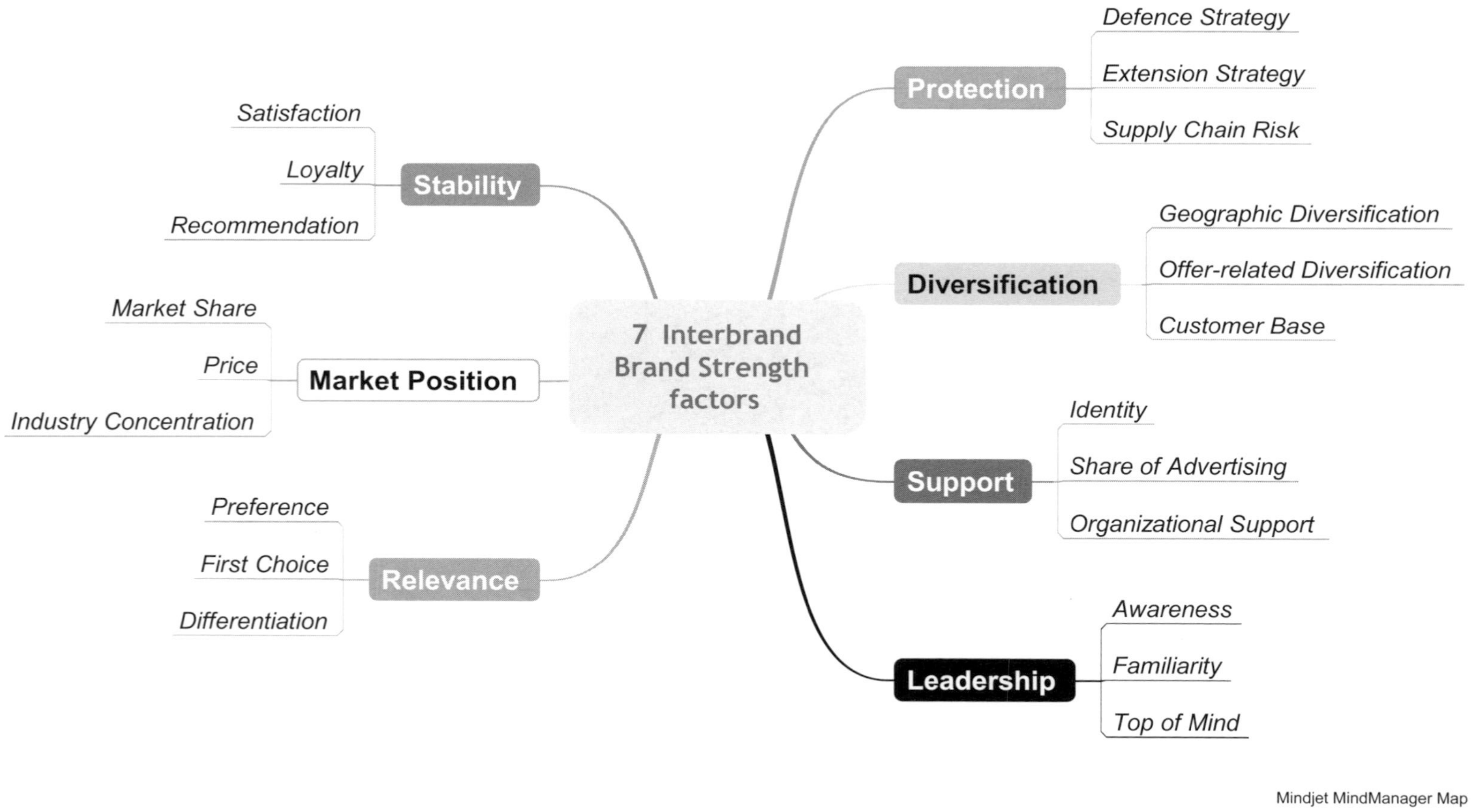

**Figure 2.11   Brand strength assessment in valuations**
*Source: Lindemann (2007)*

Mindjet MindManager Map

The mind map contains the following nodes:

**7 Interbrand Brand Strength factors** (central node)

- **Protection**
  - Defence Strategy
  - Extension Strategy
  - Supply Chain Risk

- **Diversification**
  - Geographic Diversification
  - Offer-related Diversification
  - Customer Base

- **Support**
  - Identity
  - Share of Advertising
  - Organizational Support

- **Leadership**
  - Awareness
  - Familiarity
  - Top of Mind

- **Stability**
  - Satisfaction
  - Loyalty
  - Recommendation

- **Market Position**
  - Market Share
  - Price
  - Industry Concentration

- **Relevance**
  - Preference
  - First Choice
  - Differentiation

valuations can be compared with sufficient confidence to provide insight into general trends and an opportunity to comment on the relative performance of the brands involved.

## Custom valuations

For practical purposes, many of the limitations of inaccuracy and lack of granularity in a standardized income-based analysis can be addressed by a custom valuation. This will be commissioned by the brand owner (or would-be owner) with a clear purpose in mind and conducted with full access to company data (or proprietary research) in addition to external sources of information. Most importantly, there is scope for discussion and agreement about the sensitivity of the economic use model to its inputs and about the sources of data applied in brand analysis (role of brand and brand strength assessment).

## Other dependent value

Although a valuation will indicate the brand's current worth in financial terms, it may still provide an incomplete picture of the value dependent on the brand. When a company loses a sale as a result of brand weakness, it is denied the whole value of the transaction, not just the brand earnings component identified through the valuation process. The cost of brand failure can therefore be higher than the valuation number suggests, with consequences felt throughout the profit statement or balance sheet. This is not a reason to disregard a sensible valuation, but to remember its context.

## APPLICATIONS AND BENEFITS

Operationally, valuation assists in the selection (or refinement) of relevant brand performance measures with an appropriate forward-looking component, both financial and non-financial. This can include analysis of return on brand investments. Equivalent approaches have been applied to not-for-profit brands, such as charities, where it is useful to develop a financial perspective on the brand's role as well as on its contribution to the achievement of the organization's objectives. Brand valuation is clearly of central importance in mergers or acquisitions. It has applications in licensing and in branded joint ventures. It plays a key role in intellectual property litigation and in tax matters where inter-company royalties are levied for brand use by affiliate companies.

Ambler (2003) concludes that the most reliable measure of a brand's performance remains its ability to shift economic demand *today*, coupled with an understanding of its identifiable strengths and weaknesses – which can include its sustainability or untapped potential.[43] Nevertheless, the due diligence and fresh perspectives associated with a carefully customized valuation should contribute to brand risk management.

## Due diligence

Valuation practitioners and their clients agree that the process of brand valuation is often much more useful for the commissioning brand owner than the single-figure outcome. The process typically involves full internal and external due diligence, a review of historical performance and a comparative review of market research. As a result, the process can be revealing and instructive:

- It requires segmentation of the various sources of profit and value, so helping to create insight into the business generally.

- It tests and records for future reference key assumptions about the brand and helps to challenge a short-term view of brand investment.
- It encourages recognition of further opportunities to exploit the brand as an asset and to develop its value over the longer term.

Beyond its benefits in due diligence, the process of brand valuation has further relevance to the goals we have identified for brand management:

## Recognition

A brand valuation naturally draws the attention of an organization to the relative importance of its brand(s) as a proportion of total enterprise value. This can fundamentally alter perceptions of the role and responsibilities of brand management and establish another basis of mutual understanding between the marketing and finance functions.

## Risk focus

Systematic assessment of risk and uncertainty is a key feature of an income-based valuation, because it affects the selection of the discount rate applied to forecast earnings. This assessment helps to promote a concept of marketing practice in which fulfilment of opportunity, risk mitigation and contingency planning go hand-in-hand. As a growing phenomenon, brand valuation has also created an incentive to explore the relationship between the concentration of value in the brand asset and the volatility of share prices. This is a field of ongoing work. For example, an analysis of the shares in the S&P 500 for 2005 identified that a higher proportion of intangible value or a greater role of brand were not only associated with higher investor returns but also higher stock volatility.[44] Without going so far as to claim correlation as cause from this analysis, Haxthausen (2007) highlights the shareholder perspective on brand risk mitigation:

> As companies refocus on activities that generate competitive advantage, they deliver higher returns to shareholders. But their risk profiles also change. On a risk-adjusted basis, these companies often don't deliver additional value to shareholders, because an increase in volatility has offset the increase in returns. The challenge is to better manage the intangible assets, to reduce the risk associated with them.[45]

This view follows Madden, Fehle and Fournier (2002), whose earlier study had, by contrast, identified higher returns but lower volatility in a portfolio of heavily advertised brands during the period 1994–2000:

> One implication of the present work is that we move toward a deeper understanding of brands within the framework of risk management ... 'Brand' is typically conceptualized as an asset to be valued, or worse still, an expense to be controlled – not a risk management tool to be employed within the firm.[46]

# Summary

We have now added the risk dimension to our understanding of brands:

- We have considered why and how a brand is more than a trademark or a reputation.

- We have proposed a general six-part model of brand risk.

- We have suggested a four-part framework for brand risk management.

- We have identified the connection between brand valuation and risk management.

We will now address behavioural aspects of risk-taking in business and their relevance to marketing.

# References

1   Willman, J. (2006), 'Valued Measure of Success', *Financial Times Special Report – Global Brands*, supplement to *Financial Times*, 3 April, p. 1.
2   Abrahams, D.J. (2002), 'Brand Risk', *The Marsh Topic Letter*, Number IX, Marsh Ltd.
3   Lindemann, J. (2007), *Brand Valuation: The Economy of Brands*, Interbrand.
4   Haig, M. (2003), *Brand Failures: The Truth About The 100 Biggest Branding Mistakes Of All Time*, Kogan Page Ltd.
5   Haig (2003), op.cit.
6   Nielsen BuzzMetrics (2007), 'BlogPulse™ Stats', 5 July, www.blogpulse.com.
7   Pringle, H. and Gordon, W. (2001), *Brand Manners*, Wiley.
8   Sull, D. (2006), 'Difficult Decisions for an Uncertain World', *FT Mastering Uncertainty Part 1*, supplement to *Financial Times*, 17 March, pp. 2–3.
9   Economist Intelligence Unit (2005), *Reputation: Risk of Risks*, The Economist Intelligence Unit, p. 2.
10  Economist Intelligence Unit (2005), op cit., p. 2.
11  Clifton, R. and Maughan, E. (2000), 'Introduction', in R. Clifton and E. Maughan (eds) *The Future of Brands: Twenty-Five Visions*, Interbrand and Macmillan Business.
12  Ambler, T. (2003), *Marketing and the Bottom Line*, FT Prentice Hall, p. 43.
13  Aaker, David A. (1991), *Managing Brand Equity. Capitalizing on the Value of a Brand Name*, The Free Press, p. ix.
14  Aaker (1991), op cit.
15  Aaker (1991), op cit.
16  East, R. (1997), *Consumer Behaviour – Advances and Applications in Marketing*, FT Prentice Hall, p. 133.
17  Podolny, J.M. (2005), *Status Signals: A Sociological Study of Market Competition*, Princeton University Press.
18  Blau, P.M. (1964), *Exchange and Power in Social Life*, Transaction.
19  Podolny (2005), op.cit.
20  Podolny (2005), op.cit.
21  Podolny (2005), op.cit.
22  Podolny (2005), op.cit., p. 255.
23  Podolny (2005), op.cit.
24  East, R., Hammond, K. and Wright, M. (2007), 'The Relative Incidence of Positive and Negative Word of Mouth: A Multi-Category Study', *International Journal of Research in Marketing*, Volume 24 (Issue 2), pp. 175–184.
25  Podolny (2005), op.cit.
26  Tripas, M. and Gavetti, G. (2000), 'Capabilities, Cognition and Inertia: Evidence from Digital Imaging', *Strategic Management Journal*, 21 (October–November), pp. 1147–1161.
27  McDonald, M., Smith B. and Ward, K. (2006), *Marketing Due Diligence: Reconnecting Strategy to Share Price*, Butterworth-Heinemann, p. 114.
28  Pringle, H. and Gordon, W. (2001), *Brand Manners*, Wiley.
29  Pringle and Gordon (2001), op.cit.

30  Ambler (2003), op.cit.
31  Aaker (1991), op cit., p. 157.
32  Aaker (1991), op cit., p. 149.
33  Aaker, David A. (2002), *Building Strong Brands*, Free Press Business.
34  Zaman, A. (2004), *Reputational Risk – How to Manage for Value Creation*, FT Prentice Hall.
35  Matthews, R. (2007), 'How to Work a Rumour Mill', *Financial Times*, 28 June.
36  Marsden, P., Samson, A. and Upton, N. (2005), *Advocacy Drives Growth: Customer Advocacy Drives UK Business Growth*, London School of Economics and The Listening Company.
37  Interbrand (2007), *All Brands Are Not Created Equal: Best Global Brands 2007*, Interbrand in association with BusinessWeek.
38  Brand Finance (2006), *Global 100 Banking Brands Index: An Annual Review of the Top Banking Brands in the World*, November, Brand Finance plc.
39  Lindemann (2007), op.cit.
40  Millward Brown Optimor, http://www.millwardbrown.com/Sites/Optimor/Content/Knowledge Center/BrandzRanking2007.aspx.
41  Dorffer, C. (2007), 'Brand-Driven Shareholder Value Creation', *European CEO*, May–June, pp. 47–49.
42  Lindemann (2007), op.cit.
43  Ambler (2003), op.cit.
44  Haxthausen, O. (2007), 'Risk Jockey', *Marketing Management*, March–April, pp. 35–38.
45  Haxthausen (2007), op.cit., p. 36.
46  Madden, T.J., Fehle, F. and Fournier, S.M. (2002), 'Brands Matter: An Empirical Investigation of Brand-building Activities and the Creation of Shareholder Value', working paper, Harvard Business School, p. 24.
47  Ambler (2003), op.cit.

# Snakes and Ladders

## MARKET RESEARCH

### Identify Key Uncertainties and Assumptions in the Brief

Researchers – and the recruiters of respondents – always need a brief that gives them a profound understanding of research objectives. It is not enough simply to give the agency details of a new product concept and a concise definition of its intended customer segment. Particularly if there has been no previous round of qualitative research, the brief must provide reasonable insight into all important assumptions and hypotheses. By definition, these are the uncertainties that the research should be aiming to explore. If the research team lacks this awareness, there is a real possibility that the research will be biased or inadequate, whether in questionnaire design, recruitment of respondents or reporting.

### Do Not Assume that Measurements are Comparable

When brand data sets are compared, it is not uncommon that the measures turn out to be inconsistent, for example in terms of underlying segmentation or time periods covered.[47] Since conclusions may then be misguided, it is always worth checking that data can legitimately be compared.

### Ensure that Someone Who Conducted the Research Presents It

Since a presentation of research results will affect business decisions, one or more of the practical researchers on the team must be in the room – no matter how senior the client audience. This becomes vitally important when findings are ambivalent and therefore risky. At such times, a client requires and deserves the highest degree of transparency and well-informed advice in their interpretation of output.

### Always Check that Conclusions are Consistent with Detailed Findings

There can be a degree of well-intentioned rhetoric in research report writing. A wise client therefore:

- reads the questionnaire or discussion guide before the presentation of results and attends some of the focus groups, if there are any

- insists on a complete set of unedited verbatim quotes from respondents

- looks at the detail behind averaged numbers that are central to interpretation

- requests that all charts show absolute sample sizes, not only the percentage splits, reducing the temptation to draw spurious conclusions based on small numbers

- asks 'What's the filter?' when presented with any slicing of data that has led to a research conclusion. It can be important to know (and not assume) what parameters have been included or excluded when data are interrogated or segmented.

### Be Clear About the Sensitivity of Quantitative Scales

An audience of decision-makers (particularly one of non-marketers) needs a prior appreciation for the statistical significance of quantitative findings, bearing in mind considerations such as sample size and the assessment scales used. This is an important matter for case-by-case determination. For example, if it is true that people rarely give top marks or '10 out of 10' in a questionnaire, a respondent rating of 'excellent' may be represented by an apparently lesser outcome in the range 8.0–8.6. Similarly, a small move in the data may signal worthwhile progress, especially in stationary and mature markets.

# **3** *Learning to Take Risk*

So far we have been looking at risk from the corporate and brand perspectives. The third perspective is a behavioural one: how we perceive risk and how we act on those perceptions.

In this chapter we will:

- suggest why it is helpful to learn to take risk
- review typical attitudes to risk and their implications
- describe some common risk behaviours in decision-making
- consider the challenges of learning from failure.

## Why learn?

To marketing people not yet familiar with risk management, it is easy to assume that its focus is predominantly one of risk avoidance rather than risk optimization. The former strategy would have you take no risk at all. The latter starts from a premise that there is no reward without risk. The challenge is to get the identifiable balance of risk and reward right, consciously, whether in strategic, operational or financial terms. To counter the narrow view, risk management professionals draw an analogy between their function and automotive brakes. On the face of it, they concede, brakes were invented to make cars slow down and stop. But they suggest a wider and more positive interpretation: that a set of well-maintained brakes makes it possible for you to drive your car faster and go to places where you could not otherwise venture. By extension, acquiring risk literacy is learning how to take risk, not simply avoiding it.

In the early pages of this book, we argued that risk-taking is what marketers generally and legitimately do. Since many marketing applications of risk thinking are in strategic and tactical decision-making, we have also argued that a marketing strategy should be complemented by a risk strategy (or an explicit risk component of the wider strategy) that identifies the key risk-related choices and assumptions being made (see Chapter 1). Risk literacy is finally a matter of making *better-informed judgements* about risk or uncertainty, supported by concepts and techniques that create useful insight and suggest an appropriate practical response. Such judgements invariably involve both our attitude to risk (personal and corporate) and the application of experience (direct or indirect). Learning to take risk ought therefore to involve induction in three areas and in the order suggested here:

1. an appreciation of the human factors at work in risk-taking;
2. a familiarization with conceptual frameworks suitable for risk assessment, in conjunction with the terminology that applies;
3. a selective introduction to methodologies for more structured modelling of risk (usually quantitative or semi-quantitative), including some useful approaches that may require an amount of specialist support in use.

# Human factors

It is helpful to start on the path towards risk literacy with a review of the human factors associated with risk-taking, before considering the other concepts and techniques that we shall be going on to review. It may prompt you to reinterpret your own experience of risk, adding a degree of self-awareness to the way you think about risk in general and some risks in particular. An understanding of human factors will also improve your sensitivity to the decision-making styles you encounter in others.

Another practical reason for considering human factors at the outset is that they are relevant to the way people apply the risk assessment tools and techniques that we shall be going on to review. A number of these tools accept subjective input and all of them require thoughtful interpretation of output. It is as well to be introduced to these risk assessment methodologies after acquiring an appreciation for some of the 'psychological' issues associated with their use. To adapt a famous phrase: where evaluation of risk is concerned, 'chance favours only the prepared mind'.[1]

There are two particular aspects of risk perception that should interest marketers. The first is how human psychology influences the way in which we apply our experience when decisions are not clear-cut, when information is incomplete and data absent. The second is how individuals and teams can best learn from experience – their own and that of others – especially when things have not gone according to plan. We need to consider how subjectivity influences the interpretation of facts and the drawing of inference. These influences naturally arise when we contemplate risk and uncertainty.

## RISK ATTITUDE

It is a familiar idea that different people will interpret the same facts differently. In conversation we will often hear it said that 'So-and-so is a glass-half-empty person', by which we mean that they tend to be naturally pessimistic rather than optimistic in a given situation or when confronted with a choice involving uncertainty. In risk management we need to explore these differences of interpretation more deeply. People's attitude to risk (or 'response to uncertainty') has a natural influence on the way they perceive opportunity, as well as the attention they pay to the assessment and proper management of risks.[2] Importantly, organizations also have risk attitudes, borne of their culture, experience, strategic choices and the personality mix of those who make the decisions, influenced by outsiders such as investors.

An essential point about risk attitude is that it is a perception of reality, not reality itself:

> *Risks are not concrete entities like computers or motor vehicles, which can be studied largely without subjective bias. Risks cannot be measured in objective, unambiguous terms, for any assessment of them is based on perceptions that are neither neutral nor value free.*[3]

It is therefore no surprise that individuals are not always consistent in their attitude to risk and may not even conform to a single stereotype at a particular moment. Different people and different organizations may perceive the same risk or uncertainty in different ways at different times and behave accordingly. A person's normal attitude to risk can be affected by circumstance to produce a reaction quite out of keeping with their characteristic behaviour. This is especially so when circumstances are unfavourable or hostile.[4]

Perception of risk alters according to the potential returns and the existence of alternative courses of action. But the resulting choices may not always appear rational. For marketers involved in risky new product developments, the way in which individuals and teams act in the face of irrecoverable project costs ('sunk cost') is an important demonstration of how risk-taking behaviour departs from standard rational theory.[5] It is not only pride which inhibits the exit alternative when a project runs into difficulty and makes marketing managers reluctant to accept the judgement that an attempted turnaround is not worthwhile.

## Risk attitude spectrum

People's attitudes to risk lie along a continuum. At one end, there are those who enjoy taking risks; at the other end, those who prefer to avoid them. Leaving aside the extremes of risk paranoia and risk addiction, a four-point classification is conventionally used to characterize (if oversimplify) the typical risk attitudes and likely behaviours of both individuals and organizations. Strictly speaking, of course, we diagnose most reliably after the fact, because actual behaviour is the best indicator of relevant attitude.

The four types along the continuum are these:

- the risk-averse
- the risk-tolerant (the central majority)
- the risk-neutral
- the risk-seeking.

*Risk-averse* individuals tend to have more faith in facts and less confidence in speculation. They are usually pessimistic in quantitative projections, evidenced by their production of wide ranges in forecasting outcome, along with a focus on other indications demonstrating high uncertainty. They tend to emphasize the extent of potential downside, rather than its likelihood of occurrence. They are typically assiduous managers of risk, impatient to see exposures substantially reduced and often critical of existing risk management approaches. Consistent with their cautious attitude, the classic risk-averse individual tends not to be aggressive in pursuit of opportunity.[6]

*Risk-neutral* individuals are dispassionate about risk. In essence, risk-neutrals think in terms of 'return on risk', rather than risk in isolation. They accept risk in the short term if there is a longer-term justification for accepting the exposure. To that extent, risk-neutrals exploit risk and will manage it creatively and strategically to pursue opportunity and fulfil objectives.

*Risk-tolerant* individuals accept risk but, in essence, ignore it. Risk professionals are worried by risk-tolerants, because their composure means that they may not fully appreciate or manage the significant risks their business projects face.

*Risk seekers* are aggressive in their pursuit of opportunity, considering the risks to be part of the challenge. Forecasts and update reports are optimistic, with narrow ranges in quantitative projections, demonstrating confidence in assumptions and plans. Contrary to their risk-averse opposites, risk seekers tend to emphasize the low probability of downside events and outcomes. They will tend to use more short-cuts and make faster decisions. Risk seekers are not usually committed to proactive risk management, preferring to rely on contingency plans and existing processes.[7]

Figure 3.1 illustrates how risk-aversion and risk-seeking attitudes are similarly reflected in the behaviour of organizations. Note in particular how organizational expectation can affect the behaviour of individuals.

Among the most widely cited work in the field of risk attitude are the studies by Daniel Kahneman and Amos Tversky. These two psychologists demonstrated how difficult it was, even for the most sophisticated individuals, to make consistent and rational risk-related choices. In a well-known experiment, Kahneman and Tversky (1979)[8] offered their subjects a choice:

- they could accept a guaranteed payment of $3000, or
- they could gamble on an 80 per cent chance of winning $4000 and a 20 per cent chance of winning nothing.

Bear in mind that the subjects were not asked to risk any of their own money, so that under no circumstances could they have ended up worse off than when they started. The probability-weighted value of the gamble was $3200 (0.8 * $4000 + 0.2 * $0 = $3200). There was a risk of making nothing, but the gamble quite clearly offered a very good chance of making the full $4000. Nevertheless, 80 per cent of the participants opted for the safe alternative and took the guaranteed $3000.

Now Kahneman and Tversky applied the same mathematical probabilities to a prospect of loss rather than one of gain. This time they offered participants a choice between:

- a certain loss of $3000, or
- an opportunity to gamble on an 80 per cent chance of losing $4000 and a 20 per cent chance of losing nothing.

| | Risk–aversion | Risk–seeking |
|---|---|---|
| Risk thresholds | Low thresholds; reduce readily | High thresholds; resist pressures to reduce |
| Financial objectives | Low targets; no stretch goals | High targets; perhaps unachievable |
| Contingency budgets | High; increase readily if off-target | Underprovide and underspend |
| Employee risk-taking | Penalize employee risk-taking | Discourage time on risk management |
| Investments | Cautious; forego opportunity | Overconfident; risk-reward ratio unclear |
| Portfolio management | Prefer low risk and low return | Prefer high risk and high return |
| Strategic stance | Maintain status quo | Responsive stance; innovate |
| Risk management | Overinvest; conscientious | Underinvest; spend on fire-fighting or crisis |

**Figure 3.1   Influence of organizational risk attitude on strategic decisions**

*Source: Hillson and Murray-Webster (2005)*

When the tables were turned in this way, 92 per cent of participants decided to risk the 80 per cent prospect of a $4000 loss, because the gamble gave them a 20 per cent chance of avoiding the certainty of a $3000 loss.

The experiment, corroborated in subsequent work by Kahneman and Tversky and others, demonstrated a tendency for people to be risk-seeking when prospects of loss feature most prominently, whilst avoiding risk in a situation where a mathematically attractive gamble involves trading off a certainty of lesser value. In essence, Kahneman and Tversky had shown that prospects of loss have a more powerful effect on behaviour than equivalent prospects of gain. It is this 'asymmetry' that helps explain why individuals or groups find it so hard to abandon a failing project with a low chance of recovery, especially where they have been personally associated with the initial commitment and there is already a high sunk cost. It is far easier for a subsequent team to make the more rational evaluation, write off the sunk cost and stop the losses.

## Other influences

In the corporate context, the 'official' definition of success can affect managers' perception of risk and their willingness to take it. The budget as personal target is a good example. Budgets are the demon of the Beyond Budgeting Round Table, a thought-leading research collaborative committed to the abandonment of budgets as a management device. Hope and Fraser (2003) believe that unless managers are incentivized in ways that are independent of the biases of budget setting, and are rewarded according to relative measures of competitive performance, the delusions that result may be crippling.[9] In high-growth markets, for instance, it is quite possible for a manager to exceed a soft budget handsomely, yet fail to capitalize on a fleeting market opportunity that presents itself.

Whilst self-awareness coupled with a high emotional intelligence may enable some individuals to alter their instinctive attitudes to risk, Hillson and Murray-Webster (2005) note that situational factors are more likely to cause individuals to adjust their normal risk attitude in response to a particular risk or opportunity:[10]

- *Sense of expertise*. Situations where an individual or a group believes it has particular expertise may lead them to perceive a greater upside opportunity and take more risk than usual.
- *Perceptions of control*. Perception of risk can be 'net' as well as 'gross'. A risk-averse individual may find a known risk acceptable, if they believe that it can be effectively managed down or transferred to others.
- *Proximity in time*. Closeness in the perceived timing of a possible risk event can intensify perception of the exposure, whilst distance in time can diminish the sense of exposure.
- *Proximity to the person*. Perception of a risk can be altered by its possible impact on the risk-taker. An impact 'closest to home' is likely to be perceived the greater risk. For example, in the case of brand launch in a single territory of a region, the regional manager may perceive the risk as lower than does the local manager – even though they are both considering the same project. An individual may also take more risk if they do not expect to be in the same job throughout the life of the project.

Edinburgh Napier
University Library

## HEURISTICS

Our lives would be very difficult indeed if we were forced to make every decision from first principles. We are bound to fall back on experience and use intuition, short-cuts or rules of thumb when we lack any other basis upon which to reach a required decision. But many of us remain unaware of the influences at work on our powers of reason. Unfortunately, it also seems to be the case that our thinking is most likely to be open to systematic bias when the stakes are high.[11]

The short-cuts we use to reduce the burden of decision-making are known as 'heuristics' (pronounced 'hew-ristics') after the work of Kahneman and Tversky in the 1970s. Whilst heuristics are said to operate systematically, that is to say habitually, they exist 'in repertory' within a given individual and are deployed according to circumstance, quite often in combination. Reflecting different attitudes in different situations, rather than a consistent personality type, heuristics also influence groups of individuals coming to collective decisions. From political history we know only too well how individual reason can be subverted by the pressures of group loyalty or a charismatic leader. The same or similar 'groupthink' effects are common in business decision-making.[12] This raises important issues for organizations that need regularly to rely on the outcomes of team deliberation – whether at board level or within functions. The key insight here is that group decisions are quite often *not* representative of the sum of individuals' points of view.[13]

### Six prevalent heuristics

If heuristics play an inevitable role in the way we make complex choices, it is worth knowing what they are. Since heuristics operate subconsciously in most individuals and groups, they are hard to identify and correct. Awareness of the common heuristic traps can nevertheless help individuals and groups to challenge their thinking, even though unlearning instinctive responses is not a sure-fire process. The role of the team leader is important, in encouraging awareness and mitigating 'heuristic risk' to the extent possible.

Figure 3.2 names the six commonly identified heuristics. To consider each in turn:

- *'Availability'*. The availability heuristic ascribes increased influence to matters that are most easily recalled. This can give adverse events that are recent or more dramatic a larger significance in risk assessment than other exposures that may be objectively greater. Similarly, people often 'overweight' new marketplace information and overreact to it.[14] They also tend to accord greater significance to events with greater emotional impact. In the case of a crisis or disaster in the public eye, this greater 'availability' can arise because the media has given prominence and added drama to the facts. Similarly, people are also influenced more deeply by events that affect them personally. Yet another manifestation of the availability heuristic is that people respond more readily to well-defined and tangible risk events than to underlying or 'erosive' risks. In brand management, as elsewhere, this can lead to inadequate focus on preventive measures, with insufficient attention to causal data in which the vulnerability or the pattern of erosion might be evident.[15] In the classic cases, steady erosion of a brand is tolerated, year on year, until there is sudden crisis and the fog clears. Then suddenly everyone sees that the writing has been on the wall for some time, with chronic inattention perhaps exacerbated by a lack of market information or the frequent reallocation of brand responsibilities within the marketing team.

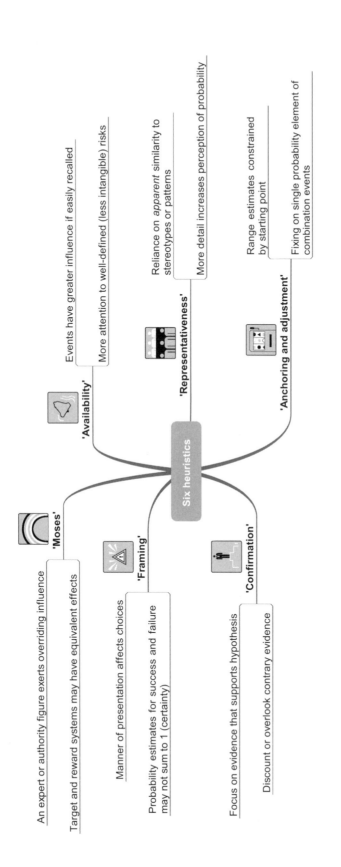

**Figure 3.2    Six prevalent heuristics**

'Moses'
An expert or authority figure exerts overriding influence
Target and reward systems may have equivalent effects

'Framing'
Manner of presentation affects choices
Probability estimates for success and failure may not sum to 1 (certainty)

'Confirmation'
Focus on evidence that supports hypothesis
Discount or overlook contrary evidence

Six heuristics

'Availability'
Events have greater influence if easily recalled
More attention to well-defined (less intangible) risks

'Representativeness'
Reliance on *apparent* similarity to stereotypes or patterns
More detail increases perception of probability

'Anchoring and adjustment'
Range estimates constrained by starting point
Fixing on single probability element of combination events

Mindjet MindManager Map

- *'Representativeness'*. The representativeness heuristic accords significance to the *apparent* similarity of a current issue to chosen stereotypes or patterns. The greater the apparent similarity, the stronger the assumption that previous experience will be a good indicator of an equivalent outcome in the current case. The difficulty here is that the stereotyping can lead to selective attention to those aspects of the current situation which most closely resemble the stereotype, potentially ignoring features of the current situation that might suggest a different outcome.[16] The heuristic therefore misleads you into assuming similarity on the basis of incomplete analysis. It can also lead you to the false conclusion that two situations share the same underlying causes, when this may not be the case. For example, what looks like a repeating and sustainable pattern of sales increase may not represent a new state of affairs, but a series of random or unrepresentative 'extreme' events that cannot be explained by recent marketing activity and will not be sustained. Conversely, the representativeness heuristic can persuade you that randomness itself will be self-correcting. If you believe that a process is random, you may look for evidence of randomness in a disjointed pattern of events, and assume that an unobserved event is becoming 'overdue'.[17] The heuristic can also affect our interpretation of strategic scenarios which present alternatives futures as the basis for present decisions. The more explicit and detailed a future scenario, the greater tends to be its assumed probability of fulfilment.[18] In fact, the laws of probability would suggest the opposite: the greater the number of uncertain details you add to a future scenario, the less likely it is to occur precisely as described. This is because the greater the number of coincidences that is required, the lower the probability of simultaneous occurrence. This example of representativeness also shows how heuristics can combine: in this case, the richness of detail in the scenario is enhancing its immediacy, so that it becomes more 'available' along the lines we have just reviewed.

- *'Anchoring and adjustment'*. The anchoring and adjustment heuristic is a common response to a difficult estimation task. Under this heuristic, people identify a range of possible outcomes by starting with a single figure and then estimate the potential variance either side of it. This has two misleading effects. Firstly, it accords the initial estimate a credibility which it may not deserve. For example, Goodwin and Wright (2004) refer to an experiment to test an anchoring influence, in which subjects were asked whether the mean temperature in San Francisco was higher or lower than 558 degrees![19] Secondly, the resulting range of possible outcomes is often too narrow, having been derived from the initial estimate. The more extreme but nevertheless legitimate values are ignored for no other reason than their distance from the number first elicited. A different demonstration of anchoring is the way in which people may estimate the probability of outcomes involving more than one event. There are two examples to consider: (1) the likelihood of alternative events ('probability of *either* Bad Thing A *or* Bad Thing B occurring') and (2) the likelihood of a combined event ('probability of Good Thing A *and* Good Thing B occurring'). The anchoring heuristic would lead people to fix on the individual probability of one of the chance events (for example, just A), rather than consolidating the probabilities in a mathematically correct way. The result is that the probability of combination events, such as successful completion of a multi-step project, tend to be overestimated, whereas the likelihood of alternative events occurring is underestimated.[20] In its various forms, the anchoring heuristic is said to be very difficult to overcome. Efforts to decouple one's thinking from an earlier single-figure estimate may serve only to reinforce the anchoring effect.

- *'Confirmation'*. The confirmation heuristic describes the tendency we have to spot the evidence that supports our own assumptions, whilst overlooking or discounting the evidence that does not. This is a common error in the interpretation of market research, for example, and the risk is self-evident. In general, the confirmation heuristic leads us to have an ill-founded confidence that the favourable outcome is more likely than the unfavourable one, even in the face of contradictory findings. The risk of falling into the confirmation trap can arise when there is uncritical reliance on a decision-support model ('garbage in, gospel out'). There are two complementary approaches that can help minimize confirmation traps. The first is to declare strict criteria for a decision upfront, so that there is somewhat less temptation to be selective in reviewing the evidence. The second approach is to reverse the burden of proof. The starting assumption is that the undesirable outcome holds true. Only when there is sufficient evidence to support the alternative, desired course of action is the decision made to proceed on that basis.

- '*Framing*'. The framing heuristic describes the influence of presentation on the choices people make. In other words, the way you ask the question affects the answer, even where the underlying realities remain the same. For example, a promotional effort for a brand will either succeed or fail to meet its objectives. These two outcomes embrace 100 per cent of the possibilities. Logically you would expect that separate estimates of probability for success and failure by the same individual would also sum to 100 (or 1, which is how 'certainty' is usually expressed in the language of probability). In practice, the framing heuristic disturbs this consistency. People frequently respond differently to the same question, depending on whether it is expressed in negative or positive terms. One additional observation, supported by the framing heuristic, is that when people ascribe probabilities to 'events', what they are really doing is ascribing a probability to a description of an event – even if the description is implied, unconscious or undeclared to others.[21] It means that differences in unexplored estimates of probability between individuals can be explained by the different 'movies' running inside their heads, rather than by their having made probability estimates for the same scenario. This can make discussion of risk events amongst colleagues before an attempt to reach consensus important for two reasons. The first is that everyone can contribute their particular insight and experience to an understanding of the risk; the second is that there is a greater chance that everyone is considering a comparable version of events.

- '*Moses*'. This biblically named heuristic accounts for the nature of conformist thinking by individuals, where an authority or an authority figure exerts an overriding influence. The decision-making process is subverted by a predisposition towards outcomes that will satisfy the values held by the influencer. The influencer can be a subject-matter expert or the boss, embodying a corporate philosophy ('We will only invest in markets where we are going to be #1'). An equivalent influence can also come about where a reward system encourages particular behaviours, or where an established 'way of doing things' constrains free thinking. Where substantial risk-taking is encouraged, there may be pressure on individuals to conform, without proper regard to foreseeable downsides, which might be considered 'negative thinking'. Conversely, a risk-averse management may discourage the marketing group from ever presenting a plan that had the potential to take a new market by storm. In common with the other heuristics reviewed here, the antidote is imperfect. Nevertheless, an attempt to counteract the Moses heuristic is worthwhile where feasible. For example, the influential leader of a decision-making group stands a better chance of receiving honest and well-considered recommendations from subordinate colleagues if the leader's own underlying attitude is declared upfront, at the same time as giving colleagues express reassurance of the leader's commitment to achieving a consensus view of the matter under consideration (even if a consensus-based decision may not follow).[22]

## Other decision models

In their comprehensive review of decision analysis, Goodwin and Wright (2004) identify a number of other heuristics that are often employed when people have to choose between alternatives under uncertainty:[23]

- *'Recognition'*. A heuristic which gravitates towards the familiar. People often come down in favour of an alternative they recognize, especially in fields where they lack confidence to make the decision on any other basis.

- *'Minimalist'*.[24] Assuming that the alternatives qualify through recognition, the choice is then finalized on the basis of a randomly selected attribute.

- *'Take the last'*.[25] Under this heuristic, people apply the same single criterion they used successfully last time, otherwise defaulting to a 'minimalist' tie-break, i.e. by picking another attribute at random.

- *'Lexicographic'* (or hierarchical).[26] This approach ranks attributes according to their importance and then makes a selection according to which alternative offers the most important attribute. Where two options both offer the most important attribute, the tie is broken according to which of the alternatives performs best on the second attribute. As Goodwin and Wright (2004) point out, this formula is 'non-compensatory'. It creates no scope for trading off performance in higher-ranked attributes for good (or better) performance in lower-ranked attributes.

- *'Semi-lexicographic'*.[27] An approach that establishes a margin within which key attributes are considered to be tied, so that the choice is made on the basis of the next-highest attribute. For example, a campaign manager could decide that reach was more important than frequency in a communication plan, but that the choice between two proposals within 5 per cent of each other on reach ought then to be determined by frequency. There is a problem with methodologies such as this one, which can lead to selection by reason of an 'order effect'. Since items have to be compared in pairs for the purpose of elimination, you can find yourself arriving at different results according to which pairs you begin with. This is an example of Condorcet's Paradox, described in 1785 by the French mathematician, philosopher and political scientist, the Marquis de Condorcet (1743–1794). In a logical analysis of majority voting, he showed how it would be quite possible for people to prefer candidates A to B, B to C, but C to A.[28] If you were to begin a process of elimination by comparing A to B, C would win. If you begin by comparing B to C, A wins.

- *'Elimination by aspects'*.[29] Alternatives are first of all eliminated if they fail to match a declared standard for the most important attribute. The remaining alternatives are finally reduced to a single winning option by applying the same elimination approach against each successive attribute. So, having eliminated some alternatives that failed to qualify on the most important attribute, the elimination process continues to its second stage by reference to the second most important attribute. As in a lexicographic selection, the weakness in this approach is that it provides no opportunity for trade-offs between attributes. Any compensating strengths on lower-ranked attributes would not save an alternative from elimination against a single higher-ranked attribute.

- *'Reason-based choice'*. A variant of the 'framing' heuristic described earlier. Here the decision-maker seeks to rationalize a decision by providing reasons for it. The heuristic problem arises because there is often inconsistency in the weighting of key attributes according to whether the question to be answered concerns acceptance or rejection. *Positive* attributes are given greater weight when deciding whether or not to *accept* something, whilst *negative* attributes are given greater weight when deciding whether or not to *reject* something.

- *'Satisficing'*. In many decision-making situations, there is time pressure or some other limit on completing an exhaustive search for the 'ultimate' solution. For example, there are only so many agencies you can invite to pitch for an urgent project, before feeling the need to pick one. The satisficing heuristic responds to dilemmas of this kind by selecting the course of action which meets a minimum requirement or aspiration, adjusted in light of the search experience ('It's true they've not done international work, but at least they're familiar with our category'). The theoretical shortcoming of the satisficing approach is that the order in which options arise determines selection. Unless the options reviewed up to that point have been representative of the full range of what is available (whether by accident or design), there may be preferable alternatives 'out there' which have not yet been considered when the decision is made.

## 'Groupthink'

All other things being equal, a group decision should reflect the richness of experience and perspective offered by the group's members. People are also more committed to a collective course of action when they have had some part in the deliberation. As we have already seen, one way of counteracting the heuristic bias in an individual's thinking is to involve others in the process. However, heuristics also exist that are specific to collective thinking. Groups tend to coalesce in a number of ways that dilute or repress the independence of thought that the individual members of the group are supposed to provide.

Thinking that is the product of a group dynamic and which subverts the critical thinking of individuals is known as 'groupthink'.[30] It most often shows itself when a group comes towards the end of its decision-making process. Group heuristics tend not to occur in isolation: there may be combinations of heuristics at work that reinforce or trigger others.

There are four particular manifestations of 'groupthink' that the risk-literate marketer should be conscious of:

- *'Conformity'*. Members of a group tend to abide by the group's accepted norms when coming to a collective decision. At first sight, this is an unsurprising feature of group behaviour. After all, good teamwork requires a degree of alignment. However, alignment has gone too far when it impairs critical thinking that would ultimately benefit the group. In practice, the 'gravitational pull' of corporate culture generally induces conformity of risk behaviour. If a firm's culture is risk seeking, then a project team's plan will usually be risk seeking, because that is the best way to secure approval and a licence to proceed. Even if some members of the group dissent initially, the pressure to reach consensus will gradually direct the group to make the conformist decision. Where there is no effective 'loyal opposition' within a group, it is more likely to reinforce its own prevailing attitudes, more likely to resist deliberate change and less likely to evolve in response to new challenges, especially those which require a fundamental review of underlying assumptions. Creating meaningful opportunities for uninvolved colleagues (or friendly outsiders) to critique a plan makes an important contribution to risk management. This often requires support by the risk-literate leaders and managers of the business. Without this support, the desire to belong and a fear of ostracism may conspire to reduce the candour and value of the exercise.

- *'Cohesion'*. Membership of a group is reinforcing. This reinforcement may improve morale at the expense of critical thinking, so that cohesive groups will not accept criticism implying the vulnerability of their decisions.[31] Negative or critical feedback will be neutralized.

> *One of the most common norms appears to be that of remaining loyal to the group by sticking with the policies to which the group has already committed itself, even when those policies are obviously working out badly and have unintended consequences.*[32]

  Even in the face of failure, groups will often hold beliefs that justify their collective actions and will tend to resist evidence contrary to their established perspective on reality.[33]

- *'Moses'*. We have already noted how this heuristic can account for conformist thinking in individuals, influencing their decision-making by explicit or implicit reference to expectations of an authority figure. The same applies to groups.

- *'Shifting'*. One fascinating characteristic of 'groupthink' is that collective positions can progressively become more extreme than the average attitude of its members, whether in risk-taking or in risk avoidance.[34] Depending upon the direction of movement, the phenomenon is either referred to as 'risky-shift' or 'cautious-shift'.

## Conclusion

Heuristics are a means by which individuals and groups cope with uncertainty and respond to reality. They are an inevitable feature of the way we think and co-operate. To the extent that they run the risk of blind-siding us, a degree of self-awareness will help us to decide when to touch the brakes and look to the left and right before we and our colleagues proceed.

Sometimes you will need to look back – and learn from failure.

# Learning from failure

Whilst defeatism is not a quality to be encouraged amongst marketers, it is important that people should find an effective way of learning from experience and applying its lessons in practice. This is a very important area of risk management. Not all mistakes are catastrophic and expensive, but some most certainly are. From a marketing management perspective, to learn from past failure or disappointment is to increase the probability that a comparable brand project will succeed. The obvious ideal is to identify unnecessary and avoidable errors or omissions before they occur, by consciously applying whatever hindsight is (or might be) available to us. Yet even though hindsight is perhaps 'one of our most important and most costly information sources', it is striking how often organizations and individuals appear not to learn as best they might from failure or near-failure.[35] All too often the reasons for operational or strategic failure seem to have been self-evident after the fact.

Unfortunately, experimental studies confirm that people do not enjoy learning from negative events, even when there is benefit for them in doing so.[36] According to Middlestaedt (2005), less than 10 per cent of 500 managers surveyed over a two-year period claimed to have undertaken *any* structured review of past decisions including forecasts.[37] As a consequence, object-lessons are likely to have gone unacknowledged and unlearned.

Case studies can be a great help. It is clearly less expensive to learn from other people's failures than your own. However, in situations where managers are unaided, they regularly fail to identify illuminating lessons of failure beyond their particular industries, irrespective of whether the circumstances of the case might be similar to their own.[38] This is partly a function of time and resources, but it is also a matter of *perception*. Managers make mistakes that they would plainly perceive to be mistaken in other contexts. They fail to recognize a pattern of errors or simply rationalize them away.[39] According to Ambler (2003), an apparently high failure rate of marketers who move from one sector to another also serves to reinforce a common view that marketing failures in other sectors have little relevance to one's own.[40]

The question is how we can make hindsight work harder for us in our assessment of risks to the brand and in our plans to address them. In particular, we need to consider the problem in an organizational context, where effective learning from failure does not happen automatically. Organizations (and their teams) need mechanisms for 'generalizing' their own experience and the experience of others, so that it can be prudently applied in future decisions.[41] Whilst powers of perfect prophecy are not on offer, there is evidence that a commitment to engage in systematic learning from failure is worthwhile. Toft and Reynolds (1997) provide a detailed study of organizational learning from adverse events.[42] The recommendations presented in this chapter draw substantially on their insights.

## PRACTICAL CHALLENGES

Regrettably, crisis is often the sole catalyst for attempts at fundamental review and commitments to real change. It seems that only disaster itself is certain not to be ignored. Even then, effective learning from failure is not easy, certainly not at the organizational level. It is invariably the case that the most dramatic organizational failures flow from a combination of technical and cultural causes.[43] This means that any serious attempt at learning from the experience requires that both sets of issues should be taken into account, something that is not easy to accomplish. Employees and the organization may be unable to explain what their culture actually is; individuals may be discouraged from being sufficiently candid. The personal and political influences on decision-making within organizations may be too difficult to discuss openly, unless a clear-cut breach of standards or public scandal make it safer (or mandatory) to do so.

For as long as they remain unaddressed, a number of other reasons can conspire to frustrate proper learning from hindsight in the corporate context:

- *No means of creating insight from bad experiences.* Learning from failure remains superficial if there is no systematic process for assessing what really happened and drawing useful conclusions. The immediately obvious errors or misjudgements can mask underlying root causes, which may require a more thorough review to reveal them. This is especially true because failure invariably arises for a combination of reasons, no single cause being sufficient to have caused the (system) failure that ensued.

- *Presumption of irrelevance.* As we have seen, the further removed from an adverse event personally, and the less emotional impact it makes upon them, the greater the tendency of individuals to discount the value to their organization of learning from it.[44] Failure is often ignored if those in authority believe that the failure was simply a case of bad luck or due to other external factors that they believe could not have been mitigated.

- *No means of dissemination.* A company is composed of individuals, each making decisions. Unless the company finds a reliable way of disseminating experience, there is nothing to stop similar processes elsewhere in the organization failing in the same way. Similarly, organizational learning evaporates all too easily as people leave.

- *Cultural resistance to change.* Valuable lessons can be identified in theory but ignored in practice. In some cases, the strength of an organization's culture can be a weakness in attempting to learn from experience. Organizations with powerful and focused cultures tend not to consider alternatives, so that they may resist challenges to the status quo. Hierarchical or consensual organizations may be defensive or slow to react to bad news.[45] There is evidence that the closer the misadventure to the accepted mission of the organization, the less likely it is that a disaster will result in a change of philosophy and related business practice ('These are the risks we are in business to take'). The experience is that only organizations 'whose cultural expectations have suffered the largest surprise' will undertake the more radical review of their operations.[46]

- *Modified definition of success.* Managers may reinterpret objectives or results to give the appearance of success, when the unalloyed facts may be rather different.[47]

- *Opaque decision-making.* It is clearly harder to develop insight into the circumstances leading to an unfortunate outcome, if the way decisions were made proves to be unclear. There may be a tendency for people to frustrate analysis of what truly occurred by adjusting recall of their own predictions with the benefit of expedient hindsight: the 'I-knew-it-all-along' effect.[48]

- *Fear of sanction.* Self-preservation being a powerful instinct, the fear of sanction can be a thoroughly effective disincentive to openness. Even an organization that believes in allowing employees 'permission to fail', understandably issues only a limited licence to do so. Apparent tolerance of error does not in itself ensure that the most serious omissions are comprehensively confessed.

- *Distance in time.* Finally, unless the lessons of a particular case have been embodied in new standard practices, people's awareness and sensitivity to the lessons of experience will diminish with time and the vital lessons will be forgotten.

## INCREASING PROBABILITY OF SUCCESS

A deliberate and sustained effort to improve the quality of hindsight achieved after unexpected failure can benefit an organization or a team in a number of different ways:

- It helps to identify the combined root causes of a particular failure as well as its triggering event(s). By addressing root causes, there is a greater possibility of avoiding comparable failures in future and improving performance across a wider area of activity.

- It encourages a habit of 'active foresight', so that there is a greater readiness to recognize latent errors as projects proceed and to respond more quickly in ambiguous situations.[49]

- It helps to reveal the significance of *behavioural* factors, including both the conduct of individuals and the extent of organizational influence (which could either have been too great or too small).

In order to secure these benefits, there are three useful steps to take. We will describe each of them in outline and then consider them in more detail.

1. *Avoiding classic pitfalls.* There are some commonly recognized but repeated causes of operational failure. These are failures of process or people or both. The likelihood of operational failure increases significantly if these classic pitfalls are present.

2.  *Organizations as 'systems'.* System thinking (a term we will define) can help us to get somewhat closer to identifying the nature of a complex failure and to specifying the context within which it took place.

3.  *Reviewing chains of events.* Organizations can generate valuable insights from failure, if they reconstruct the relevant chain of events and then add the benefit of hindsight to each significant act, fact or omission. Making this kind of commitment to assess failures may involve overcoming some cultural roadblocks that we will need to touch on.

## Avoiding classic pitfalls

Untoward operational events always have more than a single cause, although analysis of past cases suggests that there are some persistent contributors. Figure 3.3 lists a number of these by way of a cautionary checklist.[50] On the printed page, these classics may not seem novel or surprising to the experienced marketer. In practice, their implications are regularly glossed over or ignored.

The risk-literate approach to the problem is *systematically* to check for the existence of the common pitfalls, to assess their specific implications for the project in question and then to *follow through* by taking steps to address them. Judgement needs to be applied; the exercise will be easier said than done in some situations. However, little may be achieved without a conscious effort to take stock.

It is worth making a particular comment on rule-breaking, which includes failure to observe marketing best-practice recommendations. The existence of rules can create a false sense of security in the minds of managers. It is often clear after the event that chronic rule-breaking was a significant contributory cause of failure.[51]

Mittelstaedt identifies other warning signs of incipient error, which it would be equally sensible not to ignore (see Figure 3.4).[52]

## Understanding systems

Like marketing science, risk management is much concerned with cause and effect. At its best, risk thinking should go beyond identification of immediate causes ('proximate causes') and strive for an understanding of the wider context and other contributing factors. In short, risk thinking involves system thinking. Scientists refer to 'systems' when they describe the way in which elements or events, each contributing to a common outcome, behave differently in their current combination than if each were to be operating alone. The importance of such holistic insight has became central to much modern analytical thought, not least in the assessment of markets and customer behaviour, as well as in the evaluation of operational and behavioural risk.

In particular, system thinking recognizes that:

*   minor events within a system can provoke a significant chain reaction within the system as a whole

*   one component in a system may act in such as way as to modify other components

*   when a system fails, it may not be possible to identify a single precipitating event amongst the combination of causes.

A single issue or event may have no impact initially, but tip the balance to create catastrophe (or 'system failure') as the problem accumulates. Alternatively, a single action can create

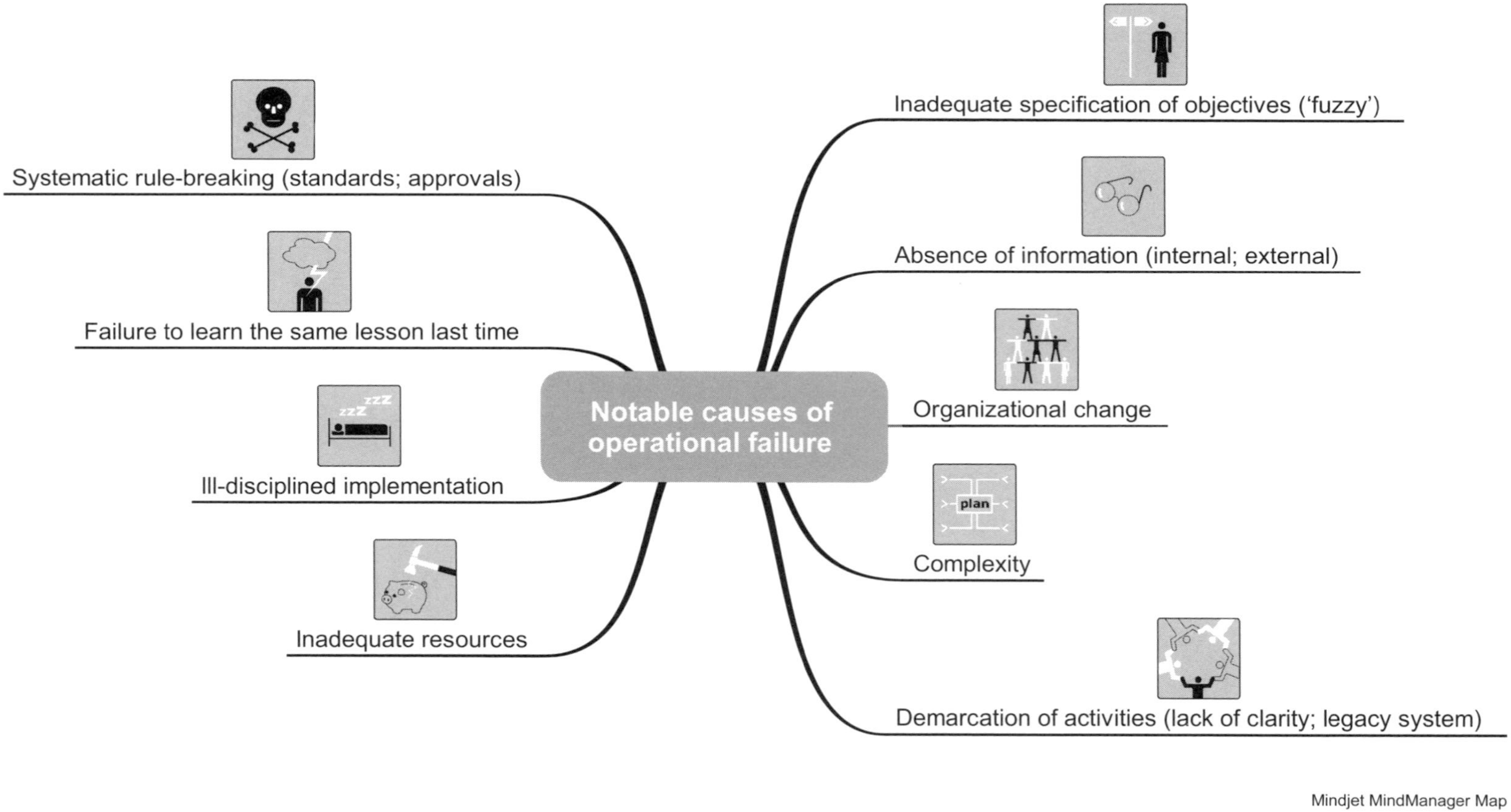

**Figure 3.3    Notable causes of operational failure**

*Source: After Toft and Reynolds (1997)*

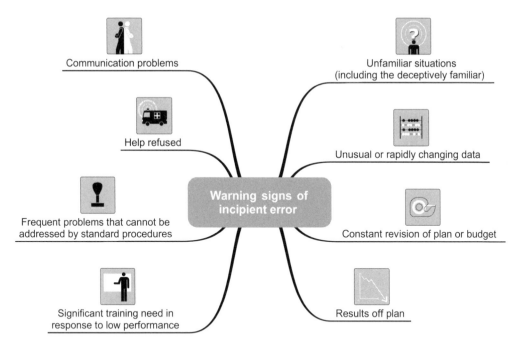

Mindjet MindManager Map

**Figure 3.4    Warning signs of incipient error**
*Source: After Mittelstaedt (2005)*

dormant or latent errors that go undetected until another triggering event occurs.[53] This is sometimes known as 'creeping catastrophe'.[54] For example, failure to monitor how a trademark is being managed by an overseas licensee may have no effects today, but vitally impair future efforts to enforce exclusive rights. The matter may not emerge until the relationship with the licensee comes under review for quite different reasons.

In a marketing context, there is also a useful distinction to be drawn between 'closed systems' and 'open systems'. A closed system is not connected to any other system, so that performance management need take no account of external influence. By contrast, an open system is always connected to the wider environment and so continues to be influenced by it. Generally speaking, any system that includes people will be an open one, such as a market and all the actors in it. This makes it impossible to predict local outcomes with absolute certainty, even though it may be perfectly reasonable and necessary in practice to attempt estimations. For a company, its 'system' comprises all of its functions, processes and resulting interactions. The unique properties of the system emerge from this combination of elements, reflecting the organization's distinctive set of culture, competence, strengths and weaknesses.

The characterization of a brand and its components in Chapter 2 is also a partial description of an open system. System thinking (by whatever name) helps marketers to project their imaginations into the worlds which their customers inhabit, so that needs and solutions, risk and opportunities, are all considered within an attempted model of the context. Since open systems cannot be controlled, it may be difficult to explain good and bad outcomes with precision. For example, a fashion brand might succeed or fail for reasons that we could not have predicted and cannot fully explain.

The Austrian-born biologist Karl Ludwig von Bertalanffy (1901–1972) developed the idea that any two systems with markedly different origins (for example, sociological and chemical) might still have much in common as systems, notwithstanding their evident differences otherwise.[55] The resulting insight has been extended into analysis of operational failure by Toft and Reynolds (1997). They show how two apparently different organizations in completely different industries can share modes of failure, provided they also share relevant characteristics *as systems* (technically known as 'organizational isomorphism').[56] The similarity of the relevant systems in the two organizations would suggest the possibility that a reported chain of events in the first organization might be replicated in the second at some future time, irrespective of the other differences between them. For example, the challenges of crew co-ordination in the cockpit of airliners may hold valuable lessons for business managers. Just as the negative effect of hierarchy on good communication between senior and junior pilots needs to be consciously addressed for flight safety, so the possible effects of an authority figure's influence should be taken account in the interpretation of market facts. (This is the 'Moses' heuristic we considered earlier.) Without going to extremes, it suggests that there is value in understanding our own organization – or a particular activity – as a system. The value lies in increasing our sensitivity to cases of 'system-equivalent' organizations in any field of activity, from which to draw object-lessons that will improve our own chances of success. In reviewing the reported facts of a story, the sort of questions to ask might therefore be: 'Do we rely on the same inputs or equivalent structures, processes or techniques? Could they fail in our case, so as to affect us in the same way?'[57] Pattern recognition is an important feature of analysis and learning.[58] As marketers we are accustomed to a literary diet of case studies that helps us to develop useful generalizations about brand strategy and tactics. These tend to accumulate in our minds as one-line rules of thumb. Helpful though these generalizations are, the heuristic that they represent may also lead us to miss some of the more elusive risk-related value to be extracted from a particular case. Appearances can deceive and assumed similarities may be spurious. Nevertheless, by consciously breaking out of conservative pattern thinking, to explore a wider range of validated patterns from other relevant or stimulating situations, we may be able to identify not only new exposures, but new opportunities.[59]

## Reviewing chains of events

Whilst acknowledging that no two events are exactly alike in every detail, Toft and Reynolds (1997) suggest a powerful (admittedly simplifying) device to model and interpret the chains of events that lead to failure.[60] Figure 3.5 illustrates the iterative approach in schematic form.

Insights are created by distinguishing between events or activities believed to be satisfactory or sound *before* the failure and those conditions which were hidden or only partially understood at that time. By clustering components of a completed schematic into logical event chains, suitably captioned for clarity, it becomes easier to see causes and effects and to draw meaningful conclusions with hindsight. The key is to undertake the process in three distinct steps:

1.  Establish the chronology, identifying any implicit or explicit assumptions that prevailed as events unfolded.

2.  Go back over the chronology, adding evidence of 'erroneous beliefs, assumptions, hidden events or poor practice' that become apparent after the event ('Revelations').[61] Look for insights from what occurred.

3.  Set down the vital lessons to be learned ('Hindsight') and the practical recommendations that flow from them.

**Step 1 – Establish chronology**

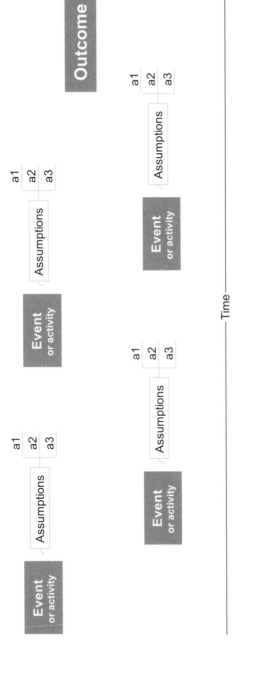

**Step 2 – Look for hindsight**

**Step 3 – Act on insights**

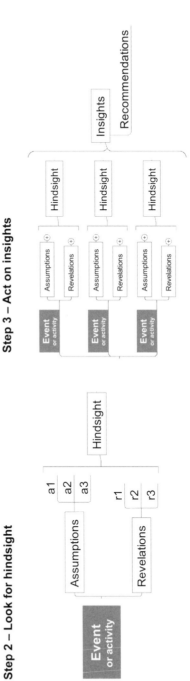

MindJet MindManager Map

**Figure 3.5    Reviewing chains of events**

*Source: After Toft and Reynolds (1997)*

The review of events may be helped along by considerations such as:

- the context within which activities were undertaken (business environment, culture, pressures, ambitions)
- how decisions were arrived at
- the degree to which risks were explicitly or implicitly assessed
- whether rules were, or were not, respected
- the extent to which signs of incipient failure were (a) present (b) perceived and (c) acted upon.

In common with all such exercises, a certain amount of revision and refinement may be necessary until the model achieves its ultimate clarity and insight.

## BEST WAY FORWARD

The best advice certainly argues against a permanent state of inquisition, but suggests that effective learning from failure in organizational contexts arises when, in policy terms:

- there is visible sponsorship and genuine interest from senior management (important, as ever)
- there are systematic post-implementation reviews of all significant projects (especially long-term capital projects, where the real lessons may not be clear without tracking back through the entire history)
- there is a willingness to apply resources to learning from near-misses, not just full-blown failures.

Where the right policies are in place, the most constructive and helpful hindsight is more likely to emerge when:

- there is an initial review only with those immediately involved
- there is importance given to preservation of original decision support documentation, not just internal 'pitch documents'
- there is recognition of what went well, not just what went badly
- there is positive recognition for the individuals who contribute openly and constructively to the process of learning from hindsight.

# Summary

We have considered some of the ways in which nature contrives to make people act inconsistently when they evaluate risky or uncertain courses of action:

- We have reviewed the human factors relevant to risk assessment, including the role of heuristics in decision-making under uncertainty.
- We have suggested that the most effective assessment of risk and opportunity should take account of systems not single causes.
- We have identified the features and benefits of efforts to improve hindsight.

In the next chapter we will develop our familiarity with different concepts of probability and risk.

# References

1   Generally (though not universally) attributed to the French scientist Louis Pasteur (1822–1895) during his address given on the inauguration of the Faculty of Science, University of Lille, 7 December 1854: 'Where observation is concerned, chance favours only the prepared mind.'

2   Hillson, D. and Murray-Webster, R. (2005), *Understanding and Managing Risk Attitude*, Gower Publishing Ltd.

3   Toft, B. and Reynolds, S. (1997), *Learning from Disasters – A Management Approach: Second edition*, Perpetuity Press, p. 1.

4   Hillson and Murray-Webster (2005), op.cit.

5   Bernstein, P.L. (1996), *Against the Gods The Remarkable Story of Risk*, John Wiley & Sons, Inc.

6   Hillson and Murray-Webster (2005), op.cit.

7   Hillson and Murray-Webster (2005), op.cit.

8   Kahneman, D. and Tversky, A. (1979), 'Prospect Theory: An Analysis of Decision under Risk', *Econometrica*, Volume 47 (Issue 2), pp. 263–292.

9   Hope, J. and Fraser, R. (2003), *Beyond Budgeting – How Managers Can Break Free from the Annual Performance Trap*, Harvard Business School Press.

10  Hillson and Murray-Webster (2005), op.cit.

11  Bernstein, P.L. (1996), *Against the Gods The Remarkable Story of Risk*, John Wiley & Sons, Inc.

12  Janis, I.R. (1982), *'Groupthink': Psychological Studies of Policy Decisions and Fiascoes*, Houghton Mifflin.

13  Hillson and Murray-Webster (2005), op.cit.

14  De Bondt, W. and Thaler, R. (1985), 'Does the Stock Market Overreact?', *Journal of Finance*, Volume 40 (Issue 3), pp. 793–805.

15  East, R. (1997), *Consumer Behaviour – Advances and Applications in Marketing*, FT Prentice Hall.

16  Hillson and Murray-Webster (2005), op.cit.

17  Goodwin, P. and Wright, G. (2004), *Decision Analysis for Management Judgment – Third Edition*, John Wiley & Sons Ltd.

18  Goodwin and Wright (2004), op.cit.

19  Quattrone, G.A,, Lawrence, C.P., Finkel, S.E. and Andrus, D.C., 'Explorations in Anchoring The Effects of Prior Range, Anchor Extremity and Suggestive Hints', unpublished manuscript, Stanford University.

20  Goodwin and Wright (2004), op.cit.

21  Shafir, E. (1993), 'Choosing versus Rejecting: Why Some Options are both Better and Worse than Others', *Memory and Cognition*, Volume 21 (Issue 4), pp. 546–556.

22  Goodwin and Wright (2004), op.cit.

23  Goodwin and Wright (2004), op.cit.

24  Gigerenzer, G., Todd, P.M. and the ABC Research Group (1999), *Simple Heuristics that Make Us Smart*, Oxford University Press.

25  Gigerenzer et al. (1999), op.cit.

26  Tversky, A. (1969), 'Intransivity of Preferences', *Psychological Review*, Volume 76, pp. 31–48.

27  Tversky (1969), op.cit.

28  Condorcet, Marquis de (1785), *Essai sur l'application de l'analyse à la probabilité des décisions rendues à la pluralité des voix.*

29  Tversky, A. (1972), 'Elimination by Aspects: A Theory of Choice', *Psychological Review*, Volume 79, pp. 281–299.

30  Hillson and Murray-Webster (2005), op.cit.

31  Goodwin and Wright (2004), op.cit.

32  Janis (1982), op.cit.

33  Mintzberg, H, Ahlstrand, B. and Lampel, J. (1998), *Strategy Safari: The Complete Guide Through the Wilds of Strategic Management*, FT Prentice Hall.

34  Hillson and Murray-Webster (2005), op.cit.

35  Toft and Reynolds (1997), op.cit., p. 24.

36  Wason, P.C. (1960), 'On the Failure to Eliminate Hypothesis in a Conceptual Task', *The Quarterly Journal of Experimental Psychology*, Volume 12, pp. 129–140.

37  Mittelstaedt, R.E. (2005), *Will Your Next Mistake Be Fatal? Avoiding the Chain of Mistakes That Can Destroy Your Organization*, Wharton School Publishing.

38  Toft and Reynolds (1997), op.cit.

39    Mittelstaedt (2005), op.cit.
40    Ambler, T. (2003), *Marketing and the Bottom Line*, FT Prentice Hall.
41    Toft and Reynolds (1997), op.cit.
42    Toft and Reynolds (1997), op.cit.
43    Toft and Reynolds (1997), op.cit.
44    Toft and Reynolds (1997), op.cit.
45    Mittelstaedt (2005), op.cit.
46    Toft and Reynolds (1997), op.cit., p. 73.
47    Levitt, B. and March, J.G. (1988), 'Organizational Learning', *Annual Review of Sociology*, Volume 14, pp. 319–340.
48    Fischoff, B. (1975), 'Hindsight is not Equal to Foresight: The Effect of Outcome Knowledge on Judgment under Uncertainty', *Journal of Experimental Psychology: Human Perception and Performance*, Volume 1, pp. 288–299.
49    Toft and Reynolds (1997), op.cit.
50    Toft and Reynolds (1997), op.cit.
51    Toft and Reynolds (1997), op.cit.
52    Mittelstaedt (2005), op.cit.
53    Toft and Reynolds (1997), op.cit.
54    Zaman, A. (2004), *Reputational Risk – How to Manage for Value Creation*, FT Prentice Hall, p. 242.
55    Bertalanffy L. von (1950), 'An Outline of General System Theory', *British Journal for the Philosophy of Science*, Volume 1 (No. 2), pp. 139–165.
56    Toft and Reynolds (1997), op.cit.
57    Toft and Reynolds (1997), op.cit.
58    Clemons, E.K. (2006), 'Past Experience Points the Way to the Future', *FT Mastering Uncertainty Part 1*, supplement to *Financial Times*, 17 March, pp. 6–8.
59    Wind, J. and Crook, C. (2006), 'Changing Mental Models in an Uncontrollable World', *FT Mastering Uncertainty Part 1*, supplement to *Financial Times*, 17 March, pp. 10–11.
60    Toft and Reynolds (1997), op.cit.
61    Toft and Reynolds (1997), op.cit., p. 47.
62    Smith, A.K., Bolton, R.N. and Wagner, J. (1998), *A Model of Customer Satisfaction with Service Encounters Involving Failure and Recovery*, Report No. 98-100, Marketing Science Institute.
63    East (1997), op.cit.
64    Dubé, L., Schmitt, B.H. and Leclerc, F. (1991), 'Consumers' Affective Response to Delays at Different Phases of a Service Delivery', *Journal of Applied Social Psychology*, Volume 21 (Issue 10), pp. 810–820.
65    East (1997), op.cit.
66    Halstead, D. (1993), 'Five Common Myths about Consumer Satisfaction Programs', *Journal of Services Marketing*, Volume 7 (Issue 3), pp. 4–12.

# Snakes and Ladders

## CUSTOMER SERVICE FAILURES

### Customer Perceptions of 'Justice' May Guide the Best Response

A study by Smith, Bolton and Wagner (1998) affirmed that customers attach significant importance to their perception of what is 'fair, right or deserved' in assessing the effectiveness of recovery from a service failure.[62] Customers consider that three aspects of justice apply:

- *distributive justice*: assessing the outcome in terms of benefits received, such as compensation or reinstatement
- *procedural justice*: assessing the fairness with which any policies and procedures were applied
- *interactional justice*: assessing the quality of the personal treatment they received following the service failure or complaint.

The principle of justice also appeared to reflect a reciprocal standard for the equity of compensation. Whilst compensation was always important, it appeared possible for providers to *overcompensate* customers, to the point where their overall satisfaction might be reduced, compared to those who felt their compensation had been a fair and proportionate reflection of their 'loss'.

The recommendations that flowed from this study were:

1.  In their regular surveys of customer satisfaction, companies should specifically explore customer perceptions of the fairness with which complaints have been handled, not merely whether the outcome was worse or better than expected.
2.  The handling of service recovery and complaints should set out to discover and emphasize whichever aspect of justice is most likely to concern the customer.
3.  In cases where a customer's 'loss' is comparatively small, there may be a diminishing return to the provider in giving excessive compensation, matched by a wasted opportunity to provide customers with a lower-cost response more in keeping with their actual demands.

### Managing Delay Requires Special Attention

Service providers, especially individual employees, may have quite different perceptions of delay from their customers and therefore fail to appreciate the dissatisfaction caused.[63]

Delay is best tolerated when customers understand the reason for it or have been led to expect it. In general, delay is less well accepted when it occurs at the beginning or at the end of a service than during the actual process of service provision.[64] However, some 'standardized' ways of dealing with delay, such as music on helplines, may be counterproductive if they communicate management's acceptance of the delay as normal, rather than something to be reduced or avoided.[65]

### Overreaction Exacerbates Minor Dissatisfactions

There is a risk that excessive apology for minor failings in performance will draw attention to something that customers would normally have overlooked or accepted.[66] The overreaction may create an unnecessary sense of dissatisfaction. Service people must possess sufficient customer insight to gauge the nature and materiality of the failing in each case.

# **4** *The Language of Risk*

Having considered some of the human factors at work in risk-taking, we turn again to risk itself. In order to explore and understand risk, it helps to know the language.

In this chapter we will:

- recap and supplement our definitions of risk and uncertainty
- describe the essential rules of probability and the practice of probability assessment
- describe ways of translating risk attitude into numbers to help with decisions.

## Introduction

It would be unusual if anyone reading this book did not have a lay person's understanding of what 'risk' and 'probability' mean. But there are good reasons for marketers to acquire an enlarged concept of risk:

1. *Insight.* Familiarity with the central concepts of risk should improve your ability to evaluate the opportunities and uncertainties you perceive. This does not mean that you will suddenly know the unknowable, but you may understand what you know (or do not know) better than you did.

2. *Confidence.* Theory does alter facts or the future. All the same, a command of risk concepts and their practical application should help you to take and avoid risks with greater decisiveness and acceptance.

3. *Communication.* If you speak the language of risk, this can only assist you in communicating the extent of due diligence that has gone into your plans and recommendations. Of course, this assumes that there is substance behind the words.

## Useful distinctions

### RISK AND UNCERTAINTY

From the outset, it will be useful for us to understand the technical difference between risk and uncertainty. We will be using a distinction widely applied, first proposed by the economist Frank Knight (1921).[1] It may be hard to respect this distinction with faultless consistency in general discussion, but the conceptual difference matters in risk management.

*Risk* is the term applied in situations where an actual outcome is unknown, but the range and likelihood of possible outcomes is known (its *probability distribution*). By this definition, it is clear that risk can include positive as well as negative outcomes.

*Uncertainty* applies in situations where there is no known probability distribution for the range of possible future outcomes – or no defined outcomes at all. In practice, uncertainty can arise because we do not have information that exists elsewhere. Uncertainty is often a characteristic of new and evolving market situations, such as those faced by marketers. It is also a feature of the qualitative judgements that are common in management – for example, about the effectiveness of one innovation strategy compared to another.

We can simply live with the uncertainty, assuming we can afford it. Alternatively, we can attempt a speculative model of outcomes by reference to proxies, patterns and parallels. In the latter case, we are attempting to turn uncertainty into something *artificially* akin to risk. This may be a necessary device to secure the confidence, co-operation and contribution of others in the firm. On occasion it may be no more than a useful way of expressing 'degrees of comfort' with an uncertainty ('I think there's an 80 per cent chance this agency idea will work out really well'). There is nothing wrong with making these subjective estimations for decision-making purposes – in fact, it can be very helpful – provided there is full disclosure of assumptions and a recognition that the underlying uncertainty remains.

Resolving uncertainties into actual or pseudo-certainties, so that an organization can plan effectively, is a source of influence for the functions that do so.[2]

## CLASSIFYING RISKS

Figure 4.1 shows an accepted four-way classification of risks: *financial, strategic, operational* and *hazard*. There is some overlap between the last two. Hazard risks are usually those in the physical environment, such as fire, flood or food poisoning. As its name suggests, an operational risk is one that arises from human behaviour and the nature of an organization's systems or processes.

This conventional classification helps organize our thinking about the sources of risk, although it is possible for all four exposures to combine. A wrongly managed preparation process (operational risk) can turn a food contamination exposure into an actual event (hazard risk). If we were unprepared and uninsured, the resulting product recall could have a very large

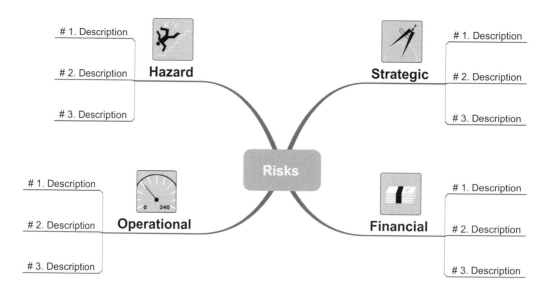

Mindjet MindManager Map

**Figure 4.1    Classification of risks**

impact on our profits and balance sheet (financial risk). It could prevent us from realizing our brand plans (strategic risk). This example shows why it is necessary to distinguish between *cause* and *effect*, and to be aware that an exposure in one area can compound the risk in another. For example, we may have a wrongly managed process because we are short of funds in the training budget. This is the purpose of 'root cause' analysis (see Chapter 5) or dependency modelling (see Chapter 6), which set out to identify ultimate sources of exposure that may prove to affect the business in a number of ways. In our example here, shortage of funds may also be affecting marketing research budgets and management's attitude to commercial risk-taking (perhaps, as we saw in Chapter 3, causing them to assume too much risk).

## DETERMINISTIC OR STOCHASTIC?

When we create a spreadsheet model to estimate demand or predict other outcomes, we often start by building a *deterministic* model. This delivers a single value for every output variable each time we run the model. When it is appropriate to make the upgrade, a *stochastic* model (pronounced 'stock-astic') helps us take a more insightful account of risk. In particular:

*   A *deterministic model* assumes a chain of causation: that one thing will lead to another. For example, IF there are 100 000 potential customers AND we achieve a strike rate of 10 per cent, THEN we will make 10 000 unit sales. It follows that an ambitious deterministic model of market demand might attempt to describe the complete sequence of causes and effects that will turn a citizen into a long-term profitable customer. However, a deterministic model does not take inherent account of the risk or uncertainty in any of the value inputs to the model. It simply requires a value input at each step in its calculation. Moreover, the model remains deterministic even if some value inputs are conditional upon another value ('IF retail distribution is greater than 65 per cent THEN increase marketing expenditure from $X to $Y'). It is possible, of course, to run the same model a number of times, in order to see how changes in certain variables affect the outcome. This can be a simple and uncomplicated way of testing for sensitivity to changes in important variables. However, this kind of scenario analysis draws no statistical conclusions: it simply presents you with two or more sets of results, each having an apparently equal chance of occurring.

*   A *stochastic model* is specifically designed to take account of uncertainty in calculating its outputs. Whereas a deterministic model can only accept a single-value input for each step in its calculations, a stochastic model can accommodate inputs that are expressed as ranges (or 'probability distributions' – see below). In effect, a stochastic model enables us to enter risks instead of assumed certainties into many of our calculations. It does mean that the outputs from stochastic models require some statistical interpretation, because they do not present an unequivocal single answer. But for those of us who assume business risks for a living, this more sophisticated approach can offer great insights. It allows us to take transparent account of risk (including any true uncertainties expressed as risks), so helping us to explain to others the complex risk considerations underlying a preferred course of action.

# Probability

Since so many of the formal and informal techniques involved in risk thinking call for arithmetic expressions of probability, it is worth reminding ourselves of the basic rules and other practicalities. The rules govern how to express likelihoods on a consistent basis and how to calculate the probabilities of two or more events in combination.

## EXPRESSING PROBABILITIES

Given a finite number of possible outcomes, probability describes the likelihood of a given outcome as a proportion of all the possible outcomes that are relevant to the assessment. So, if there are three equally possible outcomes for a new brand project (e.g. 'launching', 'postponing', 'terminating'), each clearly has a one-in-three chance of occurrence. Most of us will be used to referring to probability (or likelihood) in percentage terms ('There's a 33 per cent chance the plan will go ahead'). Arithmetical probability is usually expressed on a scale of 0–1, so that a 33 per cent chance is the same as a probability of 0.3. The probability of an event which has a 50:50 likelihood of occurrence is 0.5. Expressing probabilities on this 0–1 scale makes them much easier to use in spreadsheet models and in other forms of decision analysis. The conventional way of notating a simple probability is $p(A)$, where $p$ is the probability that A will occur.

## Certainty

An outcome which is certain to occur has a probability of 1. It follows that you cannot have a probability that exceeds 1 (greater than absolute certainty) or a probability less than 0 (less than absolute impossibility).

It is said that the *complement* of 'X happening' is 'X not happening'. Since it is logically certain that one of these two events will occur, the probability of two complementary events must always sum to the value 1. It can improve your perspective on one complementary risk (A) to calculate the probability of its inverse (B), by simple subtraction:

$$p(B) = 1 - p(A)$$

For example, a group of colleagues may forget that a 0.2 probability of failure (20 per cent chance) is still far less than the complementary 0.8 probability of success (80 per cent chance).

## Odds

There is, of course, another way of describing the chance of an event occurring. The *odds* on an outcome expresses likelihood too, but in the form of a ratio: the probability of occurrence divided by the probability of non-occurrence. To take our simple three-outcome example: 'The odds of our ever launching are 2:1'. In risk management we usually prefer to work with probabilities, rather than odds.

## COMBINING PROBABILITIES

Risk assessment frequently involves combining probabilities, because we are considering a number of risks at the same time. Even when we are not applying probabilities in a structured quantitative analysis, but using them to express intuitive judgements, it is helpful to understand whether we should be adding them or multiplying them. Choosing the correct arithmetic operation clearly matters. Assume the example below applies to the same two-component risk and note how the answers differ:

$$p(0.5) + p(0.5) = 1, \text{ but } p(0.5) * p(0.5) = 0.25$$

Here are the two rules.

## Addition rule

Where events are *mutually exclusive*, you add the probabilities to combine them. Two events are said to be mutually exclusive if the fact of one event occurring means that the other event cannot occur. Alternative outcomes connected with the word 'OR' are added together. For example, the probability that our competitor will introduce its new product into our domestic market this year or next year will produce two mutually exclusive estimations. The competitor can only introduce the product once (for the first time, at least), so the two events are without doubt mutually exclusive. So, if you think that the probability of our competitor launching this year is 0.5 (i.e. a 50 per cent chance) and the probability that they will launch next year is 0.33:

$$p(\text{competitor launches this year } \textit{or} \text{ next year}) = p(0.5) + p(0.33) = 0.83$$

In the case of *mutual exclusivity/independence*, bear in mind that these two concepts are not equivalent.[3] By definition, independent events are *capable* of occurrence without any effect on the probability of the other's occurrence – even though we may be interested to know their aggregate probability of occurrence. By contrast, mutually exclusive events are actually dependent, because the occurrence of one precludes the occurrence of the other.

There is an important gloss to the addition rule, which deals with situations of overlap, where events are independent and no longer mutually exclusive. Let us stay with the risk of competitor launch, but alter the scenario. This time, you see three possibilities:

- that they launch against us in country A next year (event A: 0.5 probability)
- that they launch against us in country B next year (event B: 0.2 probability)
- that they launch against us in countries A *and* B next year (event C: 0.1 probability).

Consider the Venn diagram in Figure 4.2 that Schuyler (2001) recommends for visualizing combinations of events and probabilities.[4] The rectangular field in the entire diagram represents an 'event space' and all the alternative outcomes under consideration should feature within it. In this case, you will see events A and B represented, with the prospect of simultaneous launch indicated by the overlap at C. The design of the 'event shapes' within the boundaries of the space is not critical, but they should be drawn roughly proportional to the probability of the corresponding event. If the alternative events within the space represent the entire range of possible outcomes, their probabilities must sum to the value of 1, being the value we are obliged to give to total certainty.

What now is the probability that our competitor will launch anywhere next year? The answer is not 0.8, but 0.6. If you look at the Venn diagram in Figure 4.2, you will see that you overstate the combined probability if you simply add the probabilities of all three events A, B and C. By failing to take account of the overlap represented by launch C, you will have double-counted to the extent that the two events A and B are not mutually exclusive.

Here is the gloss to the addition rule expressed in notation:

$$p(\text{competitor launches next year in A } \textit{or} \text{ B}) = p(A) + p(B) - p(A \textit{ and } B)$$

$$= 0.5 + 0.2 - 0.1 = 0.6$$

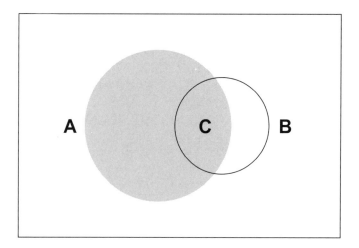

**Figure 4.2     Venn diagram of possible outcomes**

*Source: After Schuyler (2001)*

We have now determined that the probability of our competitor launching this year or next year is 0.6. Since 'total certainty' must always have a value of 1, it follows by subtraction that all of the unconsidered alternatives in connection with our competitor's launch must have a combined probability of 0.4, the difference between 1 and 0.6. Where the probabilities of all the possible outcomes for a particular event add up to 1, it is said that the list of possible outcomes is *'exhaustive'*. However, if the sum total of all probability estimations exceeds the value 1, you will have to revise one or more probabilities downwards or exclude some inapplicable events. Conversely, a sum total of less than 1 may indicate that you have not yet considered all the possibilities.

## Multiplication rule

In considering the risk of success or failure in a marketing strategy, we often need to think about *joint probability*. This is the likelihood that two or more events will occur in combination or in series. For example, take the probabilities that we will achieve BOTH the target test results for our product ($p=0.7$) AND target retail distribution ($p=0.8$). In this case, assuming that the two events are independent, we multiply the two probabilities in order to determine the likelihood of their joint occurrence:

$$p(\text{target test results } and \text{ target distribution}) = p(D) * p(T) = 0.7 * 0.8 = 0.56$$

If there were more than two chance events in the risk scenario, their not being mutually exclusive, we would just keep multiplying. The compound effect of joint probabilities in a high-risk sales plan may be quite sobering if you include all the critical factors for success. Conversely, the probability of a severe downside risk is substantially reduced if it depends for its occurrence on a large number of other chance events. In a similar vein, the occurrence of a second event may be described as being *conditional* upon a first. For example, consider the probability that we will achieve sales of more than 2000 units of a new item this season [$p(A) = 0.7$] and that *as a consequence* a known competitor might imitate the concept next year

[$p(B) = 0.5$]. In this case a somewhat different logic applies, because B will not occur unless A occurs. To express the logic of the calculation in the notation of probability, we have:

$$p(A \; and \; B) = p(A) * p(B|A) \text{ where the '|' sign means 'given that ...'}$$

In practice, however, we still multiply the prerequisite and the dependent probabilities to arrive at the joint probability, so that:

$$p(A \; and \; B) = p(A) * p(B|A) = 0.7 * 0.5 = 0.35$$

## PROBABILITY AND CONFIDENCE LEVELS

Probability is not the same as a confidence level, even though we might accept them as synonymous in normal usage ('We're confident that the focus groups will go well'). To be more technically precisely, we can express a probability that the value of an outcome will fall within a given range, accompanied by an expression of confidence that our estimation is a reliable one. Consider the difference between these two statements:

'We are 100 per cent confident in our assessment that the campaign will be 0 per cent successful.'

'We are 0 per cent confident in our assessment that the campaign will be 100 per cent successful.'

The first statement communicates something deceptively equivalent to a probability estimate, because 100 per cent confidence suggests that no other outcome is expected. By contrast, the second statement makes it perfectly clear that there is a complete lack of confidence in the information currently available to us, but it says nothing about the probability of success that we might ascribe if better information came along.[5] So, neither of the expressions of confidence in this case can be a probability assessment.

(Later in this chapter we will come across the term *confidence interval*. This is a way of qualifying 'the certainty of a probability' – in other words, the likelihood that the probability of a particular unknown falls within a defined range of probabilities.)

Indications of confidence level are very important in statistical sampling, such as in market research, where inferences are drawn from a population sample with a certain degree of confidence that they are true. At the risk of confusion, confidence factors (CFs) can be expressed in the same way as probabilities on a scale 0–1, though more usually in percentages when they appear in business research. A CF of 1 means 'The information on the behaviour of this variable is true'; a CF of 0 means 'The information on the behaviour of this variable is not worth anything'.

From time to time, you will find it useful in practice to probe an expression of probability for its associated confidence level. At that point the significance of the distinction will become clear: it is a first step in deciding whether or not to invest in acquiring more information.

For a full discussion of the theoretical and practical issues involved in statistical sampling, see Wisniewski (2006).[6]

# Expected value and volatility

We need to be able to apply probabilities to alternative outcomes arithmetically, even if such numbers represent 'degrees of belief' rather than hard data. *Expected value* and *volatility* are two practical indicators of comparative risk. They are central to risk thinking, and it is a good idea to consider them together.

## EXPECTED VALUE

At its simplest, expected value (EV) is a future outcome multiplied by its probability of occurrence. When the outcome is monetary, it is often referred to as *EMV* (expected monetary value). For example:

$$\text{EMV} = p(.5) * \$10\ 000 = \$5000$$

It follows that expected value can also be the weighted average (or 'mean') of *all* considered outcomes for a single project or an event, where the probability of each outcome is the weighting factor:

**Project A**

| | |
|---|---|
| Outcome 1? | $2k  * $p(.4) = \$0.8k$ |
| Outcome 2? | $18k * $p(.5) = \$9.0k$ |
| Outcome 3? | $30k * $p(.1) = \$3.0k$ |
| | |
| EMV(A) | $= \$12.8k$ |

You apply the same calculation to different projects in order to compare, each of them with an entirely different range of possible outcomes and associated probabilities. In this way, the expected value calculation allows you to reduce a range of assumptions, which may be difficult to assimilate otherwise, into a single indicator for each project or event.

Consider this example:

| **Project A** | | **Project B** | |
|---|---|---|---|
| Outcome 1? | $2k  * p(.4) = \$0.8k$ | $5k  * p(.2) = \$1.0k$ | |
| Outcome 2? | $18k * p(.5) = \$9.0k$ | $17k * p(.5) = \$8.5k$ | |
| Outcome 3? | $30k * p(.1) = \$3.0k$ | $20k * p(.3) = \$6.0k$ | |
| | | | |
| EMV(A) | $= \$12.8k$ | EMV(B) | $= \$15.5k$ |

All other things being equal, a risk-neutral person (i.e. someone looking at risk entirely rationally) would prefer Project B, because it has a higher expected value or probability-weighted return. As a point of detail, if both scenarios returned *negative* expected values, a risk-neutral comparison would logically favour the lower one.

The reference to 'expectation' should not be taken literally. Firstly, expected value does not need to equate to a feasible value in the range of possibilities. For instance, one can arrive at an expected value of 6.5 for frequency of audience exposure to an advertisement, even though this would be a physical impossibility. More importantly, expected value is a statistical indicator: it is unlikely that the expected value will turn out to be the figure actually achieved, especially if you have only one 'throw of the dice'. In essence, expected value is the *anticipated average outcome*, assuming an opportunity to re-run history many times. Expected value calculations are therefore at their most statistically accurate when applied to consolidations of multiple risk events, because the dispersal of outcomes progressively averages out. Nevertheless, using expected value as a simple subjective risk indicator is a better way of beginning to compare a number of risky alternatives than taking the mid-point (median) of probable values or relying solely on a 'most likely' outcome as a basis for decision-making. Expected value adds insight to risk-taking, even when it is only a calibration of 'gut feel'.

In practice, expected value calculation is a convenient way of checking that the assumed risk mix within a brand plan is in balance. A simple way of going about this is to calculate the expected values for likely causes of variance, above and below the brand's volume and financial commitments (or other performance standard, provided one compares like with like). You draw up a balance sheet listing all the significant risks and opportunities relative to your objective and compare the respective sums of their expected values. Figure 4.3 shows a simplified example. In principle, a brand plan is in 'risk balance' if the expected values for upsides and downsides appear to cancel out. The same principle applies across a portfolio of brands.

Expected value theory has also demonstrated its relevance to the analysis of consumer behaviour, for example in the work of Edwards (1954)[7], Rosenberg (1956)[8] and Fishbein (1963).[9] They studied consumer attitudes to the overall 'benefit package' provided by goods or services. Their work showed that this aggregate attitude score could be reconciled with separately elicited factors for evaluation of each benefit and a respondent's estimations of its *likelihood of occurrence* in each case: thus an 'expected-value theory of attitude'.[10] Behavioural theory offers different perspectives on consumer behaviour, but the application of expected value is not without precedent and authority.

## VOLATILITY

The limitation of expected value estimation is that whilst it does enable a comparison of returns (one expected value versus another), it does not take account of inherent differences

---

*Illustrative*

| **Opportunity** | EV | **Risk** | EV |
|---|---|---|---|
| Demand exceeds forecast by $100k (p = 0.1) | $10k | Bad weather reduces offtake by $500k (p = 0.02) | ($10k) |
| Major customers add $1MM sales (p = 0.05) | $50k | Stock shortfall leads to $200k lost sales (p = 0.04) | ($8k) |
| Total upside (EV) | $60k | Total downside (EV) | ($18k) |

Expected value of sales variances (net) = $60k - $18k = $42k

**Figure 4.3    Brand risk balance sheet**

in risk. In itself, expected value does not reveal how much risk is being taken to secure the anticipated return. For example, it is possible to adjust the marketing mix for a project in such a way as to hold expected value constant but simultaneously increase both the upside and downside exposures. The unaltered average masks the shift in extreme values. Volatility is a key measure of this risk, the extent to which actual outcome(s) may depart from the expected value. Risk thinking about volatility is particularly concerned with *preparing for extremes of outcome*. The principle here is that if you cannot tolerate the volatility, you must do something about it.

Volatility also describes the sharp or short-term variability of outcomes over time, even if there is a steadier underlying trend. The term can be applied to the fluctuating levels of continuous demand or the changing magnitude of an infrequent, recurrent event. A volatility view of risk helps us to recognize the extent to which actual outcomes at interim intervals might depart from our average expectation (or expected value) over a longer period of exposure. It can describe upside as well as downside movement. For example, if we were using expected values to predict customer service requests in a seasonal business and then recommend investment in new service facilities, our multi-year forecasts would need to take account of the volatility of demand, in other words, its peaks and troughs: the troughs, because cash costs might exceed revenue for a time; the peaks, because (among other things) we might risk disappointing so many current customers in high season that our new product sales to them and others would not remain unscathed.

This is all business common sense, but the risk thinking provides a benchmark for corrective action. In our service example, you might, for instance, decide to modify current customers' expectation of response times or reconfigure capacity and costs to take account of the foreseeable volatility.

There are classic measures of volatility that use a statistical indicator of variance either side of the mean, the so-called *standard deviation*. However, a simple way of comparing the downside financial risk of two or more projects is to calculate the variance $(V_a)$ between expected value (EMV) and 'worst possible outcome' (WPO); then express $V_a$ as a percentage of expected value. This simplified 'coefficient of variance' (CV) allows you to compare the downside risk of the two projects relative to their expected returns. Taking our earlier projects A and B, the calculation shows how project A has not only the somewhat lower expected return, but also a higher coefficient of downside variance:

**Project A**

$V_a$ (A) = EMV(A) – WPO(A) = $12.8k - $2k = $10.8k

CV(A) = $V_a$ (A)/ EMV(A) * 100 = $10.8k/ $12.8 * 100 = <u>84%</u>

**Project B**

$V_a$ (B) = EMV(B) – WPO(B) = $15.5k - $5k = $10.5k

CV(B) = $V_a$ (B)/ EMV(B) * 100 = $10.5k/ $15.5 * 100 = <u>68%</u>

Even if you decided to go ahead with Project B, you would still need to be comfortable with the actual values involved ('Can I afford to take the downside risk?'). But the relationship between risk and reward is clearer.

It is not uncommon to identify the volatile assumptions in a marketing plan and 'hedge' them within the plan. The known high-risk assumptions in the plan are offset with conservative assumptions elsewhere.[11] For example, optimistic assumptions about price can be hedged with conservative assumptions about volume. A comparison of expected values and volatility will help to specify the extent of hedge or budget provision required. The risk balance sheet in Figure 4.3 might be used to set out the final mix that has been achieved.

Assessments of expected value and volatility are widely used in financial project evaluation to present the risk-adjusted outcomes in discounted cash flow analysis. The approach is applicable to any performance parameter that can be expressed in numbers, such as estimates of unit sales, distribution achievement, advertising reach, customer conversion rates or customer retention.

## Probability distributions

Our interest in probability can be limited to the possibility that a single event with only one possible value might occur. It will either happen or it will not, and if it happens, its value is knowable. This is called a 'binary event', because the outcome either has a value of 1 (true) or 0 (false). For example, we will either win a particular customer or we will not. It is not a complicated matter to represent these two alternative outcomes and assess their probabilities of occurrence so that their two values sum to 1 [$p$(win) = 0.7; $p$(not win) = 0.3]. But what if we actually win this customer? The immediate question will be how many units they might buy and the second question will be how much revenue these units might bring. The mix of probabilities in answer to these two questions needs to be represented in slightly different ways.

A set of possible values and probabilities for a particular outcome is referred to as a *probability distribution* and can be represented graphically according to its general type. The first example illustrated in Figure 4.4 is a *discrete probability distribution*, where the uncertain events along the horizontal x-axis have specific and indivisible values – such as the number of (necessarily whole) new customers.

The second example is of a *continuous probability distribution* (Figure 4.5). This assumes that the uncertain event could have any value within the range of values indicated on the

The probability of making a sale is 0.3 in every unrelated pitch.
If we make ten pitches, what is the probability of achieving 'x' new customers?

**Figure 4.4    Discrete probability distribution**

x-axis of the graph, such as the variable financial return from a product investment. Figure 4.5 illustrates the frequently encountered *standard normal distribution*. A symmetrical ('bell-shaped') distribution like this one is used to describe how large numbers of chance events tend to disperse symmetrically either side of their mean. An example of this would be the probability distribution of annual consumption of milk in a population, once given the average. Normal distributions are always symmetrical and bell-shaped, but they can, of course, vary in terms of their mean value and the *breadth of dispersal* of individual values around the mean. The consistent statistical relationships inherent in any standard normal distribution allow you to compare individual values from different normal distributions that would otherwise be difficult to reconcile. Each value can be expressed in the 'common currency' of *standard deviation*, even though they come from different data sets and may each have been measured in quite different units, for example age and income. Standard deviation (SD) is simply the *average deviation* from the mean for *all* the data in a given set. This means that any single value along the distribution (X) can be described in relation to the mean in units of SD: for example, X = 1.8 SD. For practical purposes this converted value never exceeds SD 3 and is often referred to as the 'Z score'. If you have the underlying value and were to look up its Z score in readily available tables, you (or someone else) would be able to re-create the entire distribution from which the single-point value had been taken. This can be useful if you have some sample data and would like to see the bigger picture.

The presentation of a continuous probability distribution in this way, with the characteristic upslope and downslope, is also referred to as a *probability density function*. The term 'density' refers to the relationship between probability and area in the graph. You will notice that the values of highest probability account for the greater proportion of the area enclosed by the distribution curve. Since the horizontal axis in a probability distribution expresses all of the possible outcomes, it follows once again that all the probabilities represented on the graph must sum to the value 1.

An alternative presentation of the same expected value information is a *cumulative probability distribution*, in which both the outcome values and their associated probabilities accumulate from left to right (Figure 4.6). For any given value on the cumulative distribution curve, we are identifying the probability that the actual outcome will have a value *equal to or*

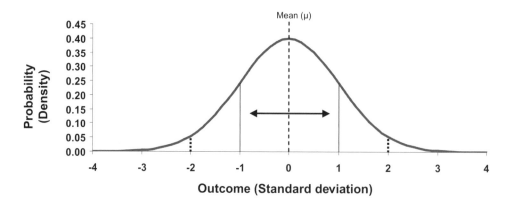

Where a Standard Normal Distribution adequately represents a risk,
68 per cent of outcomes will occur within 1 SD of the mean and 95 per cent within 2 SD

**Figure 4.5    Continuous probability distribution**

*less than* the value chosen. The same single point on the curve will also identify the probability that the outcome will be *equal to or more than* the value chosen. The pitfall in the interpretation of cumulative distributions is to misconstrue the 'equal to or less than' probability as a *chance of* achieving the single value in question. Let us assume that Figure 4.6 represents an analysis of the likelihood that we will hit a vital target number '1'. Since the dotted line in our figure shows a .84 probability of hitting this target *or less*, it follows that there is a complementary .16 probability that we will reach the value '1' or more. This means that the actual chance of achieving our objective is only 16 per cent, rather than the more reassuring 84 per cent.

On occasion, a distribution of discrete probabilities can look like a continuous probability distribution. This happens when there are so many discrete probabilities that their distribution takes on the appearance of a curve. A probability distribution for the potential unit sales of a mass-market consumer product, running into many millions, would be a case in point. Conversely, there are occasions when a continuous distribution needs to be broken down into discrete probabilities, for instance when constructing *decision trees* that model single scenarios for comparative purposes (see Chapter 6).

## Objective and subjective probabilities

There are two kinds of probability assessment: objective and subjective. Objective probabilities are so described because there is no scope for personalization of projected outcome, other than by error. In principle, two people analysing the same information in the same way should arrive at the same answers. For example, we may be able to make confident estimations of likely product returns and service requirements for a new product, because relevant failure rate data may already exist for its components. The so-called 'frequentist' interpretation of probability is based on sample data, according to the extent to which the sample can be relied upon as being representative of the real world.

Subjective probability, on the other hand, is 'an expression of an individual's degree of belief'[12] about the likelihood that a particular event will occur. Whilst we may have a sound

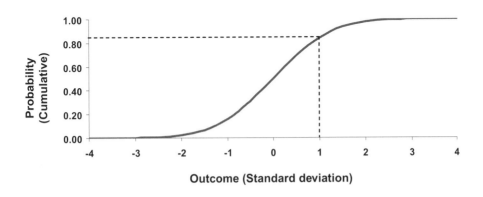

This cumulative Standard Normal Distribution shows how 84 per cent of outcomes will always have a value *less than or equal to* 1 (or its actual equivalent), assuming that the mean value is 0 (or its actual equivalent)

**Figure 4.6    Cumulative probability distribution**

basis for our beliefs, we are sometimes left with no alternative but to make such a subjective assessment. We are bound to use a subjective approach to estimating probability for one-off events ('probability of our new strategy being sustainable') or for unique events ('the likely impact of this social change on customer behaviour'). Given the distinction we have already drawn between risks and uncertainties, one-off market events are really uncertainties, even though they may embody risk: 'If this particular packaging issue isn't resolved within six months (*uncertainty*), our customer will delist the product (*risk*)'.

## WORKING WITH OBJECTIVE PROBABILITIES

Naturally, if you have good data, you should use them. Goodwin and Wright (2004) highlight two particular assumptions about the characteristics of data that should be validated before relying on them for use in objective probability calculations:[13]

*   *The equality assumption.* If you throw a single die with six faces, you know that there is a one-in-six chance (or, more precisely, a probability of 0.166666666666667) that you will throw any one of the numbers one to six. You can make this objective calculation of probability because you know that there is an equal chance of any of the six numbers coming up and you are only going to throw the die once. But if the die were loaded in favour of the six, without your knowing it, then you would obviously make an inaccurate probability assessment. The same assumption of equality applies in more complex calculations of objective probability. In order to express the likelihood of one particular outcome in relation to the total range of possible outcomes, you must either assume that each outcome is equally likely or else have simultaneous information itemizing the probability of each outcome represented in the data set. If the data fail either test, they may not be reliable.

*   *The stability assumption.* It is common to make objective probability calculations in terms of relative frequency. In other words, we calculate the regularity with which a particular event has occurred over time. However, the underlying assumption is that stable conditions have applied throughout the period during which the frequency data have been collected. We need to be sure that nothing else has changed that may affect the comparability of data for the event we are interested in. For example, change in market size, market seasonality or other competitor activity might all affect the datum in an objective calculation of frequency.

## WORKING WITH SUBJECTIVE PROBABILITIES

Marketers face a number of issues in their decision-making that call for subjective assessment of probability. Some markets experience continuous change and frequent innovative disruption, so that predictions may be uncertain. Immediate questions may be inaccessible to research techniques other than test marketing. For example, researching acquired tastes or fashions can be problematic if they depend on peer group or reference group endorsement that is not yet in place. Whilst good data collection may be technically feasible in many cases, we may decide that its cost in time and money appears to outweigh its value. Either way, we need to come to our own view on the probability of outcomes.

Let us consider three common situations that arise:

*   assessing the probability of unprecedented events

- assessing the probability of rare events
- generating subjective probability distributions.

## Unprecedented events

We sometimes make probability estimations of unique events or unprecedented recurrent events. An example of a unique event might be a named competitor exiting our market; an example of an unprecedented recurrent event would be the repurchase rate for a revolutionary online service. A good first step is to ensure that the event is truly unprecedented. You may find that your natural inclination is to adopt an 'inside' view of the issue.[14] As we discussed in Chapter 3, a limited perspective may lead you to focus on what is unique about a situation, but take too little account of what it has in common with others. Secondly, bear in mind that a time-frame is always implicit in a probability assessment. In practice, it is generally easier to estimate the probability of a one-off or repeating event in terms of its frequency within a stated time period, such as 'every year', 'once in three years' or 'once every five or ten years'. There is evidence to suggest that we are better programmed to assess the probability of events in this way.[15] It is easy to turn such an estimation of frequency into an arithmetic probability.

## Rare events

On some occasions, we may need to work in the realm of very low probabilities indeed, but without objective data to help us. Common sense or sensitivity analysis may have persuaded us that the impact of a rare event would be so great that even a remote chance of its occurrence needs to be represented in our thinking. Articulating very low probabilities, especially the significance of differences between them, can be difficult for respondents in a general risk assessment exercise. Once you get below a 0.01 probability (a 1 per cent chance), the figures become harder for non-specialists to work with. The question is how to overcome this, so that people can still express a comparative ranking in helpful terms. As we saw earlier, lower probability events are often caused by combinations of higher probability events. This means that the task of attributing probabilities to the causes may be easier than attempting a one-shot estimate of the joint probability for the outcome. Similarly, we can make a probability assessment for a rare event by identifying the probabilities for the chain(s) of events that might lead to it. A second approach adapts the kind of perceptual scale that is often used to elicit intuitive assessments of probability, as well as customer attitude in marketing research. These perceptual scales typically take the form of high/ medium/low descriptions of probability, distributed along a horizontal line, with respondents being invited to pick a point on the line that best represents their attitude. The underlying numerical probabilities (invisible to the respondent) can then be recorded and applied in any expected value calculation. In the case of very rare events, it is possible to create a consistent perceptual scale that includes an elongated low-end calibration. This produces something that people can react to intuitively, whilst capturing the fractional differences in numerical probability that are so hard to express in words. The mathematical methodology that renders this more sensitive scale uses odds and logarithms. Bunn and Thomas (1975), among others, provide further insight.[16]

## Subjective probability distributions

We may want to create subjective probability distributions for outcomes, rather than make a single-point assessment. It could be that we want to test for ourselves the reasonableness of a single-point estimate made elsewhere, or perhaps present a more complete picture of a risk to someone else. Alternatively, we could be working with a stochastic simulation of brand performance. In such cases, if we had no reliable objective data, we would need to provide subjective probability distributions for a number of variables, such as distribution achievement or the relative strength of our brand equity.

How to create such a subjective probability distribution? Above all, we want to avoid fixing initially on a single probability and making subsequent estimates that are unreasonably close to the initial figure. This would be to fall into the heuristic trap of 'anchoring and adjustment' that we described in Chapter 3.

Here are two alternative ways of proceeding. The first creates a simple 'triangular distribution' based on a selection of three values. It is often used in business project simulation models, where data may be difficult to acquire, but a 'most likely' outcome can still be identified.

To create a triangular probability distribution:

1. Identify the highest and lowest conceivable outcomes. Make sure that these extremes are true extremes, not just values for 'best likely' and 'worst likely'.[17] For practical purposes, these two extremes must sensibly define the range of possibilities. This means they must have near-zero chances of occurrence in themselves.

2. Identify a 'Most likely' value within the range and assess its probability of occurrence.

3. Plot the three points on a graph and draw straight lines to connect them (as in Figure 4.7). This turns the 'discrete' probability distribution, identifying three specific outcome probabilities, into a continuous probability distribution that associates the full range of possible outcome values with their implied probabilities.

4. Calculate the *expected value* (EV) outcome that is suggested by your three choices. In the case of triangular distributions, EV = (Max. + Min. + Most likely)/3.

5. Note the difference between the two 'tell-tale' points on the distribution: the *mode* (most likely) and the *expected value*. Note also that the chance of hitting any of the three original values is not equal.

The second approach outlined here is a brief iterative process, recommended by Goodwin and Wright (2004) after Stael von Holstein and Matheson (1979).[18] It is designed to elicit a more carefully considered picture of a risk as a cumulative probability distribution. There are six steps involved:[19]

1. Identify the highest and lowest values for the range of outcomes as above.

2. Check that this range of outcomes accommodates all conceivable values. Do this by attempting to imagine situations where the initial range estimate might plausibly be breached. Leaving a 'back door' open for the unimaginable is very important in risk thinking and is a recommended precaution in any risk modelling or stochastic forecasting. Expand the range of values accordingly.

3. Write the resulting outcome range along the horizontal axis of a graph and divide it into six or seven approximately equal intervals.

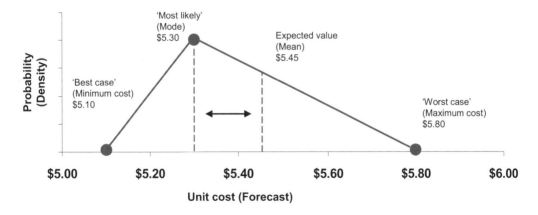

In this case of cost estimation, the difference between 'Expected value' and 'Most likely' suggests that it may be prudent to budget conservatively

**Figure 4.7     Triangular probability distribution**

4.  Estimate a cumulative probability at each of these intervals. In other words: 'What is the probability that the actual outcome will be less than (or if you prefer, more than) each interval value?' Plot the resulting values on the vertical axis of the graph and draw a curve that fits them by hand.

5.  Perform a first sense check on the probability distribution now represented by the hand-drawn curve. Do this by drawing horizontal lines from the vertical probability axis that divide the range of possible outcomes into three *equally likely* intervals. Consider this partitioned curve and see whether you (or your respondent) would be comfortable placing a correspondingly equal bet on the likelihood of the actual outcome falling somewhere within each interval. Adjust the curve to reflect any preferences that emerge.

6.  Perform a second sense check. Look for any prominent upswing on the curve. If the cumulative distribution is a good representation of the subjective probabilities, this point should identify a 'most likely' value (or mode) that feels acceptable to you or your respondent. (This would be the equivalent of the 'most likely' value chosen in the case of a triangular distribution.) If not, make final required adjustments to the curve.

## IS SUBJECTIVE PROBABILITY ASSESSMENT WORTHWHILE?

The principles in logic that underpin arithmetically expressed degrees of belief (i.e. subjective probability assessment) have been matters of considerable intellectual investment since the work of the Reverend Thomas Bayes (1702–1761) was published posthumously in 1764. We have no need to detail the academic discussion of so-called 'Bayesian analysis' here, except to say that the mathematical principles are sound and have stood the test of time. Bayes' Theorem still provides us with an authoritative rule to adjust subjective probabilities in the light of new evidence or information. This rule is particularly helpful when a source of information, such as market research, cannot be 100 per cent reliable but still indicates that we should be modifying our earlier view (see Chapter 6). As it happens, Bayes' Theorem has also been used for automatically updating e-mail anti-spam filters in response to the characteristics of newly emerging threats (it does this by continuously updating the probability that an unknown e-mail source is likely to be spam).

The perceived worth of an expected value calculation naturally depends on the presumed quality of input. There may be a concern that making seemingly overelaborate subjective estimates of probability will be a hollow exercise.

East (1997) provides us with some initial insight into the process of subjective assessment. Based on comparisons with objective data, it seems that a subjective weighting often occurs at around 0.15 objective probability. This means that people in general tend to 'enhance' objective probabilities of 0.15 *or less*, so that subjective estimations express a somewhat greater likelihood than the objective data. Conversely, at 0.15 objective probability or higher, people tend to 'depress' an objective likelihood, sensing a lower probability than is suggested by the unseen data.[20] Whether this weighting tendency matters in practice is a key question. In reviewing the considerable body of research in this area, Goodwin and Wright (2004) conclude reassuringly that:

> ... *such judgements rarely need to be exact ... [S]ensitivity analysis often reveals that quite major changes in the probabilities are required before it becomes apparent that the decision-maker should switch from one course of action to another.*[21]

In other words, the predictable error in subjective probability estimations may not matter. However, checking the sensitivity of important decisions to variations in subjective expectation is not a step to omit.

Although we discussed the biases to which human judgement can fall victim in Chapter 3, it would be wrong and ridiculous to suggest that we should therefore decide nothing. In practice, it is clearly better to express a degree of belief in an outcome than to make no judgement at all. As an offset to our cautionary tale of heuristics, there is evidence to suggest that individuals *with relevant experience* (in Bayesian terminology good 'reference priors') will make independent estimates that are surprisingly representative of the actual possibilities.

In their experimental study, Griffiths and Tenenbaum (2006) were interested to see how accurately 350 people could estimate actual outcomes based on a single piece of interim information.[22] For instance, they asked participants to estimate the total box office intake for a movie that had already grossed $10 000 000, without telling them how long it had been running. What emerged from the answers to nine distinct questions on various subjects was that the distribution of people's judgements was collectively remarkably close to the distributions of actual data drawn from objective sources, notwithstanding that the benchmark distributions were each rather different. In one interesting exception (as it happens, the life expectancy of ancient Egyptian pharaohs), participants' estimates were incorrect, but the pattern of incorrect estimates was nonetheless appropriately distributed (i.e. would have exhibited an appropriate shape plotted on a graph, even though the numerical estimates were adrift). To summarize two of the conclusions drawn by Griffiths and Tenenbaum:

- People's cognitive (i.e. information-processing) judgements are not *inevitably* based on heuristics that take no account of relevant frames of reference.
- To the extent that people's limited base of knowledge and experience may otherwise cause them to make wildly inaccurate predictions, a strategy of 'prediction-by-analogy' offers a useful way of making the required judgements.[23]

Experience and experiment have given us good reason to apply the mechanisms of subjective probability assessment in decision-making. Even under conditions of complete uncertainty, the approach offers a way of recording and comparing important assumptions.

# Beating the averages

During the course of his study into physical inheritance between fathers and sons, the British scientist Sir Francis Galton (1822–1911) observed that tall fathers did not consistently produce tall sons. In fact, Galton demonstrated quite the opposite: that the adult sons of taller or shorter men were closer in height to the male average than their fathers had been. By this discovery, Galton established what is now the important principle he first described as *regression to the mean*: namely, that in the long run you cannot beat the averages. Individual events that are higher or lower than the average tend to be followed by events that are closer to the average. Provided that comparable events of any kind are truly independent of each other (such as lottery draws or the amount of toothpaste individuals use every day) and are observed in sufficient numbers, you would find the observations distributed symmetrically around their average. This is the bell-shaped 'normal' distribution illustrated in Figure 4.5.

In the present context, we are not concerned with the statistical principles applied in finding and fitting 'regression lines' to sets of data, to prove the point. Spreadsheet packages largely automate the process once the technicalities are understood.[24] Meanwhile, a conceptual understanding of regression to the mean has some value in brand risk management. When finance directors take a cynical view of ambitious marketing plans in the absence of any apparent familiarity with the detail, it is often their intuitive respect for regression to the mean that causes them to take the conservative line.

## STATIONARY AND NON-STATIONARY MARKETS

A stationary market is said to exist if the number of consumers exiting the market is compensated for by the number entering it, so that the volume of market transactions does not materially alter.[25] Value growth may track economic expansion or retail price inflation, but the drivers of demand remain essentially unchanged. The structure and relative stability of a market has implications for the risk assessment of marketing plans.[26]

- *Predictability*. Even stationary markets will lose and regain approximately 15 per cent of their purchasers in any single year.[27] Provided that there is nothing to disturb the underlying equilibrium, it is possible to make reasonably safe assumptions about overall volume, price, costs and profits. In particular, regression suggests that the long-run performance of a branded business in a stationary market will be more predictable and less uncertain than might be suggested by short-term fluctuations of commercial results.

- *Performance correction*. In a stationary market, regression suggests that it may be reasonable to expect a run of below-average performance to be correctable, assuming the relative qualities of both product and marketing effort are maintained. After all, the principle of regression holds that neither above-average nor below-average performers will sustain their off-average positions indefinitely. So the probability of success in ultimately correcting sales underperformance, at least for a time, may be good. (It is another matter whether the correction will have been achieved profitably or efficiently.[28]) In stationary markets, it is remarkable how long-established brands survive, even when they are managed inconsistently. The rub comes when the market is no longer stationary. We will come to that.

- *Marketing efficiency.* It is quite natural for marketers to propose business development goals. However, to the extent that they are not assuming an increase in the physical distribution of the product, regression may frustrate their efforts to redistribute market share on a *sustainable* basis. There is considerable evidence that under truly stationary market conditions, a substantial proportion of marketing investment produces no more than a transitory and unprofitable diversion of custom.[29] Promotional investments may simply enhance distributor margins, while competing brands fight to protect their current market positions on steadily worsening terms of trade. This is not to suggest that maintenance of brand momentum is futile – it is necessary – but that the forecast of financial returns on effort and investment need to fall within realistic bounds if the structure of demand is known to be (or expected to be) stationary.

- *Above-average growth.* One of the classic, if paradoxical, indicators of risk is when a brand experiences extraordinary growth that cannot be adequately explained. Where stationary market conditions suggest that regression to the mean might prevail, then there is good reason to expect the pattern of unexplained growth to end. You should not assume that your marketing efforts have established a new market equilibrium *without reason*. It is a common feature of heuristics to ignore regression to the mean, and (for example) to persuade oneself that a series of successful volume-building promotions has resulted in a sustainable upward adjustment to market position.[30] Seasonal merchandise businesses, for example, may drive substantial increases in wholesale and retail stocks, but see disappointing offtake in consumer sales. The result can be either heavy retail discounting after the season or negative brand revenues as customers press the company to accept unsold stocks. There is doubtless truth in the old adage that 'inventory pressure sells', but a probability-based assessment of possible outcomes in such a situation offers an approach to achieving the right commercial balance.

- *Reconfiguration.* Markets evolve, resegment and respond to innovation or crisis[31] in ways that can make them 'averse' to the current mean and open to reconfiguration around a new mean. In the words of Bernstein (1996), the strategic question is whether '[a] trend ... has a higher probability of continuing than reversing'.[32] Market instability clearly creates both opportunities and risk for incumbent brands and new entrants. One particular circumstance worth noting is that it may only be a *portion* of the market served by the brand that is undergoing immediate change. This has two implications. First of all, the more stationary part of the market may respond less readily to an innovation, but remain predictable otherwise. The risk here is that investments to exploit emerging trends may not show rapid or encouraging returns. Secondly, outcomes in the evolving ('non-stationary') part of the market may be much more uncertain than pressured or inexperienced marketers are prepared to acknowledge, strategically and operationally.

  When a previously stationary market reconfigures, traditional brand leaders may find that strategic myopia catches them out. Their ingrained respect for regression has gone too far. Scenario planning recognizes the possibility of a meaningful market shift and its potential variants (see Chapter 5). In the short term, comparing stationary market assumptions with actual outcomes is one way of detecting fundamental change that calls for action.[33] Hindsight often reveals that the firms which needed this advice most are the ones that ignored it. The 'psychology' of an organization is akin to the psychology of an individual: ultimately, it has to want to change. Risk literacy helps.

## INTERPRETING REGRESSION

An awareness of regression to the mean doubtless adds to risk insight, but it may not always be easy to apply in practice. Bernstein (1996) explains why regression should not be mechanically interpreted and slavishly applied:[34]

- The concept of regression describes an envelope of expected performance, but does not necessarily predict *rate of regression*. Where the process of regression is slow, it may lack sufficient momentum to resist a sudden shock that disrupts its progress. Conversely, the pace of regression may be so strong that 'matters do not come to rest once they reach the mean', but fluctuate around it to confound our interpretation.[35]

- Finally, the regression itself may not merely be volatile, but may be supplanted by a set of 'new normal' conditions that we cannot yet make out.[36]

Regression to the mean remains a powerful reference point in risk thinking, because it tests and tightens assumptions in marketing plans.

# Risk thresholds

Knowing how much you can afford to lose (or would be prepared to lose) is important, if you want to take risk rationally and confidently. This applies equally to individuals and organizations. In financial services businesses, these limits are very much in evidence, but all organizations require them. An explicit risk threshold, rather than an overriding desire for 'peace of mind', might even determine whether or not an individual buys travel insurance.

There are two kinds of risk threshold: tolerance and appetite.

- *Risk tolerance* defines the extent of loss (or adverse variance from any benchmark) that an organization or an individual can *objectively* withstand. A business can set risk tolerance in a number of ways: by reference to earnings, loan covenants, share price or balance-sheet strength. Risk tolerance for a firm is most often set in terms of profit or earnings impact, because this is a central measure of performance and a common denominator across functions within the business. It is said that risk tolerance is typically between 17 and 20 per cent of net worth for an organization or an individual.[37] Operationally, the concept of risk tolerance can be adapted and adopted as an *action standard* for any decision or intervention. One can establish a tolerance for movement (or 'drift') in any indicator that can be measured or usefully estimated, for example market share drop, customer complaint or departure from specification. Even diverse measures, such as employee turnover or product functionality, can be transposed onto an approximate scale of financial impact or worth, for reconciliation and ranking against other risk issues.

- *Risk appetite* is a qualification of risk tolerance that reflects the *risk attitude* of the risk-taker. It is often influenced by external perception or expectation, with reputational considerations featuring largely. A reckless risk seeker may have an appetite for risk that far exceeds their risk tolerance. On the other hand, it would not be surprising to find that a risk-neutral manager had a risk appetite that was approximately equal to their risk tolerance.

## SETTING FINANCIAL RISK THRESHOLDS

A company with a coherent risk strategy will relate its risk tolerance to its competitive stance. If all of your competitors are willing (and able) to take more risk, this tells you something.

Both risk tolerance and risk attitude can alter with circumstance. As a firm's financial strength waxes and wanes, its risk thresholds may change. Generally speaking, however, a company will set and communicate a standard risk threshold as a basis for risk assessment throughout the firm. Although it will be referred to as risk tolerance, it is very likely to be reflective of risk appetite. If a company can afford to lose $50 000 000, but would prefer not to lose more than $20 000 000 for reasons of investor credibility, the lower figure will determine the benchmark.

Whilst a corporate risk tolerance will be immediately relevant to the assessment of big risks and the aggregation of exposures across the firm, divisional or functional management generally needs a different figure that is relevant and proportionate to the scope of its own activities. There are a number of ways to achieve this 'cascading' of risk tolerance. Here are three examples:[38]

- *For revenue divisions.* Apply an analysis of past performance to determine critical thresholds: for example, '3–5 per cent fall in profit-from-operations versus prior year'.
- *For non-revenue divisions.* Identify a 'critical function surplus'. Risk tolerance is equal to a division's cost budget less an amount that would ensure continuity of its absolutely critical function(s).
- *General risk-adjusted approach.* Allocate a proportion of the corporate risk tolerance according to the size of divisional budgets, adjusted by a factor for divisional differences in inherent risk. 'Inherent risk' is a way of describing the division's desirable or unavoidable risk profile. One way of achieving this adjusted allocation is to calculate the risk tolerance twice: (1) an allocation based on budget and (2) an allocation based on a simple 3-2-1 rating for the inherent risk in each division (high-medium-low). Then average the two results.

## USING RISK THRESHOLDS

Sensing the aggregate risk being assumed or controlled by the marketing group is a fundamental discipline of risk management. You may recall that *expected loss* is the term used to describe the expected value of any adverse impact, which would need to be set off against your risk threshold in the relevant period. In principle, the net expected value of all identified exposures should not exceed your allocated risk tolerance (although it may be challenging and unnecessary in practice to attempt the perfect aggregation mathematically). It is advisable to leave a safety margin for the 'unknown unknowns' – losses that you could not predict. If you are taking a risk that exceeds your own group's tolerance, it is likely that you will need to make someone else aware of it. The escalation of critical risks, so that they are regularly reviewed on the corporate 'risk radar', is a discipline common to all good risk assessment processes.

## FUNDING SPECULATIVE OPPORTUNITIES

Comparison of high-value, high-risk opportunities is more constructive if parties to the discussion can relate them to the whole firm's tolerance or appetite for risk. This would be especially relevant if a speculative opportunity were not expected to make an immediate positive contribution to the firm's profits or had significant downsides.

# Expected utility

As we have seen so far, expected value and volatility allow us to compare the actual or assumed riskiness of alternative decisions and outcomes. But these indicators do not necessarily help a decision-maker to understand their own attitude to risk in current circumstances. The same financial (or non-financial) risks can have a different value or usefulness to different people at different times. *Utility* is the term used to describe such a subjective measure of value. As such, it translates a series of 'objective' outcomes (e.g. profit returns or product benefits) into their relative worth to a particular individual or organization, according to their own current yardstick.

The utility that a decision-maker places on particular risks can be approximated by inviting them, in effect, to consider the minimum 'price' at which they would notionally 'sell' their chances of securing the range of risk outcomes presented to them. The most common technique adjusts the value of a potential outcome so that it is 'discounted' (worth less to the seller) if the seller is averse to the perceived risk, but 'enhanced' (worth more to the seller) if the seller has appetite for the perceived risk. Now, instead of multiplying the potential outcomes by their probabilities of occurrence to calculate their expected values, you multiply the utilities (i.e. the risk-attitude-adjusted outcomes) by their probabilities, to produce an *expected utility* for each decision alternative. You have simply replaced the original (money) values with a relative measure that reflects not only their (money) value but also the decision-maker's attitude to the risk of achieving them.

To be clear about this, let us consider the different responses one might expect from people who are risk-neutral, risk-averse or risk-seeking:

- *Risk-neutral.* If someone is risk-neutral, it means that they would be *indifferent* to a choice between gambling on the expected value of a risk and accepting a sum equal to the expected value in cash now. In other words, if you offered them the option of accepting *either* $5000 in cash *or* cost-free shares in a business venture where there was a 0.5 probability of securing a $20 000 return and a 0.5 probability of personally underwriting a $10 000 loss, they would regard each choice as equally attractive. This is because both options have the same expected value. Here is the simple calculation:

$$(\$20\ 000 * 0.5) + (- \$10\ 000 * 0.5) = \$10\ 000 - \$5000 = \$5000$$

- *Risk-seeking.* If you offered a risk-seeker the same investment opportunity on identical terms, they would feel less concerned about the $10 000 loss than their risk-neutral colleague and more attracted to the chance of the high return. You would probably need to offer the risk seeker more than $5000 in cash, for them to forgo the opportunity of greater gain promised by the investment. In light of the best available outcome (the $20 000 gain), $5000 in cash is worth less to the risk seeker than it is to the person who is risk neutral.

- *Risk-averse.* A risk-averse individual will clearly be more concerned about the downside than the upside. On their scale of value, they will make an intuitive downward adjustment to the expected value suggested by the investment. In terms of our example here, it means that they would be satisfied with *less* than $5000 as an alternative to taking the gamble.

## UTILITY IN PRACTICE

In practice, formal estimations of utility are not common. Much of the time you will find that expected values have no need to be adjusted for utility, especially when the assessment of expected values has been your own. Intuition, experience and an ability to articulate risk attitude replace the structured process of estimation. For present purposes, it is nevertheless a useful exercise to work through one of the less complicated approaches. It will help to crystallize much that we have reviewed in this chapter.

There are a number of ways to elicit a required utility function. Farquahar (1984) considers a number of these.[39] The methodology we shall review is not difficult, though experience suggests that it does require a degree of risk literacy to be successful, and the result of such an exercise will only be an approximation.[40] Even so, this well-recognized method can help to clarify feelings about risk when faced with the figures.

Let us put ourselves in the situation illustrated in Figure 4.8.

In this case our sales colleagues have presented us with two opportunities, each involving a separate client: Blue Chip and Big Deal. We can only afford to invest in one of them. Although our colleagues feel that each opportunity is most likely to return the same profit ($40k), our discussions indicate that Big Deal has much greater risk: it may produce substantially higher or lower profits than Blue Chip. However, Big Deal is a newer customer and we are keen to build the relationship. Since we did not make the initial profit forecasts, we are undecided about the relative risks. On this occasion, we would like to develop some insight into our feelings about the mix of risk and reward in each proposal. In practice, what we now need to do is to turn the expected values that have been presented to us into expected utilities, so that our current attitude to risk can be more clearly understood as an influence on our decision.

The simple technique we will use is recognized for the general insight it provides and is known as the *certainty equivalence approach*. Figure 4.9 provides a template, already completed for illustrative purposes, based on our current example. By now, it may not surprise you that the approach sets out, in effect, to discover the minimum 'price' at which we would 'sell' the opportunity to invest in each of the proposals now before us.

There are three parts to the template and it is completed from left to right. On the far left-hand side is the utility scale, which does not need to be modified. It identifies five standard

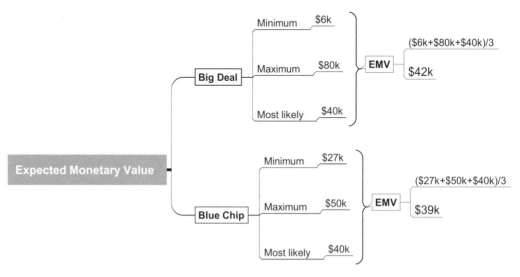

Mindjet MindManager Map

**Figure 4.8    Two risky proposals: expected values**

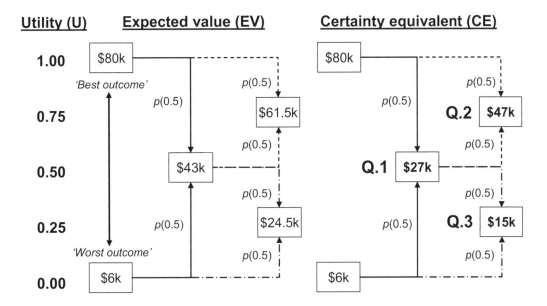

**Figure 4.9    Certainty equivalence approach**

utility intervals, from 'Best outcome' to 'Worst outcome'. The utility curve we develop and plot from these standard intervals will enable us to read off utilities for the actual expected returns promised by each transaction and calculate expected utilities accordingly. The second part of the template ('Expected value') steps through the process of calculating the unadjusted expected values that correspond to the five standard utility intervals on the scale. These need to represent the full range of outcomes across every decision alternative under review. As it happens, the two extreme values for best and worst outcome are to be found in the Big Deal proposal. We write these two values in the appropriate boxes: $80k and $6k. Next, we need to calculate the expected values for the remaining standard positions along the utility scale. The template shows that this is accomplished in two stages. Firstly, by calculating the mid-point value for the entire range:

$$\text{EV at U}(0.50) = (\$80k*\ p(0.5)) + (\$6k*p(0.5)) = \$43k$$

The final step is to complete the remaining two expected value boxes, so that we have expected value figures that sit in horizontal alignment with the 0.75 and 0.25 values on the Utility scale. We approach these second and third calculations in just the same way as the first. The only difference is that the mid-point value we have just calculated ($43k) must be one part of the 50:50 calculation in each case:

$$\text{EV at U}(0.75) = (\$80k*\ p(0.5)) + (\$43k*p(0.5)) = \$61.5k$$

$$\text{EV at U}(0.25) = (\$43k*\ p(0.5)) + (\$6k*p(0.5)) = \$24.5k$$

We now have an expected value aligned with each of the five points along the utility scale. Moving to the right-hand section of the template, we need to determine the 'certainty equivalent' values (CE) for each of the three expected values that we have newly calculated on the left-hand side. (By definition, we already know the certainty equivalents for the two extremes of expected value, $80k and $6k.)

There are three near-identical questions to ask (Q.1–Q.3), bearing in mind that each question will ask the respondent to evaluate a 50:50 gamble between two values. The first question (Q.1) is:

'*What is the minimum price at which you would forgo a 50 per cent chance of making $80k and a 50 per cent chance of making $6k?*'

The question is aiming to identify the necessary cash compensation for the gambling opportunity. In other words, how much we would rather have in cash now, to tip the balance in favour of *not* taking the risk as described. The named amount becomes the certainty equivalent of the gamble, which is then no longer available. In our case, you can see from the figure that $27k would be the minimum acceptable price at which we would 'sell' the gamble's expected value of $43k. The second and third questions are the same, but this time it is our newly stated 'certainty equivalent' for a utility of 0.50 ($27k) that becomes one of the two possible outcomes in each of the gambles. The second question (Q.2) is therefore:

'*What is the minimum price at which you would forgo a 50 per cent chance of making $80k and a 50 per cent chance of making $27k?*'

We have completed the template in the figure, which shows that CE at U(0.75) = $47k and CE at U(0.25) = $15k.

(It is important to remember that the second and third gambling choices are determined by our response to the first question, so we need to take time to reflect before giving our first answer.[41] Keep in mind also that the way questions are asked can influence the way they are answered.)

With this information, we can now produce a graph of our utility function (Figure 4.10).

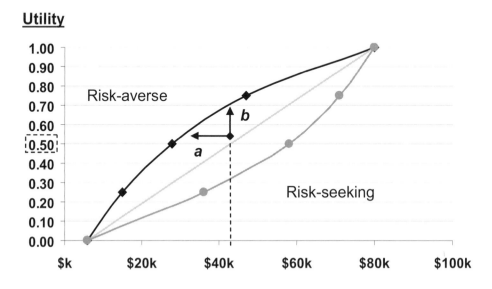

## Utility

Risk-aversion discounts gambles (*a*), whilst placing higher utility on 'cash in hand' than an equivalent sum gambled for greater gain (*b*)

**Figure 4.10    Utility functions**

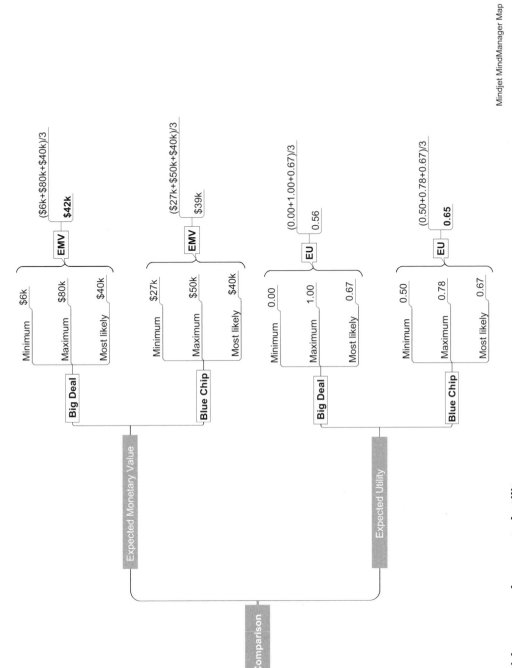

Mindjet MindManager Map

**Figure 4.11    Two risky proposals: expected utility**

You will see that there are three lines on the figure: the heaviest line is the utility function resulting from the elicitation process we have just completed. You will notice that it is concave to the straight grey line underneath it. The straight line represents a risk-neutral attitude, the subjective worth of any dollar amount in cash, up or down, being precisely equal to its expected value in the gamble. By contrast, we are clearly risk-averse. After all, we were prepared to forgo an expected value of $43k for just $27k in cash. Although the gamble promised up to $80k, the prospect of only making $6k weighed more heavily in our attitude to the overall risk. The utility we produced through our answers is a classic presentation of risk aversion. As the graph shows, risk aversion devalues a gamble (at *a*), whilst putting higher utility on 'cash in hand' than an equivalent sum put at risk for greater gain (at *b*). The line below the risk-neutral line represents the opposite case of risk seeking. In particular, you will notice that in both cases the distance between the risk-neutral line and the other two lines tends to be greatest at the mid-point between the two extreme values. This is not surprising because 50:50 is, by definition, the position of least certainty between two complementary probabilities. Any other mix is moving closer to one or other outcome. The visible difference between the two non-neutral attitudes is that the risk seeker perceives *higher* utility, not lower utility, in the opportunity to make money by taking risk.

Returning to our case, an adjustment of the two opportunities for our attitude to risk reverses their ranking. Figure 4.11 (see previous page) shows that Blue Chip has the higher expected utility for us, even though it has a somewhat lower expected value. Unless we decide that our risk aversion should be ignored, we will probably decide in favour of this less risky course of action. But there is no automatic obligation on us to do so. What we should do, however, is to *understand* our attitude to risk as revealed through the exercise and to make our final decision equipped with the additional insight that we have acquired.

## Summary

We have now defined some of the key concepts of risk and risk thinking:

- We have reviewed the rules and practice of probability estimation, with emphasis on the role of subjective assessments.

- We have considered the insights offered by expected value, expected utility, volatility and regression to the mean.

- We have suggested that explicit risk thresholds add an important perspective to decision-making.

  In the next chapter we will consider the identification and management of risk.

## References

1     Knight, F.H. (1921), *Risk, Uncertainty, and Profit*, Houghton Mifflin.
2     Piercy, N. (1985), *Marketing Organisation: An Analysis of Information Processing, Power and Politics*, George Allen & Unwin.
3     Schuyler, J. (2001), *Risk and Decision Analysis in Projects*, Project Management Institute.
4     Schuyler (2001), op.cit.
5     Schuyler (2001), op.cit.

6    Wisniewski, M. (2006), *Quantitative Methods for Decision Makers – Fourth Edition*, FT Prentice Hall.

7    Edwards, W. (1954), 'The Theory of Decision Making', *Psychological Bulletin*, Volume 51 (Issue 4), pp. 380–417.

8    Rosenberg, M.J. (1956), 'Cognitive Structure and Attitudinal Affect', *Journal of Abnormal and Social Psychology*, Volume 53 (Issue 3), pp. 367–372.

9    Fishbein, M. (1963), 'An Investigation of the Relationships between Beliefs about an Object and Attitude toward that Object', *Human Relations*, Volume 16 (Number 3), pp. 233–40.

10   East, R. (1997), *Consumer Behaviour – Advances and Applications in Marketing*, FT Prentice Hall.

11   McDonald, M., Smith B. and Ward, K. (2006), *Marketing Due Diligence – Reconnecting Strategy to Share Price*, Butterworth-Heinemann.

12   Goodwin, P. and Wright, G. (2004), *Decision Analysis for Management Judgment – Third Edition*, John Wiley & Sons Ltd, p. 75.

13   Goodwin and Wright (2004), op.cit.

14   Goodwin and Wright (2004), op.cit.

15   Gigerenzer, G. (1994). 'Why the Distinction between Single Event Probabilities and Frequencies is Relevant for Psychology and Vice Versa', in G. Wright and P. Ayton (eds), *Subjective Probability*, John Wiley & Sons.

16   Bunn, D.W. and Thomas, H. (1975), 'Assessing Subjective Probability in Decision Analysis', in D.J. White and K.C. Bowen (eds), *The Role and Effectiveness of Theories of Decision in Practice*, Hodder and Stoughton.

17   Schuyler (2001), op.cit.

18   Stael von Holstein, C-A.S. and Matheson, J. (1979), *A Manual for Encoding Probability Distributions*, SRI International.

19   Goodwin and Wright (2004), op.cit.

20   East (1997), op.cit.

21   Goodwin and Wright (2004), op.cit., p. 76.

22   Griffiths, T.L. and Tenenbaum, J.B. (2006), 'Optimal Predictions in Everyday Cognition', *Psychological Science*, Volume 17 (Issue 9), pp. 767–773.

23   Griffiths and Tenenbaum (2006), op.cit., pp. 767–773.

24   Wisniewski (2006), op.cit.

25   East (1997), op.cit.

26   McDonald et al. (2006), op.cit.

27   East (1997), op.cit.

28   Shaw, R. and Merrick, D. (2005), *Marketing Payback – Is Your Marketing Profitable?*, FT Prentice Hall.

29   Shaw and Merrick (2005), op.cit.

30   Goodwin and Wright (2004), op.cit.

31   East (1997), op.cit.

32   Bernstein, P.L. (1996), *Against the Gods: The Remarkable Story of Risk*, John Wiley & Sons, Inc., p. 178.

33   East (1997), op.cit.

34   Bernstein (1996), op.cit.

35   Bernstein (1996), op.cit.

36   Bernstein (1996), op.cit.

37   Schuyler (2001), op.cit.

38   Marsh Risk Consulting (2007), 'Divisional Risk Tolerances', unpublished paper, Marsh Ltd.

39   Farquahar, P.H. (1984), 'Utility Assessment Methods', *Management Science*, Volume 30 (Issue 11), pp. 1283–1300.

40   Goodwin and Wright (2004), op.cit.

41   Goodwin and Wright (2004), op.cit.

# **5** *Identifying and Managing Risk*

To recognize a performance risk is not necessarily to understand it. Similarly, to understand a performance risk is not necessarily to manage it well. The discipline of risk management offers a number of efficient processes and frameworks for identifying, evaluating, prioritizing and managing risks.

In this chapter we will:

- review four frameworks that help to identify and prioritize known risks
- discuss issues that arise in determining cause and effect
- outline the principal strategies available to manage risk
- describe two relevant approaches to cost-benefit analysis.

## Identifying risks

There are times when it is prudent to step back and take conscious stock of all known risks and uncertainties, so that they can be prioritized, managed and monitored. A concise and meaningful review of risks should be a standard feature of any new product sign-off, major commitment or planned response to competitive threat.

The process of identifying risks is often consultative, motivating people to contribute their perspectives and experience, whether they are directly or indirectly associated with the matter under review. Encouraging new business partners, agencies, suppliers or clients to discuss risk issues openly and in a structured fashion at the beginning of a business relationship can also help to avoid unnecessary roadblocks or misunderstandings later on. An agreement to revisit such a risk assessment from time to time creates the time and space to discuss issues that might otherwise be difficult to raise in the course of normal business dealings.

We will describe four approaches to risk identification, each different in origin, each achieving its coverage of risk issues in a different way. These techniques are useful to individuals in their thinking, as well as to groups of colleagues, though we will discuss them in an organizational context.

Here is a summary of the distinctive features of the four approaches, before we review each of them in more detail:

- *Six Thinking Hats*[*] is a flexible framework for co-operative thinking. One of its great benefits is to encourage and accommodate risk thinking in the assessment of opportunity.[1]
- *Marketing Due Diligence* is the name given by McDonald, Smith and Ward (2006) to their approach to the risk assessment of marketing plans.[2]

---

[*]     Six Thinking Hats® is a registered trademark.

- *Scenario planning* is the term used to describe a range of techniques designed to create alternative narratives of the future as the basis for decision-making in the face of uncertainty.

- *Risk mapping* is the generic term used to describe an exercise in risk identification which delivers a ranking of risks in schematic form, prioritized for management purposes. Since risk mapping is a cornerstone of corporate risk assessment, we will consider this process in greatest practical detail.

## SIX THINKING HATS

As marketers, we are positive and constructive thinkers, by and large. What we need is an intuitive way of building risk thinking into our assessment of opportunity. One effective device that meets this requirement is Six Thinking Hats.[3] This is a method for evaluating plans and ideas devised by Edward de Bono, the British psychologist first credited with using the term 'lateral thinking' to describe the way in which unorthodox thought processes solve problems.[4]

De Bono's observation of how people think and work together in organizations led him to a number of conclusions. Some of these are directly relevant to the management of risk and uncertainty:

- People should ideally be flexible in their thinking styles, but in practice they will tend to exhibit only one thinking style if they are labelled that way (e.g. optimistic, pessimistic).

- People apply their experience of the past by reference to 'standard situations' suggested by hindsight or learning. However, this may limit their capacity to think creatively. De Bono's suggestion is that '[i]nstead of judging our way forward, we need to design our way forward'.[5]

- Debate between colleagues is often competitive or overly concerned with proving the other party wrong. In practice, debate produces the best result when there is 'parallel thinking' and synergy of ideas. 'Parallel thinking' is de Bono's way of describing a process by which people consider the same aspect of an issue at the same time, albeit from their individual perspectives.[6]

- Classic random brainstorming of a problem does not guarantee or signal complete coverage of the issues, nor does it ensure that everyone contributes.

- Finally, organizational cultures tend either to discourage us from acknowledging the role of *emotion* in business decision-making or to encourage us to *justify* emotions in logic, when logic may not apply.

De Bono's response to these insights was to propose a system of six colours, each denoting a thinking style (see Figure 5.1). When a group reviews an issue or a plan, all participants are prompted to focus briefly and simultaneously on one colour-aspect of the issue at a time. By labelling each broad style of thinking as a hat and a colour, it becomes easier to ask people to think in a particular way ('What about some red hat thinking on this plan?'). Each new colour helps the individual and the group to make a clear and conscious transition from one perspective to another.

It is not only black hat thinking that is relevant to the management of risk and uncertainty. Red hat thinking enables issues of risk appetite to come to the fore. White hat thinking helps to identify requirements for better information in order to reduce uncertainties. Blue hat thinking may argue for structured risk assessment to support decision-making about particular courses of action.

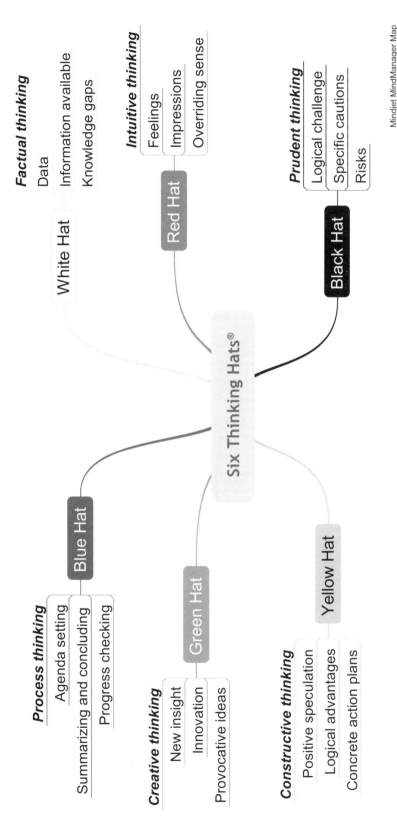

**Factual thinking**
Data
Information available
Knowledge gaps

White Hat

**Intuitive thinking**
Feelings
Impressions
Overriding sense

Red Hat

**Prudent thinking**
Logical challenge
Specific cautions
Risks

Black Hat

Six Thinking Hats®

**Process thinking**
Agenda setting
Summarizing and concluding
Progress checking

Blue Hat

**Creative thinking**
New insight
Innovation
Provocative ideas

Green Hat

**Constructive thinking**
Positive speculation
Logical advantages
Concrete action plans

Yellow Hat

MindJet MindManager Map

**Figure 5.1** **Six Thinking Hats®**

*Source: After de Bono (1999)*

The method is straightforward and non-technical. If anything, its critics feel uncomfortable with its intentional simplicity and apparent playfulness. Of course, it is not necessary actually to wear coloured hats (though some people apparently do!). De Bono's serious intention is that people should be obliged to stretch beyond their natural or default thinking styles for a time, safe in the knowledge that they will have an opportunity to contribute in their 'strong suit', if they have special knowledge or an urgent insight that needs to be shared.

Six Thinking Hats is an effective way of beginning to associate risk thinking and marketing thinking.

## 'MARKETING DUE DILIGENCE'[7]

By contrast, McDonald, Smith and Ward (2006) offer a more technical and direct approach to the risk assessment of marketing plans.[8] They argue that the seemingly intractable pattern of overambitious and underachieving marketing plans, above all for new products and services, can be ascribed to a failure of rigour in the analysis of assumptions (or the plan's 'promises') in three distinct areas:

- the nature of the market ('market risk')
- the attainable share of market ('share risk')
- the net contribution to shareholder value ('profit risk').

Their work suggests that from each of these three perspectives, there are five principal sources of risk (see Figure 5.2). The mix of the 15 risk elements will vary from case to case. Meanwhile, there are some universal causes of ill-fortune that are too often ignored:[9]

- *Inadequate customer segmentation.* Sound segmentation is the vital foundation of a good marketing plan. This is because customer segmentation defines markets not by existing products and services from a producer perspective, but by clustering customers according to their common needs and purchasing habits. Its absence suggests a lack of adequate insight into market requirements. The process of segmentation may even lead to a realization that the most appropriate definition cuts across existing product boundaries and therefore redefines the competition. Once identified, a segment can be assessed both for its accessibility and its viability: 'Can we serve all or part of this segment? Can we earn a reasonable return?' McDonald and Dunbar (2004)[10] and Weinstein (2004)[11] provide a comprehensive account of good practice in consumer and business market segmentation.

- *Inadequacy of resource.* The resources necessary to implement a marketing plan should not only be defined in relation to scale objectives ('How many customers must I reach?'), but also be proportionate to the intelligibility and strength of the offering in question from a customer point of view. It may seem obvious that a well differentiated and readily communicated product might need less intensive communication support than a more subtle or complex offering. McDonald, Smith and Ward (2006) caution that rules of thumb for the budgeting of marketing expenditure may not reflect these important differences in resourcing requirement.[12]

- *Inadequate focus on the risk in growth and change.* The greatest risks in any annual brand plan lie wherever it promises growth or involves change. The 'duly diligent' marketer will isolate and define these growth or change elements and subject the underlying assumptions to

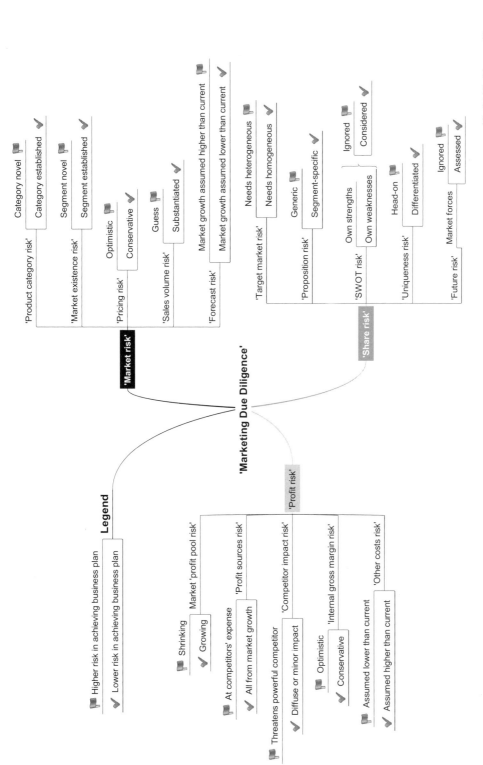

MindJet MindManager Map

**Figure 5.2**   **'Marketing Due Diligence'**
Source: After McDonald, Smith and Ward (2006)

the recommended process of 'Marketing Due Diligence'. The principle is to assess the higher risk component of the annual plan as if it were an entirely separate proposal.[13]

The 'Marketing Due Diligence' approach emphasizes that the returns promised by a plan should be commensurate with its known risk.

## SCENARIO PLANNING

Most of our day-to-day work in brand management is focused on the possibilities and probabilities of relatively short-term outcomes: next month, next quarter, next year. Yet the quality of some decisions can only be judged against an interpretation of the future. All too often, future perspectives remain implicit, incomplete or unchallenged, managers maintaining their belief in an 'official future' that is questionable in the light of experience or events.[14] There may be changes in the business environment that are collectively acknowledged within the firm, but are inadequately addressed.[15] By default, companies may put the wrong priority or time-scale on known issues, misjudging their ability to deal with them in an unspecified future.[16] In the face of technologically driven change, for example, there is a common tendency to overestimate the short-term implications of the change, but misjudge its long-term impact.

Making sense of the future is therefore a very important strategic and risk management task, but one that can be frustrated by combinations of inertia, hubris or lack of effective process. The purpose of scenario planning is to create a pertinent set of 'negotiated futures' as the context within which managers across the firm can evaluate decisions for their longer-term impact and appropriateness. Since the process is founded on an acceptance that no one can predict the future with certainty, the development of scenarios readily accommodates contributors' different perspectives and insights. It obliges managers both to articulate and challenge their assumptions about the future, whilst helping in some measure to counter 'groupthink' by allowing minority opinions 'airtime'.[17] This is not only helpful to colleagues in developing a common view of what might lie ahead: it has also been used by business-to-business service firms to enable customers to describe and share their own outlooks and expectations.[18]

The narrative form of final scenario output does not require a technical understanding of probabilities or decision analysis. Scenarios do not deliver expected value indications for future outcomes, but nonetheless provide a framework for risk-taking choices in the pursuit of successful outcomes. Since the future can never be certain, there is frequently a legitimate divergence of view within a single organization. With an articulate and accepted view of alternative futures, it becomes easier to accept the need to prepare for low probability and worst-case events or to spot the early signs of change in a particular direction:

*[A] portfolio of mental models allows us to improve our response to change and engage in 'impossible thinking' that can enable a shift in mental models to identify hidden opportunities and threats. Actions that would have been considered impossible based on current models become possible with this shift in thinking.[19]*

Pierre Wack is credited with the early application of formal scenario planning for business at Royal Dutch Shell. More than 30 years after its first introduction, Shell still applies scenario planning to the evaluation of all major projects. As a complement to the normal due diligence, projects requiring substantial investment are assessed for robustness under each of three alternative futures that the company has established as part of its wider planning process. A strategy that depends upon the certainty of a single predicted business environment is judged to have insufficient flexibility to be viable over the term of investment.

Rather than being an amalgam of incompatible inputs, a single scenario is usually one of several stories, each internally consistent and distinct from the others. A particular scenario may not have a high probability of occurrence, but must be a plausible narrative account of the future. It is detailed enough to be both informative and relevant to those will refer to it. The need for plausibility means that each narrative must represent a credible combination of causes and effects within the time horizon defined for the exercise. Each scenario helps to characterize the range of developments likely to influence a critical future outcome for the firm. In aggregate, the three or four scenarios in a set define the 'space' within which the future is most likely to unfold: 'the joint impacts of many uncertainties'.[20]

Scenario planning should usually precede the development of strategies and detailed risk management plans, although the output of prior risk identification work will undoubtedly contribute to the exercise. If the aim of a scenario exercise is 'to pin down the corners of the plausible futures', the question is how best to set the boundaries.[21] Ringland (1998) describes a wide range of alternative approaches to scenario planning and its applications.[22] The most frequently cited method focuses on identifying 'driving forces'. A variant of this approach is to describe 'extreme worlds'.

## Driving forces

The 'driving forces' method prompts the creation of up to four contrasting scenarios. These are based on combinations of the *most unpredictable* of the *most critical* factors identified in the first part of the process. Schwartz (1998) provides a comprehensive review of the approach. The steps are summarized here and in Figure 5.3:[23]

1. *Define the focal issue.* This is the anchor of the process, ensuring that it keeps its relevance. In a marketing context, this would be a specific issue or decision of material significance to the branded business, rather than a general environmental question. The definition should include a time horizon that specifies the 'depth of field' for the exercise.

2. *List key factors.* These are the key factors that will determine the success or failure of a course of action or directly influence the outcome of an issue. They should be stated and listed.

3. *Identify driving forces.* These are the forces that will influence the key factors to affect outcomes. Driving forces generally emanate from the wider world or macro-environment. By definition, they are not within our control, even though we may later expect to develop strategies to exploit or mitigate their effects. The PESTLE acronym is a familiar prompt for the identification of driving forces: political, economic, sociological, technological, legal and ecological. Another stimulus is to imagine oneself at the outer limit of the scenario's time horizon and then to complete the sentence, 'If only I had known ... [that] [whether] [if] ... '.

4. *Rank the driving forces.* The identified forces need to be ranked, both for their uncertainty and their impact on the focal issue. Isolate any driving forces that are predetermined (i.e. not uncertain at all), such as demographics: these will logically need to appear in all of the final scenarios. Also remove from the collection of uncertainties any that amount to courses of action or strategic options. These do not belong in scenarios, which should encourage the development of suitable responses rather than contain them.[24]

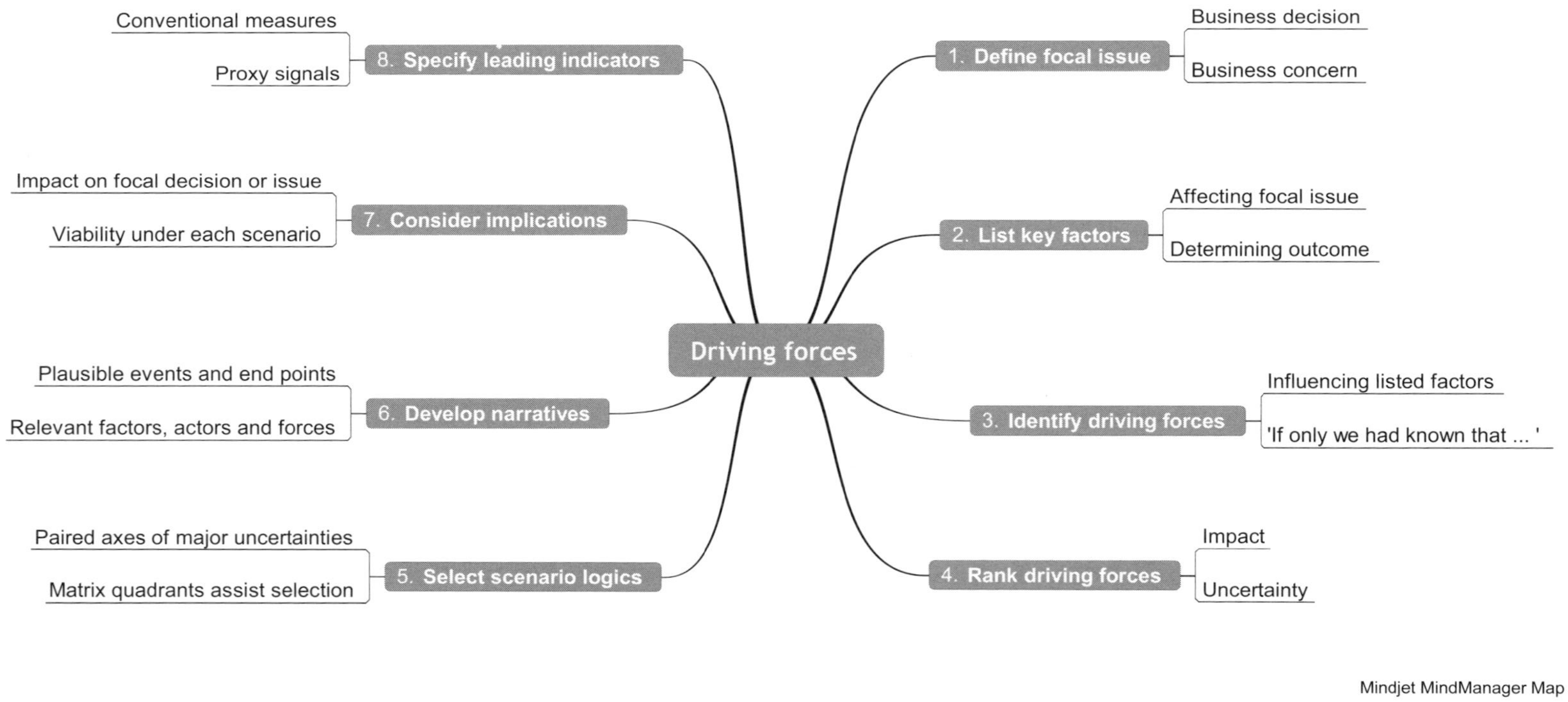

**Figure 5.3    Scenario planning – 'driving forces'**
*Source: After Schwartz (1998)*

MindJet MindManager Map

Driving forces

1. Define focal issue
- Business decision
- Business concern

2. List key factors
- Affecting focal issue
- Determining outcome

3. Identify driving forces
- Influencing listed factors
- 'If only we had known that …'

4. Rank driving forces
- Impact
- Uncertainty

5. Select scenario logics
- Paired axes of major uncertainties
- Matrix quadrants assist selection

6. Develop narratives
- Plausible events and end points
- Relevant factors, actors and forces

7. Consider implications
- Impact on focal decision or issue
- Viability under each scenario

8. Specify leading indicators
- Conventional measures
- Proxy signals

5. *Select the scenario logics.* This crucial step identifies critical uncertainties that will define and distinguish the themes of each scenario. This is an intuitive and iterative process, rather than a mechanical one. The first step is to put 'most' and 'least' impact values (*not* probabilities) on each critical uncertainty. The second step is to explore trial combinations of paired uncertainties for their coherence and relevance as scenarios, using a simple matrix such as Figure 5.4 to clarify alternatives. In the figure, the two lines joining the maximum and minimum values of each critical uncertainty, A and B, intersect. The four cells created by their intersection represent the permutations of A and B as candidate scenarios.

6. *Develop the scenario narratives.* Finalize the selection of components for each scenario by adding any other element from the original lists. It does not matter if supplementary elements are repeated across scenarios. Include the uncontrollable roles played by key actors or stakeholders in determining the course of events. Write each chosen scenario in concise narrative form, adding a descriptive title of two or three words that captures its essence. A total length of 200–300 words for each narrative would not be unusual. Check that each scenario expresses a clear and logical sequence of events and that specific cause-and-effect relationships make sense. This will establish whether the scenario is plausible. Importantly, make sure that there is sufficient contrast between each suggested scenario and that in aggregate they succeed in representing the range of possible futures suggested by the driving forces and other uncertainties.

7. *Consider the implications.* The focal issue should be reviewed in the light of each narrative in the finished set. Reconsider carefully any significant course of action that appears only to be viable under a single scenario.

8. *Specify leading indicators.* It is important to scan the environment for signals that suggest how the future may actually evolve. These key indicators or 'trigger events'[25] may be common across all scenarios or specific to some of them, as appropriate. They may be conventional measures or imaginative proxies where no direct measure exists. Consider this final step as an opportunity to create competitive insight and advantage from the exercise.

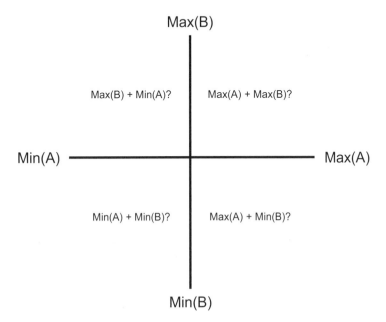

**Figure 5.4     Scenario selection matrix**

## Extreme worlds

The 'extreme worlds' approach to scenario development is broadly similar to the driving forces method we have just reviewed. There are two principal differences:

1. The ranking of factors and forces should produce two lists:
   a. those likely to have a *negative* impact on the focal issue (one extreme)
   b. those likely to have a *positive* impact on the focal issue (the other extreme).
2. The output comprises two internally consistent narratives, one of which embodies all of the 'negatively resolved' uncertainties, the other all of the 'positively resolved' uncertainties.[26]

## The Delphi alternative

Scenarios are usually developed by a group of people in joint session. The Delphi consensus forecasting technique approaches the task in a different way, by initially eliciting separate structured forecasts or estimates from *experts*. These experts are subsequently provided with an anonymous set of their combined submissions. They are asked to consider the full range of opinion expressed by their peers and to provide *revisions* to their initial estimates. An important feature of the methodology is that the participants should not consult with each other, but respond independently to the combined wisdom of the group. The recommendation that emerges is then taken to be 'best of breed' and offer the highest overall prospect of accuracy. The technique has been applied, for example, to forecasting a brand's likely sensitivity to alternative media mixes.

Delphi lacks the stimulus to imaginative thinking offered by live discussion, though the technique may arguably be a form of controlled incitement to 'groupthink', since contributors' forecasts are encouraged to converge. Nonetheless, assuming that no single forecaster has overwhelmingly superior expertise, the averaged forecast of the group will be statistically superior to any single person's view.

In its classic form, the Delphi technique does not involve a pooling of forecasting approach by contributors, merely a sharing of results. However, Shaw and Merrick (2005) describe a hybrid variant – 'judgemental bootstrapping' – in which the rounds of expert input contribute to the development of an econometric *model*, which is then used to produce the required forecast.[27]

Scenario planning cannot divine the future or make it happen. However, it can deliver an impetus for change, a clear view of strategic vulnerabilities and a greatly enriched basis upon which to identify and prioritize other risk management issues. A well-honed set of scenarios provides an efficient means of communicating relevant information about the future and promoting its consistent application in decision-making.

# Risk mapping

A *risk map* is a schematic summary of identified risks, plotted on a matrix for comparison and ease of interpretation. The risks are plotted according to their approximate expected values. One axis of the matrix shows estimated frequency or probability of occurrence, whilst the other shows estimated impact, usually financial. The highest priority exposures therefore appear in the top right-hand box. Figure 5.5 provides a schematic example.

An exercise in risk mapping provides a structured opportunity for participants to indicate all significant and identifiable risks, missed opportunities or issues that should be matters

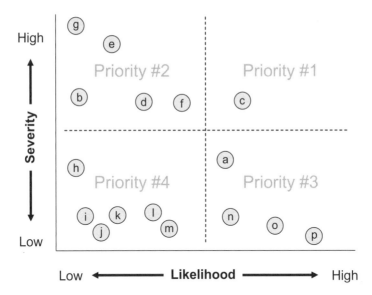

**Figure 5.5    Risk map (illustrative)**

of common concern. In formal terms, the process is a first step towards satisfying external expectations that there should be a demonstrable risk management effort in place. Risk mapping is an important complement to other risk management activities, because its focus is on prioritizing risks for practical attention and a corresponding allocation of resources.

Since the brand is implicated in many risk scenarios, a marketer's first experience of risk mapping may come about as participant in a company-wide, cross-functional risk assessment (or 'risk profiling') exercise. The marketing group may also want to run its own risk-mapping exercises from time to time. It could be that a team has already reviewed a project using Six Thinking Hats and has identified general areas of risk that now need to be specified more precisely. A structured risk assessment can also have considerable value as part of a major planning exercise or at the inception of an important business relationship. For example, sitting with a new PR agency and ranking the most important roadblocks to effective working gives both parties an opportunity to table concerns or issues in a constructive way, whilst establishing a framework for future review and stocktaking as joint activity evolves.

It is quite common to use exactly the same mapping approach for prioritization of *opportunities*. You simply alter the criteria to reflect the different perspective, ranking ideas according to their upside potential and likelihood of fulfilment within a defined time-frame.

## CORPORATE CONTEXT

Risk mapping is the first step in a widely used approach to corporate risk assessment and risk management. The exercise is usually conducted first of all at divisional or functional level, followed by a separate 'top-down' risk identification by the main board or its risk committee. The 'top-down' exercise often takes the form of a validation of the critical risk list identified in the 'bottom-up' reviews, any additions or removals being based on the wider perspective available to the board and the different impact criteria that may apply. In any event, the subsidiary groups retain responsibility for management of the critical risks they have identified, even if a number of their nominated risks do not qualify to remain on the main board's risk management agenda. The agreed ranking criteria for risk (especially financial impact) will determine whether a risk identified by a subsidiary is promoted to appear (or reappear) on the main board's 'risk radar' at a future time.

There are three other recognized components of the process that follow risk mapping:

1. A *cause-and-controls assessment* sets specific risk improvement objectives for key risks identified in the risk mapping exercise.

2. A corporate *risk register* provides a documentary summary of all risks requiring attention across the firm and the basis upon which they will be managed.

3. Regular *risk reviews* allow for the periodic assessment of progress against defined risk management goals at meetings with a specific focus on risk and its management.

The risk register and the risk review process can be described briefly. In the remainder of the chapter we will focus on the detail of the risk-mapping process and subsequent cause-and-controls assessment, because these are both activities central to risk thinking.

## Risk register and risk reviews

The corporate risk register is a maintained schedule of risks that are believed to be material to the business as a whole. The content of risk registers differs by organization. The registers are usually summary documents, in tabular form, listing the risks in whatever sequence or subdivisions make sense for practical purposes. A company-wide risk assessment process usually involves the establishment of a subsidiary risk register for each of the participating divisions and functions across the organization. A related risk management and information system may sit on the firm's intranet.

Risk registers contain some or all of the following detail on each risk in rank order:

- a reference number alongside each risk, useful in database consolidations and to avoid duplication
- a headline description of the risk (possibly consolidating similar or subordinate exposures)
- separate keyword summaries of assumed cause(s) and consequence(s)
- the risk's severity, frequency and expected value, updated as necessary: objective data or a consolidation of estimations provided by contributors to the risk mapping process.
- separately, source data and interview summaries in a similar format.

A comprehensive register might also record:

- the identity of the person ultimately accountable for management of the risk, usually at a senior level (sometimes called the *risk owner*)
- the identity of the person(s) and function(s) responsible for the implementation of the risk management and mitigation plan (sometimes called *risk agents*)
- the indicator(s) that would change the 'state of alert' or confirm actual occurrence of the risk (sometimes called *triggers for escalation*)
- a summary of time-lined actions to manage the risk, including an indication of each action's priority and the progress made to date (known as the *risk management plan*).

It is general practice to review the corporate risk register twice a year. In some organizations these reviews are conducted more frequently (i.e. quarterly) by a standing risk committee of the board.

A risk review has three fundamental purposes:

- to determine whether previously agreed risk management actions have been undertaken
- to assess whether a risk already identified should be re-ranked for either likelihood or impact, affecting its priority for management attention
- to signal any new exposures that should be taken onto the risk register.

Risk committees of the board typically focus their attention on the top ten identified risks or those considered critical to the company, with each division and function attending to its own exclusive risks in addition. These divisional risks may have lower corporate impact, but still retain their importance as key aspects of performance within the division or function.

Recognition that a market has become 'newly vulnerable',[28] and substantial changes in business operations or in the climate of external opinion may also suggest the need for an ad hoc risk review.

## RISK MAPPING PROCESS

Participants' contribution to a risk-mapping exercise can be collected in facilitated workshops or by interviewing individuals. Outside consultants can provide assistance, whether as facilitators or as subject-matter experts.

The advantages of group workshops are:

- the process can usually be completed in less than half a day, with feedback to participants at the end of the session
- a collective effort may be more stimulating to individuals and therefore more productive
- diversity of opinion and discussion ultimately produce a more rounded evaluation of key risks by individuals, whilst the use of keypads and polling software such as OptionFinder[†29] keeps participants' scoring anonymous.

On the other hand, the advantages of individual interviews are:

- imposes no theoretical limit on the number of participants or their location
- the approach offers greater freedom of expression on sensitive subjects
- the situation better accommodates the contributor's pace and thinking style
- there is a lesser propensity for individual contributions to be subverted by 'groupthink'[30] – although the 'Moses' heuristic (see Chapter 3) may still cause people to adopt a risk attitude that conforms to group expectation.

It is possible to combine these two approaches. For example, candidate risks can be collected by interview, then further discussed and ranked in group session(s) using polling software to maintain confidentiality.

---

†     OptionFinder® is a registered trademark of Option Technologies Interactive LLC.

## Participant selection

Unless the risk identification and mapping work will be followed by a more detailed assessment and action planning on the same day, participant selection should be guided by the main objective of a risk-mapping exercise, which is to identify and rank risks, not to resolve them. For a single group session, the number of participants should ideally not exceed eight to ten people. Clearly, this limitation does not apply to an exercise conducted by interview.

People should be qualified for participation in at least one of the following ways:

- they are direct stakeholders in the success or failure of the project in question
- they bring meaningful experience or expertise
- they add relevant external perspective
- they have relevant insight into the organization's operational culture
- they understand the organization's strategy and appetite for risk.

It is a good idea to limit the number of 'honorary participants', who can be consulted and engaged by alternative means.

## Preparation

Spontaneous risk-mapping sessions do not work very well. Participants must be suitably briefed in advance. They need to know:

- why the exercise is being undertaken (including who its senior sponsors are)
- why their participation is valuable
- what will happen on the day and afterwards
- what they must do to prepare themselves.

It is usual to ask participants to send the facilitator a simple list of their top five perceived risks well before the day of the session. This request for advance material is useful for ensuring that everyone has given the matter some thought before the workshop or interview takes place. It also helps the group work to achieve positive momentum more quickly, because there is something for the group to react to immediately. In an ideal world, all participants should also be encouraged to familiarize themselves in advance with the topics reviewed in Chapter 3 of this book: risk attitude, heuristics, learning from experience. This will give them an opportunity to reconsider their own experience of risk and their responses to it.

*Stimulus material.* A risk-mapping workshop is a focus group, just like any other, in which stimulus material has its place. Although a wide-ranging risk identification process cannot amount to a complete assessment of the likely causes and consequences of each candidate risk, there should be enough discussion to ensure that the subsequent scoring process by individuals will be based on a risk scenario that is broadly the same in everyone's mind. This book provides a number of risk-focused frameworks that may be helpful by way of stimulus material, whether on the day or as part of the briefing pack:

- Figure 2.6    Assessing brand vulnerabilities
- Figure 2.7    Four fields of brand risk management
- Figure 3.3    Notable causes of operational failure[31]

- Figure 4.1    Classification of risks
- Figure 5.2    'Marketing Due Diligence'[32]
- Figure 5.11    The reputation@risk[‡] model[33]

## Process management

Consistent with the underlying human factors and heuristics we considered in Chapter 3, there are some details of process to bear in mind at each of the workshop's three stages:

- engaging with the subject
- listing the risks
- rating the risks.

*Engaging with the subject.* The subject of risk needs to be approached constructively, emphasizing the complementary relationship between risk and reward, between business strategy and risk strategy, between risk management and performance management. At the beginning of the session, it can be helpful to give participants an opportunity to 'personalize' the formal definition for risk provided in the briefing documentation, so that they engage more fully with the subject. (This is not quite the same as asking if everybody *understands* the definition: they will feel encouraged to say that they do.) One way of breaking the ice is to ask people to describe the most instructive 'risk experience' they can recall in their professional lives. The case does not need to have involved them personally, but it does need to have taught them something. Be ready with your own story, if nothing is immediately forthcoming elsewhere.

*Listing the risks.* Once suitably briefed and prepared for the exercise, participants should be invited to describe each risk that they believe is important enough to merit attention. This ought to include a general indication of cause and effect: for example, 'Product recall arising from safety concerns leads to substantial loss of market share worldwide'. Some practitioners encourage groups to identify strategic risks and other external exposures first, before considering the other risk types.[34] Dealing with strategic issues at the beginning of the process tends to reinforce the positive relationship between risk and opportunity, whilst prompting the subsequent coverage of implementation risks.

All these risk statements should be listed until the schedule is considered as complete as it reasonably can be, recognizing that there will always be some risks that remain unidentifiable (the 'unknown unknowns'). Group sessions may identify 50–100 candidate risks. Individuals in interview-based exercises are usually required to identify their own top ten perceived risks, which are then consolidated to produce the collective view.

There is no obligation to use polling software such as OptionFinder[35] or any other facilitation software to capture the emerging schedule of candidate risks in group sessions. Where the number of risks identified is not likely to become unmanageable, the same general result can be achieved by inviting participants to stick self-adhesive notes onto a wallboard. Each note identifies a risk. Through further group discussion, these are then clustered and ranked. Clearly this approach does not achieve anonymity in voting and is arguably more susceptible to 'groupthink' or the influence of powerful individuals. These trade-offs may matter more in some cases than others; this is a matter for judgement by the facilitator.

---

‡    reputation@risk® is a registered trademark of Marsh Ltd.

*Rating the risks.* As we have already suggested, some discussion of the candidate risks will have helped to ensure that there is a reasonable degree of common understanding as to what each risk means. Participants should then be asked to rate each risk according to their individual assessment of its likelihood of occurrence and severity of impact on the business, should it occur. Multiplying its likelihood score by its severity score gives each risk an overall rating (in effect, a subjective value for *expected loss*). The ratings are based on scales of likelihood and severity presented to participants for this purpose. For convenience, it is common for both of these scales to be subdivided into range intervals or bands. Figure 5.6 illustrates an example in which the likelihood scale is based on frequency intervals within a relevant time-frame. This frequency approach to the estimation of likelihood is generally easier for people to relate to than an arithmetical expression of probability. Since the purpose of this foundation exercise is often to grade risks rather than to produce specific expected monetary values for each of them, it is not uncommon to assign indicative scores to each position on the two scales (e.g. scores 1–6 in Figure 5.6). Where there is reason to believe that the impact of some risks may substantially exceed the firm's risk tolerance ('Critical'), it may be helpful to add higher impact bands accordingly. The risk ranking is based on the product of the two ratings for frequency and impact: a 'critical' risk that is 'very likely' (to occur once in two years) would score 6*5=30. A more precise estimation of impact may well be necessary later on, if a risk is deemed significant enough to merit fuller cause-and-controls assessment. An alternative method of scoring is to use an alpha-numeric scale: letters for severity and numbers for likelihood. In that case a 'critical' and 'very likely' risk would be rated A5.

The most common single criterion for impact is 'profit' (earnings). The escalating thresholds of financial impact should therefore be consistent with the organization's financial risk tolerance or risk appetite. The assessment for severity needs to include the direct and indirect consequences of a risk event. For example, if a product recall delays the launch of another product, there are two costs to take into account: the direct costs of the recall and the indirect costs of delay to the subsequent launch. Bear in mind also that some high-frequency risk events may have low individual impact every time they occur, but a high accumulative impact because they happen so often. In that case, they may be more usefully assessed in the aggregate.

Some organizations find it useful to grade risks simultaneously against *three* criteria for severity, two of which are non-financial:

*   impact on short-term financial performance (i.e. levels of earnings impact)
*   impact on reputation (i.e. defined degrees of effect on stakeholder behaviour material to the organization's performance)
*   impact on 'licence to operate' (i.e. defined degrees of regulatory reaction or imposed commercial constraint).

In the case of a multiple impact rating such as this, the rating of an exposure for management attention is usually based on an aggregate of the scores for the three impact criteria multiplied by a single estimation for the likelihood of the underlying risk event.

There are two accepted calibrations for this exercise. The first gives credit for existing controls in reducing possible severity or frequency (or both), so that the scoring is based on 'current' risk. The second assumes conservatively that any form of risk control is either absent or has failed, so that the scoring is based on 'inherent' risk. Note that even where there are data for current risk, inherent risk may be unknown, perhaps unknowable, and remain a matter for subjective estimation.

One can refine the rating of risks further by considering their *control potential*. Factoring control potential into the ranking of risks adjusts their prioritization according to whether there is scope to reduce the current exposure, whether in terms of likelihood or impact. In the following example

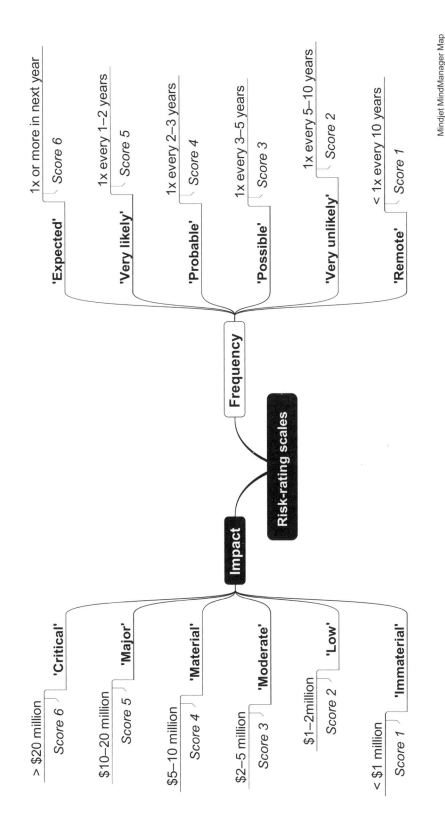

**Figure 5.6    Risk-rating scales (example)**

Risk-rating scales

Frequency

'Expected' — 1x or more in next year — *Score 6*
'Very likely' — 1x every 1–2 years — *Score 5*
'Probable' — 1x every 2–3 years — *Score 4*
'Possible' — 1x every 3–5 years — *Score 3*
'Very unlikely' — 1x every 5–10 years — *Score 2*
'Remote' — < 1x every 10 years — *Score 1*

Impact

'Critical' — > $20 million — *Score 6*
'Major' — $10–20 million — *Score 5*
'Material' — $5–10 million — *Score 4*
'Moderate' — $2–5 million — *Score 3*
'Low' — $1–2million — *Score 2*
'Immaterial' — < $1 million — *Score 1*

Mindjet MindManager Map

using expected loss (EL) and comparing two risks, risk A would be prioritized for investment in control improvement. Although it is viewed as the lesser of the two current risks, it is regarded as having greater potential for reduction through expenditure on additional controls:

Risk A: EL($50k)*Control Potential(0.5) = $25k improvement opportunity

Risk B: EL($80k)*Control Potential(0.1) = $8k improvement opportunity

In conducting their own risk assessments, the subordinate divisions or departments of an organization should adjust their impact criteria to reflect their own risk thresholds. This does not change the parent company's higher-value criteria for risks material to the whole enterprise. As we have suggested, corporate risk management generally controls for profit impact, so that risks are 'events' threatening achievement of profit targets. In that case, the marketing function should also control primarily for achievement of profit objectives, but might control in parallel for other key performance indicators (KPIs) related to demand, such as market share or brand equity. In most cases, the separate analyses will not be unrelated, of course, because profit (in principle) depends on demand.

Where a risk-mapping exercise is undertaken jointly by two different organizations, such as client and service provider, it is generally appropriate to gauge risks in terms of their impact on achievement of the principal common objectives already agreed between the two parties. However you measure success is how you should measure failure.

## Finalizing the risk map

There are then three steps to finalizing the risk map:

- consolidating and plotting participants' risk ratings
- indicating priorities on the risk map
- validating the output before wider distribution.

*Consolidating and plotting risk ratings.* Polling software, such as OptionFinder, automates the process of consolidating and plotting a preliminary risk map, although you may still want to customize the output by copying it into a spreadsheet program with graphing capability. A more sophisticated map plots each risk in three states: 'inherent', 'current' and 'managed' (current + improvement potential). This richer presentation takes advantage of the map's two-dimensional space to suggest the 'trajectory' of each risk (see Figure 5.7). It communicates visually how current or potential control improvements have been evaluated for their separate affects on severity and frequency. This is helpful because, as we have seen in Chapter 4, two expected values may appear to be identical whilst being the product of different factors. Data gathered by interview clearly require manual entry into a spreadsheet, which will then plot the basic matrix. When setting up the spreadsheet, it is helpful to adopt a layout similar to a risk register (see above), even though you may well be entering a fair number of similar-sounding risks from the different interviews. Establish whatever numbering and classification system will help you to cluster and consolidate the ratings for the various expressions of the same risk from different interviewees.

*Indicating priorities on the risk map.* Plotting the risks for likelihood and severity will usually place the highest-ranking risks in the upper right-hand cells of the matrix. For the purpose of priority action planning, you may wish to identify all critical risks exceeding a certain threshold.

Colouring the cells within the matrix is one way of achieving this distinction (Figure 5.7). In our example, the priority risks are the ones appearing in the darkest cells (if this book were printed in colour, these cells might be printed in red to denote their significance). The necessary focus on more significant exposures should not blind an organization to the existence of 'dots on the horizon'. These are lower-level risks that do not yet merit active management, but which justify regular review because of their sudden escalation potential.

*Validation of output.* Final validation of the risk map is essential before proceeding to the cause-and-controls assessment. There are two usual validation steps. The first involves the original participants, who should be given an opportunity to comment on the output before it is published beyond the group. This applies even if consensus has apparently been achieved during the course of a workshop, because participants should have a last opportunity to reconsider the risk map on their own. The second step is to ensure validation by the senior sponsors of the exercise, assuming they have not already participated in the earlier work. As we have already described, this validation by sponsors can take the form of a separate 'top-down' risk-mapping exercise, in which the map prepared by the subordinate group(s) provides the initial stimulus material to the senior one.

## Cause-and-controls assessment

Any risk identification exercise should be followed by a separate 'cause-and-control assessment' for each of the critical risks identified in the process. This involves suitably qualified colleagues (and advisers if necessary) making a more detailed assessment of the risk event, how it might come about and how its management might be improved in practice. Figure 5.8 illustrates a general template for the purpose. The approach is relevant to consideration of any important risk issue, not only those that have emerged from a larger exercise in risk identification.

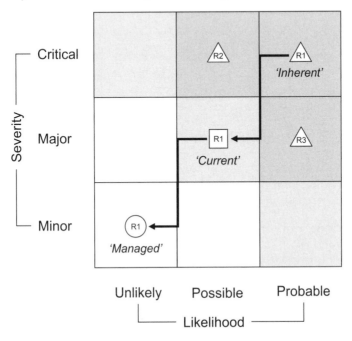

**Figure 5.7    Alternative risk map (illustrative)**

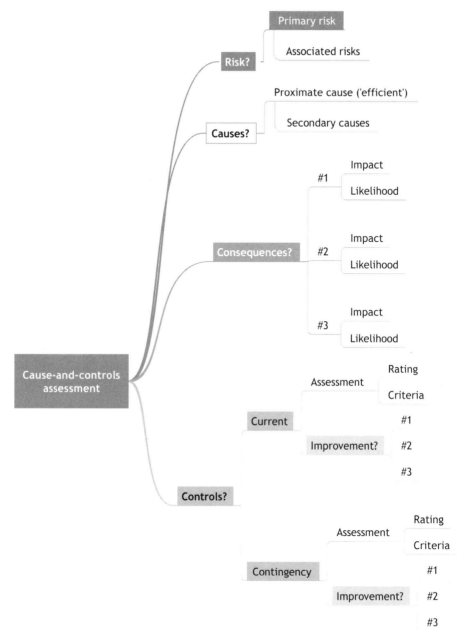

**Figure 5.8     Cause-and-controls assessment**

There are three aspects of cause-and-controls assessment that are worth considering in detail:

- structured analysis of cause and effect
- five standard strategies for risk management
- approaches to cost-benefit analysis specific to the management of risk.

## CAUSE AND EFFECT

Distinguishing between cause and effect is central to any consideration of risk. After all, without causes and effects, there would be no risk. The need for more detailed discussion about cause and effect arises on two occasions. The first is when a team makes a cause-and-controls assessment of a risk as outlined in this chapter. The second is during a chain of events analysis, after the fact, as described in Chapter 3.

Discussion of cause and effect can sometimes be confusing or ambiguous. Depending on one's perspective, effects can be causes and causes can be effects. For example, consider these three components in a situation that might arise in a contract telesales business: 'low employee morale', 'loss of sales' and 'customer complaint'. It is perfectly possible to conceive of three different scenarios, separately identified by interviewees in a risk assessment exercise, in which each component appears to play a different role:

A. *'Loss of sales causes customer complaint leading to low employee morale.'*

B. *'Low employee morale causes loss of sales leading to customer complaint.'*

C. *'Customer complaint causes low employee morale leading to loss of sales.'*

Such apparent interchangeability should not prevent us from reconciling the different perspectives, provided that our analysis begins by identifying the *ultimate effect* for which we would like to control. We work back from there, identifying the immediate causes of effects, the causes-of-those-causes and so on, using a variant of the dependency modelling approach we describe elsewhere in this book (see Chapter 6). Figure 5.9 suggests a framework for detailed discussion of cause and effect. We need to consider some of its terms.

### Risk events

We have already defined 'a risk' as a situation in which the actual outcome is unknown, but the probability distribution of possible outcomes is known. When thinking about cause and effect we need to define more precisely the situation in which at least *one* of the possible outcomes is assumed to have become certain (or has a probability of 1). This is the so-called 'risk event', when the risk materializes and becomes an actuality. A risk event can be an occurrence, an altered state or an altered process. Applying this event-driven logic, *known situations are inadequate descriptions of risk*, even though they may evidently create or explain risk. For example, 'bad quality today' is not a risk, because quality is already known to be bad. What is true is that bad quality today *implies* a risk event with foreseeable effects, but neither the risk event nor the effects have yet been defined. In this case, bad quality would sit as an 'explanatory feature'[36] on the left of our framework in Figure 5.9. Of course, this does not alter the case that bad quality is undesirable and needs to be improved. However, in risk management we are ideally concerned to make a rational allocation of resources against unknowns. Unless we complete the picture, we may not be able to judge how much emphasis to place on the separate management of causes, event and effect. For example, a product recall by a car-maker is a risk event requiring dedicated contingency planning. By contrast, the sudden falling-out-of-fashion of a clothing brand is a risk event that can only really be managed in terms of its causes and its effects.

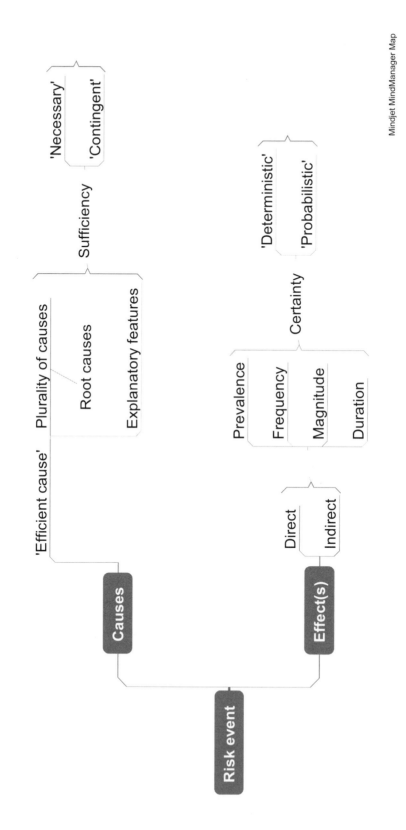

Mindjet MindManager Map

**Figure 5.9** **Cause and effect**

## Causes

The causes of risk events are events too: occurrences, altered states or altered processes. Logically, there is said to be only one immediate cause for a risk event, the so-called 'efficient cause'. It is generally the cause with the clearest one-to-one relationship with the effect, even though a risk event cannot have a single absolute cause. This means that the efficient cause is often (though not always) the 'proximate' cause – the most immediate in the chain of causation. The precise distinctions are made in order to improve understanding of the precipitating causes and to separate them from the inducive facts, circumstances and other secondary causes, which do not directly bring about the risk event, even if they facilitate it. The distinction may matter, because achieving some control over the precipitating causes (if identifiable) may be more practical and effective than attempting control over a range of facts, circumstance and contributory factors. By way of a simple example, making it difficult for children to remove caps on household bleach is easier for manufacturers to control than is the accessibility of bleach bottles in the nation's shops and homes.

## Explanatory features

Strictly speaking, facts and circumstances are not considered to be causes, even though they may be extremely important in explaining causation.[37] This is because facts and circumstances are not 'events' – unless they change, in which case an event has occurred. However, facts and circumstances may still need active management to prevent adverse outcomes (or bring about favourable outcomes). For example, an organization's culture is often mentioned as an explanatory feature of risk-taking behaviour, good and bad.

## Plurality of causes

An event can have one or more alternative *precipitating* causes, each capable of bringing it about, and these need to separately identified. On the other hand, a number of individually insufficient causes may *combine* to bring about an effect, although there may still be a separable proximate cause. The existence of secondary causes may exacerbate an efficient cause or make it more or less likely to occur, raising questions of joint probability. On the other hand, individually insufficient causes may stem from small changes in a delicately balanced system.[38] As we saw in Chapter 3, a 'system' comprises all of a company's functions, their processes *and their interactions*. Consequently, it may not be possible to identify a single precipitating cause when the system fails. By extension, a new product failure can arise from the incompatibility of the components in its mix. Instead of the whole being greater than the sum of its apparently adequate parts, the parts do not add up to make an effective whole. The failure to add up is the effect and the cause may lie in the failure of the system. This makes insight into the relevant systems useful in risk management.

## Root causes

These are the indirect causes of one or more different risk events. For example, falling behind target may be a root cause of undue risk-taking in a number of areas. Similarly, the arrival of a new competitor may not only cause a direct reduction in our sales, but may also be the root cause of our increased costs and the departure of some of our best people. So-called root causes are often explanatory features of risk events, organizational culture (once again) being a common case in point.

## Effects

These make up the third category of event in a causal chain. In common with risk events and cause events, these too can be occurrences, altered states or altered processes. Since we are controlling for effects, we are interested in the measures of impact suggested in Figure 5.9: prevalence (or location), frequency, magnitude and duration. Since some risks are opportunity risks, a risk event does not necessarily produce adverse effects: they may be favourable to varying degrees. Similarly, the effect of a risk event may simply be that we are no longer at risk: i.e. that the risk has materialized but has no effects. For example, a client's audit of our procedures may come about by random selection and pass uneventfully. Bear in mind that *indirect* or *consequential* effects may outlast direct effects. For example, breach of customers' trust by a bank may result in loss of reputation that costs the firm much more than the regulator's fine.

## Sufficiency of cause

As regards cause, we need to judge whether a particular cause necessitates (i.e. must inevitably lead to) a particular outcome. The opposite case is a *contingent* view of cause, in which the stated relationship between cause and effect may be true *and* may not be true.[39] For example, in particular situations, it may *and* may not be true that dissatisfied customers voice their complaints. This insight would have implications for brand risk management, for example, if we were seeking to define a risk event according to the number of actual complaints received.

## Certainty of effect

The corollary of sufficiency of cause is certainty of effect. The first question is whether or not a single predictable effect can be *deterministically* calculated as the outcome of a defined event. The alternative case is that there is a *probability distribution* for effects, which might need to be reflected in the impact value(s) plotted on the risk map. You might estimate a high probability for the risk event, but a very low probability for one or more of its significant effects. Alternatively, some of the effects may be out of our control and others entirely manageable, with different consequences for their certainty of effect.

## ANTICIPATING CUSTOMER BEHAVIOUR

Brand risk assessment is often concerned with behavioural cause and effect, in particular the causal relationship between attitudes expressed by customers or stakeholders and their subsequent actions. The first challenge is how to deconstruct attitude; the second, how to interpret it predictively. For brand managers, the additional practical challenge is how to attempt discussion of such matters with non-specialist colleagues in the context of risk discussions. It remains impossible to make sure-fire predictions. Even so, well-founded insight, based on a reasonable model, can at least assist in the prioritization of efforts to address the uncertainties.[40]

One of the most widely accepted predictive models of behaviour resulted from the work of Fishbein and Ajzen. Known as the *theory of planned behaviour*,[41] the model builds upon Ajzen's work with Fishbein,[42] as well as Fishbein's earlier work on the expected-value theory of attitude.[43] It identifies three principal components of attitude, each having different weights in different circumstances. Figure 5.10 provides a schematic representation of the comprehensive review provided by East (1997) and is explained here:[44]

- *Attitude to expected outcomes.* A person's attitude to an action by them is based firstly on their intuitive consolidation of the action's various expected outcomes ($A_b$). Work by Ajzen (1991) indicates that the consistency between people's so-called 'global variable' for attitude and the sum of their expected outcomes ('the sum variable') can be quite low when measured under experimental conditions, exhibiting a typical correlation of 0.5.[45] This should not discount the importance of a global measure of attitude as an indicator of intention to act. East (1993) suggests that it may be possible to obtain better correlations if the global variable is subdivided and matched to appropriate subsets of the respondents' salient beliefs – such as the short- and long-term consequences of the action in question.[46]

  Importantly, we should not expect high correlations between people's attitudes to things and their actions towards those things. To desire something does not inevitably mean that you will buy it (a personal Boeing jet); to dislike something does not mean that you will not buy it (root canal treatment). On the other hand, *an attitude to a behaviour*, such as buying the object, should prove to be consistent with that behaviour. This is because the attitude to buying the object is based on top-of-mind beliefs about the value and personal relevance of buying it ('Root canal treatment will stop my tooth from hurting'). This is why buying intention has long since become a standard question in marketing research. Meanwhile, general attitude surveys should be interpreted with care, unless they are supplemented by directly relevant behavioural questions.

- *Subjective norm.* Intention to act is also affected by another global variable, referred to as 'subjective norm' (SN). This variable reflects the extent to which a person's inclination to act is based on the influence of other persons who are important in their lives. This aggregate influence operates internally, without actual reference to those persons.

- *Perceived behavioural control.* The third determinant of intention to act, taken together with attitude and subjective norm, is 'perceived behavioural control' (PC). This is a person's

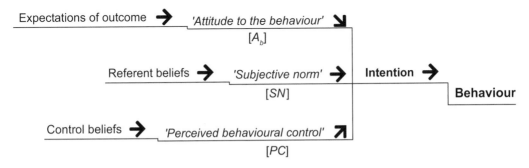

Mindjet MindManager Map

**Figure 5.10    Theory of planned behaviour**
*Source: After East (1997)*

own view of their ability to take an action. It can reflect a person's confidence[47] as well as their freedom or capacity to act. The addition of PC substantially improves the prediction of intention.[48] In practice, there appears to be little overlap between PC and either $A_b$ or SN.

- *Role of experience.* Measures of customer experience or degree of expertise may improve the accuracy of behavioural predictions. East (1997) suggests how the basis of a customer's choice may evolve with their experience in certain markets, becoming more independent and driven predominantly by $A_b$ and PC. The same experience effect may occur generally as a new category matures.

Once again, in this context, we see that definitions of cause and effect depend on perspective. As East (1997) points out, from a behaviourist perspective, thought and feelings can be effects and not causes, 'like ripples on the surface of a pond, they indicate the fish's movements but do not move the fish'.[49] More precisely, he suggests that we should not mislead ourselves into thinking that attitude data can *explain* behaviour. They merely *predict* behaviour whose actual causes will lie behind the thoughts and feelings expressed.[50] In addition, context and situation are often omitted in the search for explanations of behaviour, so that the wrong attribution is made based on a purely 'dispositional' view of cause without regard to context.[51] For instance, inertia or entrapment might be mistaken for loyalty in categories where there is high switching cost for customers, whether in time, money or inconvenience.

## Customer reaction to corporate crisis

Another problem of cause and effect in reputation risk assessment is to determine the extent to which a particular brand is vulnerable to enduring loss of franchise and custom as a result of a crisis, for example from major product failure or discreditable corporate conduct. There is evidence to suggest that the likely resilience of a consumer franchise may be explained by consumers' original 'route to persuasion'. If the original consumer persuasion was achieved through 'associations of feelings and simple responses to cues', then the attitudes formed may not be particularly resistant to counter-argument.[52] On the other hand, arguments that more fully engaged the consumers, so that their route to persuasion involved a degree of elaboration (or personalization) of the messages, may become more firmly anchored.[53] These differences are assumed to be correlated with category or segment characteristics. So, for example, snack food brands may be more immediately vulnerable than specialist dietetic brands which enter into a richer 'conversation' with consumers. This is another reason why appropriate opportunities to enrich the dialogue with consumers or customers in any category should not be lightly dismissed, even when the business is in good shape. The deeper-rooted the relationship before a crisis, the better the brand may be able to weather a future storm.

## Customer complaint

Work by Westbrook and Oliver (1991) suggests that customers may not consolidate their satisfactions and dissatisfactions with a product into a 'net' score.[54] Bad experiences, producing 'hostile' consumer response, appear to have a separate identity which is not directly offset by good experiences. Good experiences are said to be subdivided into two categories: one relating to 'surprise' (exceeding expectations), the other to consumer 'interest'. East (1997) suggests that this apparent separation has implications for the design of customer satisfaction questionnaires, and may have significance for the design of products themselves.[55]

## ANTICIPATING ACTIVIST BEHAVIOUR

One of the more edifying and potentially damaging reputational challenges an organization can expect to face comes in the form of single-issue activism. Groups with a passionate socio-political, environmental or ethical agenda can cause companies to lose control of public opinion and even their markets. Although the media has become more cautious of accepting uncorroborated claims by activist groups, the groups themselves have responded by becoming increasingly skilful in their presentation of issues.[56]

Winter and Steger (1998) have made a particular study of the patterns of activism and the ways in which firms can best anticipate the likelihood of attack.[57] They offer both insights and practical recommendations for more effective early diagnosis and positive prevention of needless escalation. They found that companies are more likely to be the subject of activist attack for three principal reasons:

1.  The company's conduct appears to set a 'bad precedent' for a whole industry.
2.  The company's conduct can be expressed as an 'issue'. Activists rarely protest against the existence of a company or simply 'what it stands for'.
3.  The company is a category leader: 'People who hate big business aim high.'[58]

Accordingly, Winter and Steger (1998) recommend the following nine-point assessment to assist companies in determining the escalation potential of any issues that they may have identified:[59]

- *Plausibility*. Are the activist arguments plausible (i.e. understandable and credible)? The burden of proof will usually be on the company to disprove plausibility, rather than on the activists to prove it.
- *Impact*. Is the issue understandable and does it evoke emotion (in the sense of being symbolic, visually communicated or 'touching')? Are there significant national or cultural differences which might cause the issue to have greater impact in some places than others?
- *Media appeal*. Is the issue media-friendly? This will tend to depend on whether the issue is 'new, extraordinary and accessible' to reporters.
- *Connections*. Does the issue connect to other issues, within or beyond the company and its industry? Connections to other issues or activist interests do not need to be logical in the eyes of the target company, but may add huge proportion to activist accusations elsewhere.
- *Lead activist profile*. How strong is the leading activist group in a campaign? Profiling this group is very important, assuming that there is more than one of them. It is the lead group's position that really determines the course of the activist campaign. Accordingly, the profile assessment should include the basis of the lead group's membership and:
  - income
  - its donors' motives
  - its internal structure (especially whether it benefits from the increased leverage that comes from effective centralized control)
  - its campaign record
  - its achievement in securing media exposure.

- *Lead activist appeal*. It is also necessary to understand why the issue might appeal to the lead activist group. In general, appeal to activists is driven by the following considerations:
  - the opportunity provided by the issue to secure a relevant organizational objective for the group (which may not share priorities with apparently similar groups)
  - the issue's symbolic value and public impact
  - its power to damage the target company without risk of generating sympathy for a weak or unjustified victim (the 'underdog effect')
  - the availability of a 'confrontational' rather than a gradual solution to the issue.

- *Company isolation*. How isolated is the target company? By and large, activists prefer to attack single companies not entire industries, even if the target is representative of the industry. Operational accidents can be inherently isolating, such as those resulting in large-scale environmental damage. This is why such unfortunate events so often facilitate an enduring activist campaign.

- *Dynamics*. How far has the crisis already evolved and what are its alternative trajectories? Important in this analysis is not only a listing of relevant events so far, but the identification of future developments that might oblige the company to alter its current position. The so-called 'take-off points' may precipitate a crisis-within-a-crisis.

- *Solution*. How easy is the solution? In general, an activist group's case is strongest where the actions demanded do not appear unreasonable from a public perspective and will not result in the company's existence being put at stake.

## BRAND IMPACT: CAUSE OR EFFECT

Brand risk assessment requires clear thinking about cause and effect, because the brand is implicated in so many aspects of business performance. Thinking about the brand in the context of a firm's 'value chain'[60] provides one approach to clarifying the analysis. This can be a useful way of tailoring a brand valuation exercise, examining the extent of brand contribution and brand vulnerability at each step along the way. We have already considered the anatomy of the brand and how this can help identify specific risks to its performance (see Chapter 2). To varying degrees, a brand's identity, presence, equity, reputation and status will influence business performance at every point in the value chain.

In general, magnitude of brand effects should be expressed in terms of the normal brand performance indicators that apply. For example, if you were using the set of non-financial measures for the customer brand suggested by Ambler (2003) and summarized in Figure 2.8 in Chapter 2, you would look to describe effects in terms of their impact on profit, customer preference, buying intention, satisfaction, loyalty, penetration or availability.[61] Similarly, effects on the corporate brand would (for example) be measured by the Reputation Institute in terms of its seven key dimensions of reputation and their subordinate components (Products/ Services, Innovation, Workplace, Governance, Citizenship, Leadership, Performance).[62] If a risk event is judged to have no material effect on the attitudes or behaviours of any stakeholder group, it follows that there is no brand risk.

Just as a brand's effectiveness needs to be assessed relative to competition, so can its structural exposure. It is a reasonable generalization that a brand with a sole equity element might be vulnerable, especially if it did not deliver a distinct emotional benefit. This is certainly not to suggest that brands should complicate their propositions or build defensive associations in every conceivable dimension. However, a brand with a well-rounded equity and underlying 'reputational capital'[63] is likely to withstand shocks better than one without any redundancy of structure. Identifying the brand's 'pillars of legitimacy and uniqueness'[64] can help to guide both current performance management and contingency planning.

We have established that there is an important difference between impact on customer attitude and impact on behaviour. This suggests that we need to be clear about the kind of brand impact we are interested in. Brand managers are inevitably interested in what people think as well as what they might actually do. This is because the worth of a brand is both short-term and long-term: it has value as an annuity and as an option. In principle, this means that adverse risk events can implicate a brand in four ways:

- It can be associated with the risk event but remain unaffected.

- Its impairment can create a sudden or gradual impact on revenue, costs or profit.

- It can be weakened by the risk event in ways that do not create immediate financial impact, but leave it less able to withstand a subsequent event.

- Its worth may be affected by changes in the availability of strategic choices or their viability.

Brands operate in marketplaces that are 'open systems' and every brand is different from another in context, character and condition. This makes it easier to describe single, generic contributors to brand failure (see Chapter 2) than to hypothesize, out of context, the variety of their combinations and consequences. Even so, some general insight into the *dynamics* of brand impact can be helpful:

- *Dormancy*. Brand risk can be accumulative. Positive equity elements and associations can gradually weaken to a point where the brand is not able to withstand a sudden shock. Some issues build invisibly before reaching a tipping point that provokes crisis. Others lie dormant like dry kindling until a corporate action causes them to escalate. For this reason it is insufficient to monitor issues that are already in sharp focus. Organizations must encourage early identification of latent issues and their assembly in a form that is easy for colleagues to consult and enrich on a routine basis, scanning the environment for weak signals of potential risks and opportunities for the firm. On occasion, it may be worthwhile attaching a more sensitive risk threshold to existing measures of brand performance, so as to trigger timely management attention to new developments.[65] In any event, brand people must contribute risk-intelligent interpretation of the mix of market information from all sources: structured research, media monitoring, blogs, customer feedback, business wins and losses. Collation of market intelligence in this way is vital. Just as in military intelligence gathering, it is the composite picture that creates the best insight and indication that an issue may shortly 'go ballistic'. Do not limit the scope of analysis to a single industry and country context: opinion formers and activists may well focus on different issues simultaneously across national or industry boundaries.[66]

- *Event chains*. Single risk events may occur in association with others, touching off a chain reaction which can make the outcomes more serious or complex. For example, product recall can lead to trade delisting, which can lead to competitive launch, which can substantially alter the market structure going forward. Having language to describe the way in which messages and opinions gather momentum is helpful. For example, Winter and Steger (1998)[67] refer to 'transmission belts' as the means by which activist groups threaten a target company through others: they secure the co-operation of constituencies with more direct economic leverage, such as customers and suppliers. Gladwell (2001)[68] describes three stereotypes that influence the formation of widespread social attitude: 'Mavens' (expert repositories of knowledge), 'Connectors' (network builders) and 'Salesmen' (active persuaders).

- *Rate of impairment.* The fastest damage to a brand can arise in the area of reputation. This is because events causing sudden reputation failure can have the most 'alarming' downside consequences for those affected. Brand equity is more likely to erode than to fail outright. Relegation in status is the longer-term consequence of either sustained loss of reputation or weakness in brand equity.

- *Rate of recovery.* Established brands can usually recover from 'equity accidents' (e.g. bad advertising) or inappropriate product extension, provided that the credibility of their core equity elements has not been irreversibly undermined. Lost status may take as long to recover as to lose. Recovery of reputation may be asymmetric, taking longer to recover than to lose. Reputation recovery may also be conditional or probationary: the damage to the brand and the business will be worse next time.

## THE REPUTATION@RISK MODEL[69]

In assessing risk to the firm's performance that may arise from weak or impaired reputation, it is often necessary to take account of complex stakeholder interactions and their financial implications. This complexity can be difficult to resolve, evaluate and communicate.

The challenge is all the greater because different functions in an organization may be accountable for different stakeholder relationships. There is practical value in establishing an integrated view of stakeholder status or exposure, so that reputation exposures can be summarized in the context of risk management review.

The *reputation@risk* assessment is based on a six-part stakeholder model. The model is represented by a memorable hexagon shape that distinguishes between two generally recognized clusters of stakeholder: the 'transactional' and the 'contextual'[70] (see Figure 5.11(A)) Transactional stakeholders are those with whom the organization has contractual relationships of a commercial nature. Contextual stakeholders are those with power to determine the organization's 'licence to operate' or strategic freedoms, even though their relationship with the organization is not contractually based. Owners and shareholders are not visibly represented in the model, because they are 'super-stakeholders' with an overarching interest in the viability of the company's relationships with the other stakeholder constituencies.

The hexagon shape (Figure 5.11(B)) is further abstracted into an 'impact icon'. In practical application, each triangular segment of the icon represents the estimated impact of an issue, action or event on the prevailing attitude or behaviour of the corresponding stakeholder(s). An intuitive colour-coding convention allows visualization of complex situations (Figure 5.11(C)). The pattern of each icon readily characterizes the nature of exposure or opportunity, whether this is most usefully expressed in terms of stakeholder attitude (e.g. 'outrage') or in terms of business impact ('high negative impact'). In cases where further quantification is unavailable or unnecessary in practice for the purpose of decision-making, this indicative colour coding will suffice.

The whole impact icon therefore reflects an integrated view of the organization's reputation or reputation risk across all relevant stakeholder groups in connection with the specific matter under review. The icon segments can be used to signal *positive* outcomes (green), escalating degrees of *negative* outcome (yellow, red, black), as well as two different states of *uncertainty* (white, blue). The colour coding also makes it possible to present a diverse mix of quantitative, qualitative, objective and subjective data. It is only necessary to agree the thresholds for moves up and down the colour scale for each stakeholder group represented in the model.

The system has application in risk assessment, scenario development, decision support, goal setting and review.

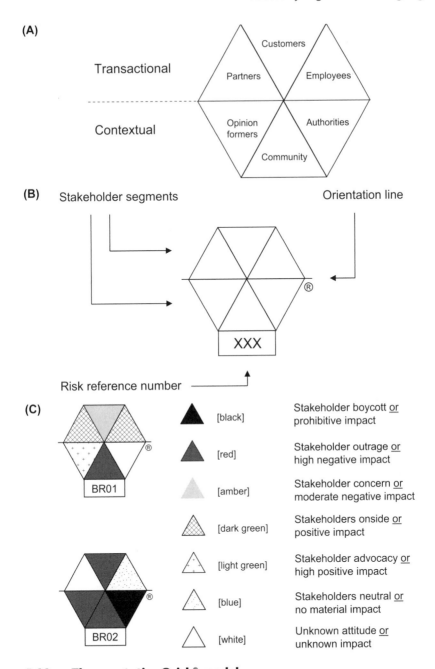

**(A)**

Transactional

Contextual

Customers

Partners

Employees

Opinion formers

Authorities

Community

**(B)** Stakeholder segments

Orientation line

XXX

Risk reference number

**(C)**

BR01

BR02

[black] — Stakeholder boycott or prohibitive impact

[red] — Stakeholder outrage or high negative impact

[amber] — Stakeholder concern or moderate negative impact

[dark green] — Stakeholders onside or positive impact

[light green] — Stakeholder advocacy or high positive impact

[blue] — Stakeholders neutral or no material impact

[white] — Unknown attitude or unknown impact

**Figure 5.11    The reputation@risk® model**

*Source: Author, reproduced with permission of Marsh Ltd*

## Managing risk

Broadly speaking, priority of management attention to risks should follow the ranking established by the assessment process. Ensuring that the right team is in place to manage a particular risk is also helped by detailed assessment of its likely causes and effects in the manner that we have described. It is a matter of identifying who in the firm (or outside it) can achieve best control over each prioritized component of cause, event and effect. 'Control' is a generic term used in risk management to describe any measure aimed at modifying favourably either the value outcome of a risk or its likelihood of occurrence. If control is not possible, then insight into a critical component of the risk is the next best thing. There is no hard-and-fast rule about who should lead the risk management effort in any particular case. In some situations, it will plainly be efficient to have a single team responsible for a number of overlapping risks, each with slightly different cause and control characteristics. In other circumstances, team leadership and overall responsibility for risk management should lie with the function having most control over the efficient cause of the risk rather than the risk event, although they may be one and the same.

In principle, the aim is to move towards an emphasis on prevention rather than cure. Even awareness of risk issues can break the chains of events and conditions that result in failure or disappointment.[71] Although one cannot hope to anticipate every eventuality, a high level of general preparedness will undoubtedly improve an organization's responsiveness, even in the face of an unforeseen occurrence.

## RISK MANAGEMENT ALTERNATIVES

Figure 5.12 summarizes the alternative responses to risk and uncertainty that would be familiar to most risk professionals. As an aid to their memorization, Rayner (2003) applies a descriptor to each of the four standard approaches that all begin with the letter 'T'.[72] We have added a fifth to the list of four – Transform:

- *Transfer.* This usually means a transfer or partial allocation of risk to another party by contractual means. Insurance is one form of risk transfer, which often involves only partial assumption of the risk by the insurers. The insured party may retain some of the lower-level financial impact as an 'excess', after which the insurance policy is said to 'attach' (respond). But transfer is not limited to insurable risks and can equally apply under various forms of commercial risk-sharing arrangement. For example, granting distributors partial reimbursement for unsold seasonal stock is one example of risk transfer back to the seller.

Mindjet MindManager Map

**Figure 5.12    The '5Ts' of risk management**
*Source: After Rayner (2003)*

Outsourcing is clearly a way of transferring operational risk – though the reputation risk will probably remain with whichever brand the end-customer perceives as the guarantor of performance.[73] If a risk has been partially transferred, it means that the original risk owner need only assume retention of the 'residual risk', for as long as both the risk itself and the transfer arrangement exist.

- *Treat.* Risk treatment describes any activity intended to alter the likelihood and impact of whatever risk has been retained. An obligation to manage a risk may remain, even if the risk has been wholly or partially transferred. Insurance companies, for example, expect that their clients should take reasonable steps both to prevent the insured events and mitigate their effects. Similarly, other forms of contractual indemnity and risk transfer may impose risk management conditions on the transferring party. For example, a licensor transferring sales volume risk to a licensee may retain the obligation to provide a certain amount of marketing support for the brand.

- *Transform.* Some risks can be substantially avoided by adopting another means of achieving the same end. For example, if there is potential conflict of interest between a client and a particular distributor, one possibility for the client is to go elsewhere. The original underlying risk no longer exists – though the new set-up will embody its own risks and uncertainties.

- *Tolerate.* In the final analysis, you may determine that you have no other option than to tolerate the risk. You may positively wish to accept it, as a means of achieving commensurately higher reward. Alternatively, the exposure may be outside your control and its effects may not be capable of mitigation. For example, minimum order quantities from licensor to licensee may create a speculative exposure which cannot be hedged to any material extent.

- *Terminate.* In some situations it may be better to withdraw from an activity altogether, rather than to continue to take on the perceived exposure. For example, a company may choose to cancel a product introduction following ambivalent test market results, rather than risk an intolerable loss or the damage to reputation that might affect trade response to a more important launch shortly thereafter.

## COST-BENEFIT ANALYSIS

A frequent challenge in risk management is how to justify expenditure on something that may never happen. A variant of the same question is how to plan and explain expenditures that reduce the variability of an intended outcome – in other words, its risk.

Effectiveness and efficiency are important measures of performance in risk management, just as they are in other aspects of marketing and business. We will suggest a practical way of addressing these cost-benefit questions, neither of them requiring total immersion in the underlying statistical theory:

- the expected value approach
- the risk efficiency approach.

### Expected value approach

This method reassesses the expected value of a risk according to the assumed effectiveness of the risk control activity. To put it another way: a financial investment in risk control is assumed to have broken even, if the cost of implementing the control is equal to the resulting change in expected value. In practice, you will probably want to set a return rate that is more attractive than break-even, but the underlying principle remains.

Simple though it is, the expected value approach is consistent with the way in which we prioritize risks in the first place, whether on the basis of objective or subjective inputs. If the original expected value estimation was a subjective one, it is methodologically sound to invite the same individual(s) to express a revised expectation on the basis of the new information provided about the *nature* of the risk controls. They make the judgement about *effectiveness* and revise their assessment accordingly.

## Risk efficiency approach

A more sophisticated measure of cost-benefit is to relate any expenditure on risk control to the changes achieved in the *volatility* of a risk outcome, not just its expected value. This is a truer measure of *risk reduction*. As you recall, two identical expected value figures can mask significant differences in underlying volatility. If you reduce the volatility, you reduce the risk, because risk is defined as the extent to which actual outcomes may depart from the expected average.

It is not unusual for us to be faced with alternative courses of action in pursuing the same marketing opportunity, each having its own expected value and its own volatility (i.e. risk profile). The risk efficiency method allows you to identify the trade-off between risk and reward, helping you to make the optimal choice suggested by the inputs. It is based on a groundbreaking and enduring insight by Harry Markowitz, published in 1952.[74] He first defined the *'efficient frontier'*, the line on a graph that marks out the best available balance between risk and reward, given a range of alternatives.

Let us take a practical example to demonstrate the principle and its application. For instance, if you were negotiating alternative distribution and promotion arrangements for one brand with a single retailer, each plan under discussion might have a different expected value in your eyes and different risks attached to it. There might be different mixes of distribution and display level, different promotional concepts, different degrees of merchandising support, demonstration, timing in relation to advertising flights and so on.

Assume that there is a base plan (A) with four alternative plans (B–E), as set out in Figure 5.13(A). You need to choose between them or negotiate adjustments that suit your appetite for financial return and downside risk. (We can make a similar calculation for upside and downside risk in combination, but the principle is easier to introduce with downside risk alone.) You have already calculated an expected return (ER) for each plan, after all control costs, by applying a triangular distribution described in Chapter 4. This means that you will have estimated a worst possible outcome (WPO) in each case. You can already compare the expected returns for their attractiveness and the absolute amounts of downside risk for their tolerability. You now want to compare the *relative* extent of downside risk as a measure of risk efficiency. One way of achieving this is to calculate the simplified coefficient of variance that we considered in Chapter 4 (CV), indexing the worst possible departure from expected return as a percentage of expected return in each case:

$$CV = (ER-WPO)/ER*100$$

So that, for example:

$$CV(\text{Plan A}) = (\$300k-\$100k)/\$300k*100 = 67\%$$

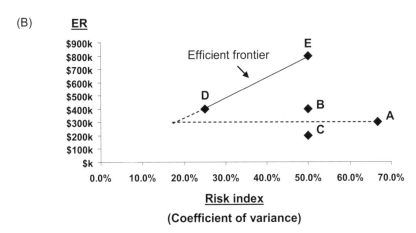

| | ER | WPO | ER-WPO | CV |
|---|---|---|---|---|
| (A) | Expected return | Worst possible outcome | Worst case variance | Coefficient of variance |
| **Base plan** | | | | |
| **A** | $300k | $100k | $200k | 67% |
| **Alternative plans** | | | | |
| **B** | $400k | $200k | $200k | 50% |
| **C** | $200k | $100k | $100k | 50% |
| **D** | $400k | $300k | $100k | 25% |
| **E** | $800k | $400k | $400k | 50% |

**Figure 5.13    Risk efficiency**

As you can see from Figures 5.13(A) and 5.13(B), the coefficient of variance allows you to compare the extent of downside risk very easily. The higher the CV, the more downside risk you would be bearing relative to the promised reward under each plan. Figure 5.13(B) shows the resulting graph, which plots expected return against coefficient of variance. It suggests that no other current plan has a balance of risk and reward superior to plans D and E, because these two plans define the efficient frontier (a straight line in our illustrative example, though more typically observed as a curve):

- Base plan A is the least attractive option, offering the second-lowest expected return for highest relative risk.
- Plans B and C offer much lower returns than plan E, but at the same relative risk.
- Plan E offers the best possible return for the same risk as B and C, provided you can tolerate the absolute amount of potential downside.
- Plan D is the next best alternative to plan E, because it offers higher rewards than either A or C and the same reward as B, but at lower relative risk.

By definition, any further alternative plan lying along the line D–E would be equally as 'risk-efficient' as plan D or plan E. In the present illustrative example, the efficient frontier suggests that plan A would only be risk-efficient if negotiations were able to secure a reduction in downside variance to approximately $60k or CV 20 per cent.

The approach described here is conservative, in the sense that it only considers a maximum downside and omits consideration of the upside variance. The more orthodox and balanced analysis would measure risk efficiency in relation to the combined upside *and* downside volatility. In such a case, where the upside variance also needs to be taken into account, the equation for arriving at the coefficient of variance and plotting the risk efficient frontier is essentially the same. The only difference is that (ER-WPO) is replaced by *standard deviation* (SD) as the risk variable in the equation. As we saw in Chapter 4, standard deviation is simply the calculated *average* deviation from the mean for *all* the data in a given set, upwards and downwards. It is beyond the remit of this book to review the mathematics involved, which are well described in tutorial works on statistics in business, such as Wisniewski (2006).[75] Meanwhile, it is reassuring to know that spreadsheet packages automate the calculation of standard deviation. Microsoft Excel, for example, offers an automatic standard deviation function suitable in our case: =STDEV(number 1, number 2 ...).[76] This function calculates standard deviation where the input 'numbers' consist of sample values from a larger data set. You would pick the alternative function offered in Microsoft Excel[§] (STDEVP), if your data were not a sample, but consisted of the entire 'population'. In our case, the three value estimations we have made are, in effect, samples from an assumed larger data set of interim values. So we enter the three estimates from our triangular distribution (minimum outcome, maximum outcome, most likely outcome), leaving the program to return the standard deviation to use in the adjusted formula:

$$CV = SD/ER*100$$

Provided one does not lose sight of the actual sums of money involved, the risk efficiency approach lends powerful insight to decisions that need to balance risk and reward.

Decision analysis tends to concentrate on financial outcomes, because that is generally the most useful yardstick for a business decision. However, it remains perfectly possible to apply any other scale of utility as a replacement for the monetary one.

## Summary

We have reviewed various ways of identifying and comparing risks and risky alternatives:

- We have seen how different methods of risk assessment can interlock and complement one another.

- We have introduced a framework for structured thinking about cause and effect, with overlays for the assessment of stakeholder attitude and behaviour.

- We have described approaches to prioritizing risks, to defining risk management strategies and to evaluating their cost against benefits.

In the next chapter we will go a step further, to model risks and the more complex or challenging risk decisions.

---

§    Microsoft® and Excel® are registered trademarks of Microsoft Corporation.

# References

1   de Bono, E. (1999), *Six Thinking Hats* ®, Penguin Books.
2   McDonald, M., Smith B. and Ward, K. (2006), *Marketing Due Diligence: Reconnecting Strategy to Share Price*, Butterworth-Heinemann.
3   de Bono, E. (1999), op.cit.
4   de Bono, E. (1967), *The Use of Lateral Thinking*, Jonathan Cape.
5   de Bono, (1999), op.cit., p. 3.
6   de Bono, E. (1994), *Parallel Thinking*, Viking Press.
7   McDonald et al. (2006), op.cit.
8   McDonald et al. (2006), op.cit.
9   McDonald et al. (2006), op.cit.
10  McDonald, M. and Dunbar, I. (2004), *Market Segmentation: How to Do It, How to Profit from It*, Butterworth-Heinemann.
11  Weinstein, A. (2004), *Handbook of Market Segmentation – Strategic Targeting for Business and Technology Firms*, Haworth Press, Inc.
12  McDonald et al. (2006), op.cit.
13  McDonald et al. (2006), op.cit.
14  Kelly, E (2006), 'The Tall Order of Taming Change', *FT Mastering Uncertainty Part 1*, supplement to *Financial Times*, 17 March, pp. 4–5.
15  Rayner, J. (2003), *Managing Reputational Risk: Leveraging Opportunities Curbing Threats*, John Wiley and Sons Ltd.
16  Zaman, A. (2004), *Reputational Risk – How to Manage for Value Creation*, FT Prentice Hall.
17  Goodwin, P. and Wright, G. (2004), *Decision Analysis for Management Judgment – Third Edition*, John Wiley & Sons Ltd.
18  Tricks, H. (2005), 'Predicting Change: Future Gazing is on the Cards', *Financial Times*, 24 October, p. 13.
19  Wind, J. and Crook, C. (2006), 'Changing Mental Models in an Uncontrollable World', *FT Mastering Uncertainty Part 1*, supplement to *Financial Times*, 17 March, pp. 10–11.
20  Winter, M. and Steger, U. (1998), *Managing Outside Pressure: Strategies for Preventing Corporate Disasters*, John Wiley & Sons, p. 64.
21  Winter and Steger (1998), op.cit., p. 67.
22  Ringland, G. (1998), *Scenario Planning: Managing for the Future*, John Wiley & Sons Ltd.
23  Schwartz, P. (1998), *The Art of the Long View: Planning for the Future in an Uncertain World*, Doubleday.
24  Goodwin and Wright  (2004), op.cit.
25  Goodwin and Wright  (2004), op.cit.
26  Goodwin and Wright  (2004), op.cit.
27  Shaw, R. and Merrick, D. (2005), *Marketing Payback – Is Your Marketing Profitable?*, FT Prentice Hall.
28  Clemons, E.K. (2006), 'Past Experience Points the Way to the Future', *FT Mastering Uncertainty Part 1*, supplement to *Financial Times*, 17 March, pp. 6–8.
29  Option Technologies Interactive, LLC, http://www.optiontechnologies.com/audience/response/optionfinder.asp.
30  Janis, I.R. (1982), '*Groupthink*': *Psychological Studies of Policy Decisions and Fiascos*, Houghton Mifflin.
31  Toft, B. and Reynolds, S. (1997), *Learning from Disasters – A Management Approach*: *Second edition*, Perpetuity Press.
32  McDonald et al. (2006), op.cit.
33  Abrahams, D.J. (2001), 'Social and Ethical Risk', *The Marsh Topic Letter*, Number V, Marsh Ltd.
34  Rayner (2003), op.cit.
35  Option Technologies Interactive, LLC, op.cit.
36  Mackie, P.J. (2005), 'Causality', in T. Honderich (ed.), *The Oxford Companion to Philosophy – New Edition*, Oxford University Press.
37  Mackie (2005), op.cit.
38  Bernstein, P.L. (1996), *Against the Gods: The Remarkable Story of Risk*, John Wiley & Sons, Inc.
39  Lowe, E.J. (2005), 'Contingent and Necessary Statements', in Honderich, op.cit.
40  East, R. (1997), *Consumer Behaviour – Advances and Applications in Marketing*, FT Prentice Hall.

41   Ajzen, I. (1991), 'The Theory of Planned Behavior', in E.A. Locke (ed.), *Organizational Behavior and Human Decision Processes*, Volume 50, pp. 179–211.

42   Ajzen, I. and Fishbein, M. (1980), *Understanding Attitudes and Predicting Social Behavior*, Prentice Hall.

43   Fishbein, M. (1963), 'An Investigation of the Relationships between Beliefs about an Object and Attitude toward that Object', *Human Relations*, Volume 16 (Number 3), pp. 233–240.

44   East (1997), op.cit.

45   Ajzen (1991), op.cit.

46   East (1997), op.cit.

47   Marsh, A. and Matheson, J. (1983), *Smoking Attitudes and Behaviour: An Enquiry Carried Out on Behalf of the Department of Health and Social Security*, HMSO.

48   Madden, T.J., Ellen, P.S. and Ajzen, I. (1992), 'A Comparison of the Theory of Planned Behavior and the Theory of Reasoned Action', *Personality and Social Psychology Bulletin*, Volume 18 (Issue 1), pp. 3–9.

49   East (1997), op.cit., p. 119.

50   East (1997), op.cit.

51   Gladwell, M. (2001), *The Tipping Point: How Little Things Can Make a Big Difference*, Abacus.

52   East (1997), op.cit.

53   See Petty, R.E., Cacioppo, J.T. and Schumann, D. (1983), 'Central and Peripheral Routes to Advertising Effectiveness: The Moderating Role of Involvement', *Journal of Consumer Research*, Volume 10, pp. 135–146; Petty, R.E. and Cacioppo, J.T. (1986), 'The Elaboration Likelihood Model of Persuasion', in L. Berkowitz (ed.), *Advances in Experimental Social Psychology*, Volume 19, Academic Press, pp. 123–205; and Cacioppo, J.T. and Petty, R.E. (1985), 'Central and Peripheral Routes to Persuasions: the Role of Message Repetition', in A.A. Mitchell and L.F. Alwitt (eds), *Psychological Processes and Advertising Effects: Theory, Research, and Applications*, Lawrence Erlbaum Associates.

54   Westbrook, R.A. and Oliver, R.L. (1991), 'The Dimensionality of Consumption Emotion Patterns and Consumer Satisfaction', *Journal of Consumer Research*, Volume 18, pp. 84–91.

55   East (1997), op.cit.

56   Ruff, P. and Aziz, K. (2003), *Managing Communications in a Crisis*, Gower Publishing Ltd.

57   Winter and Steger (1998), op.cit.

58   *The Economist* (2005), 'Runner-up, Up and Away', *The Economist*, 17 December, p. 12.

59   Winter and Steger (1998), op.cit.

60   Porter, M.E. (2004), *Competitive Advantage: Creating and Sustaining Superior Performance*, new edition. Free Press.

61   Ambler, T. (2003), *Marketing and the Bottom Line*, FT Prentice Hall.

62   Reputation Institute, 'Rankings Across Seven Categories', http://www.reputationinstitute.com-press-Rankings_Across_Seven_CategoriesFORBES21may2007.pdf.url.

63   Fombrun, C.J. (1996), *Reputation: Realizing Value from the Corporate Image*, Harvard Business School Press.

64   Rayner (2003), op.cit.

65   Rayner (2003), op.cit.

66   Zaman (2004), op.cit.

67   Winter and Steger (1998), op.cit.

68   Gladwell (2001), op.cit.

69   Abrahams (2001), op.cit.

70   Winter and Steger (1998), op.cit.

71   Mittelstaedt, R.E. (2005), *Will Your Next Mistake Be Fatal? Avoiding the Chain of Mistakes that Can Destroy Your Organization*, Wharton School Publishing.

72   Rayner (2003), op.cit.

73   Rayner (2003), op.cit.

74   Markowitz, H. (1952), 'Portfolio Selection', *The Journal of Finance*, Volume 7 (Issue 1), pp. 77–91.

75   Wisniewski, M. (2006), *Quantitative Methods for Decision Makers – Fourth Edition*, FT Prentice Hall.

76   Microsoft Corporation, http://office.microsoft.com/en-us/excel/HP052092771033.aspx?pid=CH0625 28311033.

77   Ruff and Aziz (2003), op.cit.

78   Ruff and Aziz (2003), op.cit.

79   Ruff and Aziz (2003), op.cit.

# Snakes and Ladders

## CRISIS MANAGEMENT

### Assume Human Fallibility in the Front Line

In the case of a major incident, an organization's communications infrastructure can be overwhelmed. Front-line colleagues with the least experience may find themselves fielding challenging external enquiries on their own. As part of crisis planning, provide *each of them* with a simple checklist of appropriate responses and the correct procedure for internal hand-off. The checklist needs to be immediately and reliably accessible when these colleagues answer the telephone, rather than difficult to locate on the intranet or in a remote file.

In developing question-and-answer documents to prepare suitably media-trained company spokespersons, pay particular attention to the possible sequence of follow-up questions in each case: 'What happens if they then ask ... ?'. Even a simple secondary question can baffle the unprepared.[77]

### Make Third-Party Opinion an Asset in Crisis

The trade or professional press will often be a first source of information and assistance to national media and financial analysts, when a big story breaks on a particular firm or industry. Bear this in mind in the normal course of business, keeping messages consistent in all quarters. If a crisis should occur, do not omit to include the trade press in media briefings, even though the story is not the usual 'good news'.[78]

At times of crisis, it can be very helpful to refer the media to third-party 'endorsers'. These are credible organizations and individuals, entirely independent, who would legitimately speak well of your firm's policies or conduct. They should be selected on the basis of their authority on matters that may become the subject of media interest and regularly briefed. Typical third-party endorsers might include industry analysts, NGOs, the emergency services or health and safety organizations.[79]

### Test the Plan Regularly

An untried or long-forgotten crisis management plan may not work as well as expected. Many response plans, such as product recalls, can usefully be tested in 'desktop' simulations, that take place in one principal meeting room. These day-long or half-day exercises involve all key decision-makers and collaborators, within and beyond the core crisis team, as necessary.

A good simulation exercise will:

- test the co-ordination and (to some degree) the flexibility that a real crisis would demand
- prepare those involved psychologically, helping them to develop their capacity to communicate well and make timely decisions under unusual pressure
- identify other aspects of the plan that need improvement.

A 'desktop' simulation compresses time by dividing the exercise into 'moves', each representing a further meaningful moment in the escalation of a crisis. The dramatic detail in the scenario is often developed by an external crisis management adviser on the basis of confidential interviews with people in relevant functions and at various levels in the organization. Collectively, these interviews can reveal significant operational issues and vulnerabilities, providing greater realism and a learning opportunity for those involved.

# **6** *Modelling Risks*

In the earlier chapters of this book, we focused on developing our understanding of risk and risk management, in cases where a sound perspective and the correct 'hand tools' would usually do a good job. The time has come to consider decision-making in more demanding situations, where the 'power tools' of *risk modelling* may have a useful part to play.

In this chapter we will:

- apply decision trees to the evaluation of risky alternatives
- describe a method for calculating the value of market research
- propose dependency modelling as a powerful risk management technique
- outline the role of stochastic modelling in risk simulation and analysis.

## Reasons to model risk

Even though a majority of managers claim to undertake formal forecasting, the application of quantitative modelling techniques seems to be rare.[1] Unfortunately, the evidence is that difficult forecasting decisions based *solely* on holistic judgement are unreliable. The evidence also suggests that the shortcomings of intuitive decision-making tend to be greatest when the key variables in a decision are largest in number.[2]

This is not to argue for undue complexity and the proverbial 'analysis paralysis'. The specification of a model in a particular case will depend on the demands and importance of the decision, especially the 'cost of getting it wrong'. In any event, what we need are tools without spurious refinements, which will help us to appreciate the *effect of risk* on likely project outcomes and to structure our decision-making accordingly.[3] They should provide us with a consistent approach to comparing the risk dynamics of different projects.[4] In so doing, good models can 'train habits of mind' that improve decision-making generally, not least by encouraging the identification and assessment of an alternative to any proposed course of action.[5]

The purpose of any decision support tool is not to generate a formulaic or standardized answer to a qualitative problem. Not every decision can be taken by numbers. Nevertheless, there does appear to be considerable scope for marketers, in particular, to develop the way in which they structure and describe their responses to risk and uncertainty in the areas of marketing planning, budgeting and financial performance management.

### BENEFITS OF STRUCTURED DECISION-MAKING

Risk modelling inevitably involves some commitment of time, imagination and intellect by the decision-maker, even if the model itself will have been designed in collaboration with a specialist in risk and decision analysis. Where the importance or complexity of a decision merits it, the effort is generally worthwhile. By decomposing and modelling a decision, we are able to create new insight into the problem being addressed. More specifically:

- The process of model development calls upon the decision-maker to reveal, as best they can, the *structure* of the problem to be resolved, breaking down difficult or complex issues into simpler subsets. The process in itself makes insight easier to achieve, sometimes prompting creative solutions that might otherwise have remained undiscovered.

- A decision model accommodates as much information about a problem as the decision-maker feels it is necessary to incorporate, but also indicates where more data are necessary or desirable.

- The nature and extent of risk or uncertainty are explicitly represented in a model. They are therefore more likely to be managed in practice than if they had remained implicit or ignored. Conversely, evidently bad or ill-advised courses of action are less likely to be pursued.

- An effective model helps managers to incorporate the views of others in a transparent and useable form, increasing the chances that consensus emerges 'with less heat and more light'.[6]

- A decision model is an evolving and enduring record of key assumptions. It allows for efficient review of a decision in the light of new information – and is a means of transferring knowledge to others in the future.

A marketing model of demand and financial performance is unlikely to reproduce all of the subtleties and surprises of the real world, emulating markets with perfect precision. Even so, they can establish a valid basis for decision-making and provide a valuable frame of reference as the facts unfold.[7] The mark of a good risk model is that it should lead to a *robust* decision – one which will still prove to have been reasonable, even though some of the necessary assumptions may prove to have been wrong or partially inaccurate.

## Decision trees

A decision tree is a schematic diagram of alternative scenarios and their risk components, laid out in such a way as to help calculate and suggest the best course of action. Decision trees are useful when risk decisions are difficult to make by intuition alone, for instance:

- where we are faced with a variety of final outcomes flowing from a *single decision* and we need to decide whether or not to proceed at all (e.g. the chances of 'success' or 'failure')

- where permutations of chance events will lead to a range of *interim decisions* and alternative outcomes (e.g. commercial negotiations where the other party may act or react in ways that are foreseeable but not yet certain)

- where a management decision can be isolated and reduced to its essential elements, but the business case is not yet clear for reasons of risk (e.g. whether it is worthwhile investing in imperfect market research, given what we already know).

Decision trees are expressly intended for these kinds of assessment and are able to accommodate scenarios of varying degrees of complexity within the same structure. Simple decision trees are easy to draw up by hand and work through with a calculator. More complex problems involve manipulating larger diagrams. These are most efficiently created and reviewed in a dedicated software application, such as Palisade Corporation's PrecisionTree˙ or TreeAge Pro† from TreeAge Software.[8] Such software tools are extremely useful if there are likely to be numerous revisions of a decision tree, as insight into an issue develops or as initial assumptions are overtaken by events.

## SIMPLE EXAMPLE

A tree-like diagrammatic structure makes it easy to set out alternative chains of events and calculate their joint probabilities of occurrence. For instance, assume that a customer has indicated to us that they intend to stock one of two products offered to them for listing, but are undecided as to whether they will take the new product into all stores or limit its distribution to test stores. Figure 6.1 shows a simple probability tree summarizing our own views on the prospects of securing a full listing for either of the new products in question. The diagram flows from left to right. Each individual branch of the probability tree represents a single issue or event and is labelled with its probability of occurrence where relevant. In our example, both of the two chains of events in bold type lead to the full listing we are interested in. Every outcome event ('Test stores' or 'Full listing') is conditional on the customer's initial decision whether or not to stock the product. We therefore multiply the probabilities of each event in the chain to arrive at the joint probability of the final outcome. In the present case, we know that the two chains of events in bold type are mutually exclusive outcomes: if Product A is given a full listing then Product B will not be listed at all and vice versa. This means that in order to calculate the overall probability of securing a full listing for one or other of the two products, we add the two joint probabilities of this outcome. Our consolidated view then emerges: we believe that there is a 67 per cent chance of securing a full listing for either Product A or Product B.

## DECISION ANALYSIS

The same expandable tree structure can be applied to decision analysis. In such cases, we are interested in comparing the expected values of alternative chains of decisions and chance events, not just their probabilities of occurrence. Whatever the complexity of the issue and

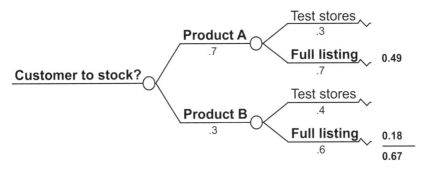

TreeAge Pro Decision Analysis

**Figure 6.1    Simple probability tree**

---

\*    Palisade® and PrecisionTree® are registered trademarks of Palisade Corporation.

†    TreeAge Pro™ is a trademark of TreeAge Software, Inc.

whatever the degree of computer assistance, the process and principles of decision tree design are the same.

## Notation

There is a conventional notation for each type of *node* or intersection in a decision tree, as illustrated in Figure 6.2.

*Squares* are 'decision nodes', points at which the decision-maker needs to make a choice.

*Circles* are 'chance nodes', denoting chance events (or risks). By definition, alternative outcomes that flow from a chance node are not dictated by the decision-maker. However, for decision-making purposes, they will each have a 'value' (or effect) described by the decision-maker, together with its probability of occurrence. Since the chance events emanating from a single chance node are assumed to be an exhaustive list of possible outcomes, their probabilities must sum to 1.

*Triangles* are 'terminal nodes', indicating the end-point of a chain of events. Terminal nodes always need to have a so-called 'pay-off' value attached to them. This value is the outcome of the particular chain of events, expressed either in money terms or in any other non-financial unit of measurement, for example a customer favourability rating. Since the decision tree will need to consolidate the pay-offs from its various branches, the pay-off denomination must be common throughout the tree. So, for example, all financial values would be in $000s or all measures of utility in terms of (say) customer favourability.

## Sequencing

Like the basic probability tree we considered earlier, a decision tree is constructed from left to right. The chaining of events is generally chronological. This is because decisions need to be made before relevant chances outcomes are known and because the probability of certain chance events can sometimes be affected by the occurrence of other events. The first node ('root node') of a decision tree must be a decision node.

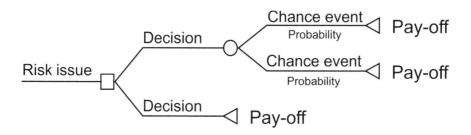

TreeAge Pro Decision Analysis

**Figure 6.2     Decision tree components**

## Branching

The branches connected to the right of a node represent the full range of alternative decisions or chance outcomes that flow from that node. Alternative decisions flow from decision nodes. Alternative chance outcomes flow from chance nodes. Branches at the extreme right-hand end of each chain of events must be terminal nodes.

Our example in Figure 6.3 illustrates a decision tree with probabilities attached to chance events and profit pay-offs attached to terminal nodes.[9] The tree expresses an international company's assessment of three principal strategic options for an overseas market: to do nothing, to enter the region by licensing or to establish its own operations. The 'do nothing' decision only has a downside (-$25 000 000), because the firm's exports to this market are tailing off. By way of second option, the licensing arrangement will either succeed or fail, but the degree of success or failure is another unknown (Major, Minor). Finally, the third option of establishing its own operations in the new region involves a secondary decision for the company: whether to do so alone or in a joint venture with a local partner. Once again, these secondary decision alternatives may succeed or fail to differing degrees. Each chain of decisions and chance events in the resulting decision tree has its own profit impact, identified at its terminal node. Each of

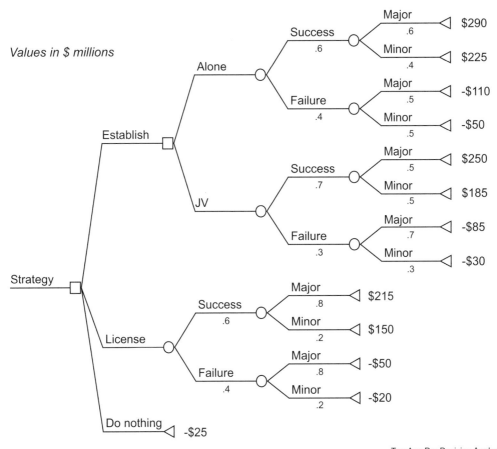

*Values in $ millions*

TreeAge Pro Decision Analysis

**Figure 6.3**     **Decision tree – before roll back**

these profit estimates amounts to the decision-maker's best estimate of outcome, assuming the chain of events in question were certain to occur.

In order to determine the best course of action, we use a technique called *roll back*. Figure 6.4 illustrates the result for the example we have been following. The process involves working backwards along each branch of the tree, from right to left, in the opposite direction to the one in which we created the tree, multiplying out the expected values for each event. The result of each calculation in our example is shown as a boxed value in the figure. At each decision node (the squares) we compare results and strike out branches offering less-than-best expected value. A sign consisting of two short bars indicates that a branch has been duly eliminated. The surviving branch is carried into the next round of roll back calculation, until the highest combination of expected values is finally identified at the initial decision node. In Figure 6.4, you will see that the 'Alone' branch has been struck out in favour of 'JV', which emerges as the best risk-adjusted decision compared to licensing, doing nothing or going it alone. To reconfirm the strategy suggested by the decision tree, we simply retrace our steps from left to right, describing the combination of actions that produced the winning pay-off. In Figure 6.4, the recommended strategy is highlighted in bold type (Strategy – Establish – JV).

## PRELIMINARY INFLUENCE DIAGRAMS

Creating an *influence diagram* is often a useful preliminary to constructing a decision tree. Its purpose is to identify the dependencies between all the decisions and chance events seen as

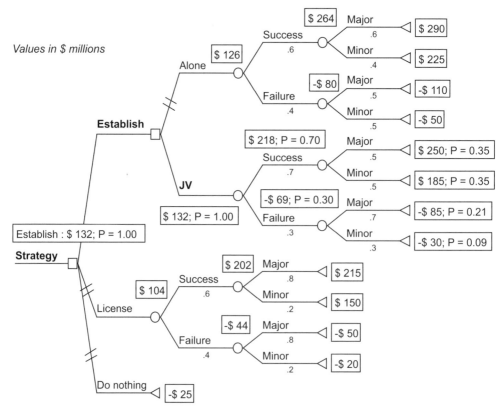

TreeAge Pro Decision Analysis

**Figure 6.4     Decision tree – after roll back**

being essential to the analysis. The finished influence diagram becomes a 'pick list' for the subsequent decision tree. Simple influence diagrams can be drawn by hand or created in many standard PC drawing applications.

Influence diagrams have a looser and less formal structure than a tree diagram. This means that they can accommodate more adjustments then decision trees before requiring a completely fresh start. It also makes them easier to use in group discussion or with colleagues who are more interested in discussing the subject matter than in learning how to use a new tool. Influence diagrams are much more compact than full decision trees, making them convenient to review and refine.

Figure 6.5 is an influence diagram of the decision tree we saw in Figures 6.3 and 6.4. The labelled squares and circles used to denote 'decision' and 'chance' nodes in decision trees are also used for influence diagrams (in our case replaced by rectangles and ovals to accommodate their labels). The pay-off objective (or 'value node') takes a diamond shape. Arrow-headed lines connect the decision, chance and value nodes to create a complete set of related events.

The specialist softwares usually offer an integrated conversion feature that automatically turns influence diagrams generated within the application into draft decision trees, subject to further inputs from the originator to ensure correct sequencing and logic. If an influence diagram cannot convert into a successful tree diagram, it will usually be for two reasons:

- *Circular arguments.* The one-way flow of a decision tree (left to right) cannot accommodate any logical loops or returns 'upstream'. This means that there can be no circular influences: a first node influencing a second node, which in turn influences the first node.

- *Disconnection.* A single decision tree can only accommodate sets of interconnected or interdependent events and actions that can roll back to a single decision. The process of creating and reviewing an influence diagram may therefore reveal the need for more than one decision tree.

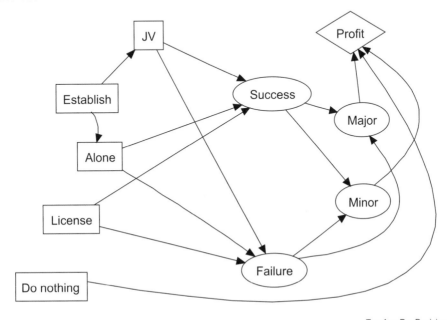

TreeAge Pro Decision Analysis

**Figure 6.5**     **Influence diagram**

## INTERPRETING DECISION TREES

Do not be seduced by the undoubted elegance of the technique into using the decision tree as a 'command instrument' telling you what you *must* do. Regard the output of a decision tree (or any other comparable model) as 'conditionally prescriptive'.[10] Provided all of the inputs and assumptions that went into the decision tree are considered to hold true, then it will be rational to follow the course of action suggested by the model. If the recommended course of action is theoretically superior by a narrow margin, test the variability of outcome according to changes in chance event probabilities.

If you have not spent enough time thinking creatively about the range of decision options available to you or the various chance events relevant to the case, then the decision model may not be serving you as well as it could. Ensure that there is clarity about the context within which the decision will be made and the overriding objectives that it will serve. There is, for example, little point in discovering which of three alternative decisions returns the highest expected value, if none of them meets corporate requirements for financial payback.

If a decision tree suggests a course of action that still runs counter to your instinct, this could be for one of three reasons:

* inadequacy of the tree's structure
* inconsistency with your risk attitude
* heuristic effects on judgement.

### Inadequacy of structure

Consider whether the structure of the decision tree is an adequate representation of the problem and the full range of decision options. There is no standard formula to apply to the design of a decision tree. However, careful reconsideration may suggest that elements are missing or that the *relationships* between the decisions and events do not accord with your view of the realities. Conversely, do not be tempted to load too much detail into a decision tree, which will rapidly expand to become unwieldy and lose its value as a tool to create insight. Remove redundant or obviously non-viable options as soon as they fail to qualify. In practice, it is rarely necessary to replicate every aspect of a situation in order to evaluate a problem in terms of its incremental impact. Consider using sensitivity analysis or a preliminary influence diagram to determine where the critical issues lie. Concentrate the scope of your decision tree accordingly.

### Inconsistency with risk attitude

The example illustrated in Figures 6.3 and 6.4 tacitly assumed that the decision-maker's attitude to risk was a neutral one and that they were therefore able to accept the downside risks associated with the decision tree's suggested course of action. It is clear that a decision tree will take no account of risk attitude unless it is instructed to do so. Since the extent of risk and opportunity is visible to the decision-maker in the pay-offs at each terminal node, the adjustment of a decision for risk attitude may be easy to make intuitively. For example, if a suggested course of action is plainly too risky on the downside, the decision not to proceed should be obvious. Supplementary tools and techniques may be helpful in the more finely balanced cases, where the model's suggested course of action might be altered by differences in risk attitude. In Chapter 3 we saw how it was possible to take account of a decision-maker's attitude to risk by converting expected monetary values into their expected utilities for the decision-maker. The same conversion approach can be used to adjust any measure of pay-off used in the decision analysis. These utilities can simply replace the financial values in the decision tree, which is then resolved as before using the roll back method we described. PrecisionTree and TreeAge Pro, for example, provide built-in features to capture a decision-maker's utility for risk ('risk preference function'), reflecting the certainty equivalent approach we outlined earlier in this book. In a software environment, it is extremely easy to test the sensitivity of the recommended decision to different risk preference functions.

This raises the practical question of dealing with two or more different utilities, in cases where a decision needs to take account of a range of pay-off attributes, such as likely profits, time to market or impact on brand equity. It is theoretically possible to convert the utility of each non-financial attribute into a monetary value, so that the decision tree is simply solving for expected monetary value throughout. This conversion approach is easy to understand, but the conversion into money value may be arbitrary and difficult for participants to accept if estimations of direct financial equivalence are not normally made. The alternative approach involves converting every attribute, including the monetary values, into utilities on their own scale. The resulting utilities then need to be recalibrated to a common scale, so that they can be added to the decision tree for roll back calculation. This can be quite a laborious procedure and is only recommended where the work involved is justified by the sensitivity of the decision. Keeney and Raifa (1993) review the theory and the practice in detail.[11]

## Heuristic effects on judgement

As a decision-maker, you may be uncomfortable with a decision tree because it is 'not telling you what you want to hear' for reasons other than risk attitude. In that case, consider whether there is a heuristic explanation for your reaction. For example, have your earlier interpretations of data been selective, or is there pressure not to reverse an earlier commitment made to a course of action which now appears to be unfavourable? (See Chapter 3 – 'Heuristics', p. 52.)

# Expected value of new information

So far, we have considered decision trees as a means of modelling alternative courses of action, based on the risk information currently available to us. By applying the simple rules of probability, we are able to identify the best risk-adjusted decision, given the information and assumptions reflected in the model. This may be enough. We may be comfortable that our assumed values for risk and uncertainty cannot be improved. After all, we may have reliable historical data that we believe will retain their validity. Alternatively, sensitivity analysis may have shown that our current course of action would not need to change, even if we set the relevant risk variables in our decision model to their maximum and minimum conceivable values.

On other occasions, however, the range of predictable outcomes may be too wide or uniformly distributed to suggest a preferable course of action. Perhaps the consequences of prediction error may be too costly, whether in terms of profit impact, lost opportunity or brand impairment. When the question of investing in market research arises, a key issue is how much it would be *rational* to spend, given that the principal purpose of the investment would be to improve existing predictions. This is a familiar challenge to many marketers and market researchers. The approach we review here helps to answer the question using a decision tree. In this instance, the technique makes it possible for us to define the value of market research in terms of its ability to reduce the cost of wrong decisions.[12] We will consider how to calculate two closely related figures:

- the expected value of perfect information (EVPI)
- the expected value of imperfect information (EVII).

The *expected value of perfect information* is the probabilistic value of new information, assuming that it would predict which current alternative plan is the best one with complete certainty. In effect, this is the *break-even point* for an investment in new information that is 100 per cent reliable. It suggests an absolute ceiling on expenditure, rather than a target cost to deliver an incremental return. All other things being equal, EVPI is therefore an expenditure that it would be theoretically 'irrational' to exceed in attempting to improve earlier predictions. The *expected value of imperfect information* is an equivalent calculation to EVPI, but takes into account the fact that the research methodology under consideration has predictive accuracy that is less than 100 per cent. This is the more common situation, of course, and the calculation will naturally produce a lower value indication than EVPI. We begin with EVPI, however, because it is the simpler calculation and a better context within which to describe the basic principles that apply in both cases.

## EXPECTED VALUE OF PERFECT INFORMATION

We cannot expect market research to change the underlying nature of a risk. We judge the value of research by its ability to deliver better information *about* a risk. Such new information is worth something to us if it increases the expected value of our decision in anticipation of actual events. Consider what this statement means in practice. Without research we may make a perfectly rational business decision, but one in which an unfavourable (or less-than-best) outcome must still form part of our expected value calculation. For example, it may be absolutely appropriate to launch into a new market, whilst still acknowledging that there is a chance that the plan will fail to deliver. If absolutely reliable research helps us to avoid making a decision from which such an undesirable result would *inevitably* flow, whilst directing us towards an alternative decision with a higher expected value, we have a basis upon which to estimate its worth. In other words, information increases the expected value of a decision when it enables us to eliminate choices (and their outcomes) which, in the absence of prior research, are 'diluting' the expected value of the best available course of action open to us. A simple worked example of an EVPI decision tree makes this clear and describes the process.

Assume we have developed a new technological product that we would like to take to market. It offers customers much lower cost over current products, by removing features that many non-users do not apparently value. We need to determine whether the market potential for the innovation is substantial enough to support a new brand or whether its lower potential means that it is best introduced as an extension to an existing branded product line. The viability of the opportunity for us turns on whether lower costs would successfully introduce a new segment of users to the category, whilst simultaneously encouraging current customers to use the product more frequently. We have calculated a net present value for profit (NPV) under each of the three scenarios represented in Figure 6.6(A). (The example values are in modest thousands for ease of comparison later in the chapter). If we launch the new brand and the market potential is high, we forecast an attractive NPV ($85 000). Alternatively, we could decide to exploit the technology under our existing brand. In that case, we estimate a substantially lower NPV ($25 000), but we see no downside. However, if we launch the new brand and market potential turns out to be low,

*Values in $ thousands*

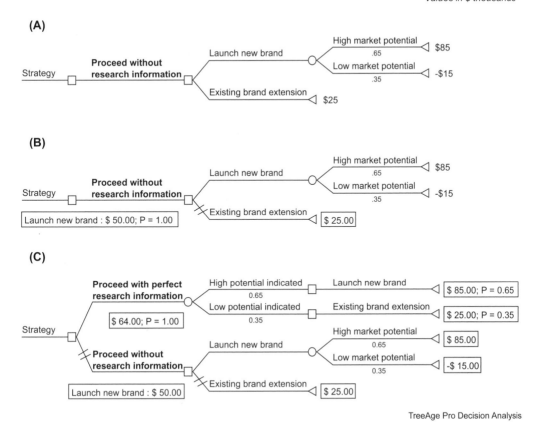

TreeAge Pro Decision Analysis

**Figure 6.6    Expected value of perfect information**

we foresee a negative NPV (-$15 000). At this point we feel that there is probability of .65 that the market can actually support a new brand. This implies a complementary probability of .35 that the new brand will fail to find a profitable market. The layout of the decision tree makes it clear that we are planning to make our decision now without research. There is only one square decision node; this is the root node of the tree, which is where we are today. When we roll the tree back to calculate its expected values, as shown in Figure 6.6(B), the outcome suggests that we should indeed launch the new brand. This is because the new brand has an expected value of $50 000, no less than twice the expected value of the brand extension alternative. If there were really no means of validating the market potential for the new technology, a decision to launch the new brand would be a rational course of action for an organization that was risk-neutral and could tolerate the downside if it occurred.

Yet if perfect information were available about market potential, how much would it be worth? Figure 6.6(C) shows that if we postponed our decision until we had this new information, it increases the expected value of our launch by $14 000 ($64 000 – $50 000). To understand this result, we need to consider the structure, assumptions and implications of the EVPI sub-tree in Figure 6.6(C), which is labelled 'Proceed with perfect research information'. Take a moment to familiarize yourself with the diagram before reading on. The layout of this sub-tree is different from the one beneath it, which continues to assume that we do not undertake any research.

You will see that the EVPI sub-tree charts two alternative chains of events as they would occur if the research went ahead. On that assumption, the research must clearly precede our strategic decision. The starting point ('root') of the EVPI sub-tree is therefore a chance node (a circle), because at the moment we commission the research, we do not know its outcome. The best we can do is to assume that the probability of either of the two envisaged outcomes being confirmed by research is the same as our current estimate of their probabilities of occurrence in real life:

$$p(\text{high potential market}) = .65$$

$$p(\text{low potential market}) = .35$$

Depending on the research confirmation we ultimately receive, there is then a single subsequent decision to be made in each case (represented by the two square decision nodes). If the research confirms high market potential, it is clear that we will launch the new brand and expect its NPV of $85 000. Since there is no better plan available in that situation, this is only rational course of action. On the other hand, if research shows that the market potential is low, it is equally clear that we will not launch the new brand, but will extend our existing brand and expect $25 000 in NPV. You will notice that the option of launching the new brand when market potential is known to be low has been excluded from the EVPI sub-tree. This would not be a logical decision after either of the two possible research results, so it is excluded from the analysis. Given what it is possible for us to assume today, the expected value of the best available decision is bound to increase if we conduct perfect research, because the prospect of such insight has enabled us to avoid taking the worst-case outcome into our expected value calculation.

Although the example is a simple one, the same principles apply when the range of alternatives is larger and the decision tree more complex. As always in a decision tree, the indicated probabilities of alternative outcomes flowing from a single chance node must always be mutually exclusive and sum to the value 1. Chance nodes must represent an exhaustive list of the outcomes material to the decision, both good and bad. Equally, decision nodes must represent all the courses of action that are being contemplated, including a 'Do nothing' option with a pay-off of '$0' where appropriate. This last point is useful to remember when there is apparently only a single course of action at the first decision node and the choice is simply between 'go' and 'no go'.

To summarize so far:

- All other things being equal, the value of information is the difference between expected value *with* and *without* the new information.

- The expected value of perfect information (EVPI) is the break-even point for investment in new information that improves current predictions to the point of assumed 100 per cent reliability, enabling identified worst-case outcomes to be avoided.

- The decision tree approach to estimating EVPI – and EVII as we shall see – is helpful operationally because it allows the decision-maker to set out and validate the realistic sequences of research outcomes and resulting decision alternatives, before using the tree to calculate and compare the estimations of expected value.

## EXPECTED VALUE OF IMPERFECT INFORMATION

We have established EVPI as an absolute ceiling on expenditure to improve expected value estimates. We now need to consider how to calculate the value of new information that is *not* going to be 100 per cent reliable in validating our current risk assumptions (EVII). Research findings can be unreliable for a number of reasons that are quite legitimate. For example, there may be a predictable error in the representativeness of research respondents drawn from a larger population. Respondents may also tend to react differently under artificial conditions from the way they would otherwise behave.

The required approach to discounting for the reliability of new information is sometimes referred to as *Bayesian revision*. Although specialist software applications greatly simplify the undertaking, it is important to understand the principles that are being applied. Without a practical understanding of the insight contributed by Thomas Bayes (1702–1761) in the theorem that still bears his name, we might be tempted simply to reduce each of the expected values in our earlier EVPI calculation by the 'headline' reliability statistic for the information in question.

First of all, by way of cautionary example of what *not* to do, let us revert briefly to our new technology case in Figure 6.6(C). In this example case, we estimated probabilities of .65 and .35 respectively, for the likelihood that the market for our new product would have either high or low potential. Since we were yet not in a position to judge whether even perfect research would actually confirm these estimates, we could only assume the same probabilities of the research validating one conclusion or the other. We calculated EVPI on that basis, effectively postponing our decision until we knew which of the two market conditions was true. So what adjustment should we make if the research is known (or assessed) to be only 85 per cent reliable? It would be *incorrect* to conclude that the likelihood of the research indicating high market potential would become .65 * .85 = .55 or that .35 * .85 = .30 would similarly become the adjusted likelihood of the corresponding indication of low market potential. The clue is that .55 and .30 do not sum to the value of 1 as they should, given that the two outcomes are supposed to be mutually exclusive and to represent the exhaustive probabilities.

One way of appreciating the *correct* approach to discounting for reliability is to 'get physical' and to follow what happens every time 100 hypothetical respondents are polled in a less-than-reliable study. Just to make the problem more interesting, let us suppose that our market research colleagues have also told us that the most appropriate research methodology happens to be *biased*. This means that it has a different likelihood of correctly identifying 'favourable' and 'unfavourable' responses. For illustrative purposes, we will assume that the research is 90 per cent reliable in correctly identifying conditions of low market potential and 85 per cent reliable in identifying conditions of high market potential.

Figure 6.7 shows what happens. First of all, we have already stated our so-called *prior probabilities* for market potential. Prior probability is the term used in Bayesian revision for the original probability assigned to an outcome, before it is adjusted in the light of further information or experience. In this case, you recall, the prior probabilities of high and low market potential are .65 and .35 respectively. They are represented by the two branches of the chance root node shown at level 2 in Figure 6.7.

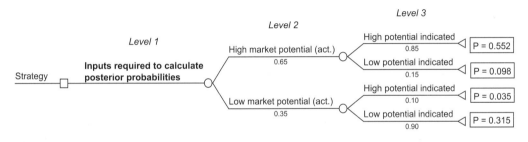

TreeAge Pro Decision Analysis

**Figure 6.7    Bayesian revision worksheet**

Now consider level 3 in the figure. If the research is only 85 per cent reliable, it means that it will *misreport* high potential conditions as low potential conditions 15 per cent of the time. In other words, for every 65 high potential indications we are expecting to find, just under ten of these will be incorrectly added to the *low* potential score. The joint probability of this incorrect outcome is therefore .65 * .15 = .098, as shown in the box to the right of the relevant pathway in the diagram [P=0.098].

We now turn to the 'Low market potential' branch at level 2 in the figure. Since the research is 90 per cent reliable in determining conditions of low market potential, it will wrongly assess 10 per cent of low potential indications as being high potential indications. The joint probability of this incorrect outcome is therefore .35 * .10 = 0.035, as shown in the diagram [P=0.035]. In our case, we would therefore expect a misallocation of approximately four of our expected 35 indications of low market potential. They would be added misleadingly to the high potential score. The figure shows the calculated joint probabilities for all four possible outcomes in the example situation: there are two anticipated market conditions (high potential, low potential), each of which will be both correctly and incorrectly reported to a different degree.

The purpose of the allocation exercise set out in Figure 6.7 is not only to illustrate a point. Since the method we will use to calculate EVII is the same as we used for EVPI, we will need to draw up a suitably amended decision tree. As before, the tree should reflect the full range of likely outcomes, with and without the unreliable market research. The tree we will use is illustrated in Figure 6.8. The sub-tree for 'proceeding without research information' does not need to be altered following our earlier EVPI assessment, but merely reproduced. However, the sub-tree for 'proceeding with imperfect information' is significantly different. At level 2 you will see that the balance of probability for the research indicating either of the two market indications has shifted. They no longer mirror our 'prior probabilities' of .65 and .35, but reflect instead the *revised* joint probabilities of these indications, given *both* the prior probabilities we assigned *and* the 'swings and roundabouts' of misallocation we have just stepped through. To make this adjustment in our case, we simply added the two joint probabilities of correct and incorrect indication for each research outcome from the diagram in Figure 6.7:

*p*Revised(any research indicating *high* potential) = .552 + .035 = .587 (or .59)

*p*Revised(any research indicating *low* potential) = .098 + .315 = .413 (or .41)

Levels 3 and 4 of the new sub-tree capture the different chains of events in these altered circumstances. (The 'high potential' and 'low potential' branches are necessarily identical in layout, so our explanation here applies to both of them.) Where research is perfect, there is no risk of misinformation if we act on an indication of high market potential. For this reason, you recall, there was only a single course of action contemplated for each research outcome in our earlier example of perfect research (see Figure 6.6(B)). However, if research is *unreliable*, we need to factor in the consequences of misinformation. We achieve this technically by adjusting each possible course of action by the expected value of our having been misled. It follows that the less reliable the research, the higher the probability that we will be misled and the closer the expected value for that decision will come to resemble a full-blown adverse outcome (in our case, the certainty of low market potential).

You will see the probabilities of misinformation at level 4 in Figure 6.8, wherever the market indication at that level contradicts its parent branch (e.g. low market potential 'actually experienced' at level 4, whereas the decision at level 2 relied on an indication of high market potential). The probabilities at level 4 are so-called *posterior probabilities*, to use another term of Bayesian revision. Posterior probability is defined as the adjusted probability of an outcome (A)

*Values in $ thousands*

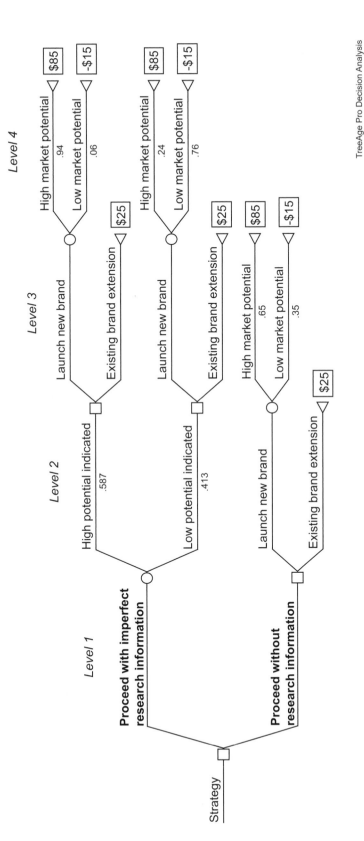

**Figure 6.8  Expected value of imperfect information – before roll back**

given new information or experience (B). In the notation of probability this is written $p(A|B)$. In our case, B is the partially reliable information provided by the market research study. Knowing the posterior probability makes it possible to answer a question such as this: 'Given that the research is unreliable by a factor of X, what is the probability that 100 respondents reported as being 'favourable' (or 'unfavourable') will actually prove to be so?' We have already entered all of the possible outcomes in the preliminary workings shown in Figure 6.7. This makes it easy to calculate the posterior probabilities for research indications of high and low market potential, without having to resort to challenging (if perhaps more efficient) mathematical formulae. We take the joint probability of each state of affairs shown at level 3 in Figure 6.7 and express it as a proportion of the revised total probability of the outcome in question, now shown at level 2 of Figure 6.8. This is perhaps easier to demonstrate than to describe:

$p$Posterior(actual *high* potential | *high* potential indicated) = .552 / .587 = .94

$p$Posterior(actual *low* potential | *high* potential indicated) = .035 / .587 = .06

$p$Posterior(actual *low* potential | *low* potential indicated) = .315 / .413 = .76

$p$Posterior(actual *high* potential | *low* potential indicated) = .098 / .413 = .24

Lastly, as before, the pay-offs for each final outcome are shown in boxes at the relevant terminal node of each chain of events (Figure 6.8). Rolling back the tree delivers the expected values of all optimal decisions, finally allowing us to compare the expected values of proceeding with unreliable research or proceeding without it. Figure 6.9 shows the result. As you would expect, the EVII is lower than the EVPI we saw earlier. On the assumptions we have made, $6700 is the maximum amount we should consider paying to improve existing information if the research is unreliable as defined ($56 700 – $50 000 = $6700). This amount is the difference shown in expected value between the two decision alternatives at the root of the whole tree ('Strategy'). Admittedly, it could be that the research has other commercial or practical value that cannot be reflected in the EVII calculation. For example, we might want the research because it is useful in creating a selling story. However, in the absence of any such collateral value, if EVII is $6700 and the research agency wants $300 000 to do the work, something in the equation is going to have to change. As ever, sensitivity analysis remains important in EVII assessments as elsewhere. Once the decision tree is set up and the principles of Bayesian revision understood, it is easy to test for alternative combinations of prior probability and reliability. This will certainly confirm your intuition: research has the highest value when you are most uncertain, and the research is also more reliable than you are uncertain. The worth of the EVII exercise is to place a specific and rationally determined money value on your 'gut feel'.

## Alternative approach to EVII

Lacava and Tull (1982) realised that managers may not have sufficient incentive to familiarize themselves with decision trees or may have difficulty manipulating prior and posterior probabilities.[13] With the needs of new product development managers and market researchers expressly in mind, Lacava and Tull created an alternative methodology, providing managers with a ready-reckoner in table form that obviates the need for time-consuming calculation. A further practical advantage of such an approach is that it is relatively easy to explain to non-marketing colleagues. The trade-off is that users are obliged to accept some fixed parameters that underlie the prepared tables.

*Values in $ thousands*

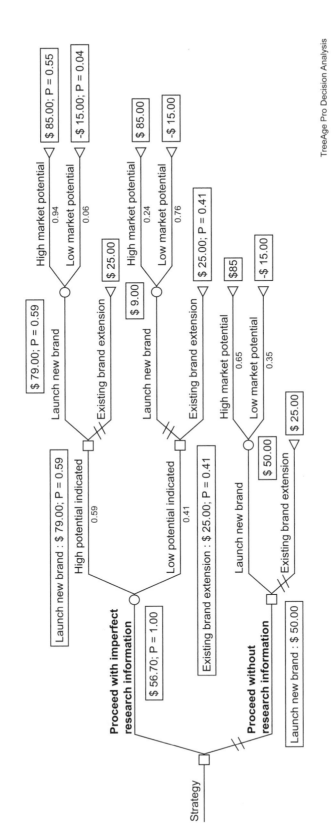

**Figure 6.9    Expected value of imperfect information – after roll back**

TreeAge Pro Decision Analysis

The Lacava and Tull method asks you to consider four indicators before looking up the answer in their tables:

- the maximum financial loss that would be tolerabie before a new product were withdrawn from the market ('maximum tolerable loss')
- the probability that this maximum amount would be lost if the product under consideration were introduced
- the probability that the product will be a success if introduced
- the accuracy with which the research is likely predict the true market state.

Figure 6.10 shows an extract from a Lacava and Tull table. The table expresses EVII as a percentage of the maximum tolerable loss, so that it can be applied to projects of any scale. This example table makes the further important assumption that the research methodology has no reliability bias, so that there is no difference in its accuracy in predicting success or failure.

To illustrate the Lacava and Tull approach in practice, suppose we believe that our new product idea has a .65 probability of success in its current form. Let us also assume that we could tolerate a loss of $1 000 000 before withdrawing a product from the market, if it proved unsuccessful following introduction. As matters stand, we believe that there is only a 0.2 probability of actually losing this amount, because our cost commitments on this project are well controlled. If the research were expected to be 85 per cent reliable, its break-even value to us would be 2.70 per cent of the maximum tolerable loss – in our case $27 000.

Lacava and Tull were able to draw some interesting general conclusions from their tables, which nicely illustrate the sensitivity of the expected value of information to changes in the reliability of research and the probabilities associated with launch outcomes. On the range of assumptions reproduced in Figure 6.10, it would theoretically never be worth spending more than 38 per cent of the maximum tolerable loss on a marketing research project, since this is the indicated maximum for EVPI. Secondly, assuming an average accepted accuracy of 85 per cent for market research and no bias, an 'expected-value decision-maker' should (on the assumptions given) never spend more than 12 per cent of the maximum tolerable loss on such imperfect information. Less favourable combinations for the assumed probability of product success and financial loss becoming intolerable indicate lower recommended research expenditure, but no EVII indication at 85 per cent research reliability exceeds 12 per cent of maximum tolerable loss in the Lacava and Tull table shown in Figure 6.10.

## Dependency modelling

Dependency modelling is a valuable technique for adding structure and relevance to the assessment of risks associated with a particular objective. The technique can be applied to a complex brand project or to the resolution of a single issue. The essence of the approach is that it focuses exclusively on the things that need to go right in order to ensure fulfilment of the stated objective (the assumed 'dependencies'), rather than by challenging you to imagine everything that might possibly go wrong.[14] By prompting a systematic identification of events that contribute to the overall outcome, dependency modelling helps to draw out the underlying assumptions and risk issues that might otherwise remain implicit and unchallenged. Grounded in the realities of a project, the technique is especially helpful in determining where the achievement of a goal might be most vulnerable to failure, and therefore the extent to which it would be reasonable to apply mitigating efforts and resources. In short, it sets performance management priorities and makes their business case.

| | P(S₁): Probability of the product's being a success (if introduced) is estimated to be | | | | | | | | | | | | |
| | 0.60 | | | | | | | 0.65 | | | | | |
| | P(L): Probability that the maximum potential loss will be lost is estimated to be | | | | | | | | | | | | |
| $1-\alpha = 1-\beta$ (%) | 0.35 | 0.30 | 0.25 | 0.20 | 0.15 | 0.10 | 0.05 | 0.30 | 0.25 | 0.20 | 0.15 | 0.10 | 0.05 |
|---|---|---|---|---|---|---|---|---|---|---|---|---|---|
| 55–65 | – | – | – | – | – | – | – | – | – | – | – | – | – |
| 70 | – | – | – | – | – | 0.50 | 1.70 | – | – | – | – | – | – |
| 75 | – | – | – | – | 2.69 | 4.27 | 4.58 | – | – | – | – | – | 0.48 |
| 80 | – | – | 0.26 | 5.30 | 7.45 | 8.04 | 7.46 | – | – | – | 0.36 | 2.97 | 3.80 |
| 85 | – | – | 8.26 | 11.34 | 12.21 | 11.81 | 10.34 | – | – | 2.70 | 6.33 | 7.48 | 7.11 |
| 90 | – | 11.57 | 16.26 | 17.39 | 16.97 | 15.58 | 13.23 | – | 5.45 | 10.86 | 12.31 | 11.99 | 10.42 |
| 95 | 15.22 | 23.24 | 24.26 | 23.44 | 21.73 | 19.36 | 16.11 | 8.55 | 17.67 | 19.01 | 18.28 | 16.50 | 13.74 |
| Perfect information | 37.48 | 34.92 | 32.26 | 29.48 | 26.49 | 23.13 | 18.99 | 32.48 | 29.89 | 27.17 | 24.26 | 21.01 | 17.05 |

**Figure 6.10   Alternative approach to EVII calculation**

Source: Lacava and Tull (1982)

The invention of the approach we will review in this chapter is credited to Professor John Gordon, who proposed dependency modelling as a new way of looking at risk.[15] The technique draws on a recognized system of logical algebraic operations called *Boolean logic*, after the Englishman George Boole, who published his thinking in the middle of the nineteenth century.

For present purposes, our assumption is that any complex dependency model would be created in a software environment, supported (at least initially) by an experienced specialist. They are likely to be working with a dedicated application such as Arium's Risk Analysis Tool, which is based on Professor Gordon's work.[16] This particular proprietary application has an interface similar to Microsoft Excel‡, so that the methods of data and formula entry would not be unfamiliar.[17]

## FORM AND CONTENT

As we saw earlier in this chapter, decision trees help managers to consider the alternative outcomes that might flow from choices and chance events along the way. Similar in form to decision trees, dependency models are hierarchical diagrams. However, they adopt a different perspective from decision trees by setting a single outcome as their starting point and then progressively identifying what needs to happen in order for the single outcome to occur. Figure 6.11 illustrates the intuitive 'Sticky Steps' variant of dependency modelling suggested by Obeng (1996) as a planning tool.[18] Figure 6.12 represents the beginnings of an equivalent quantitative model showing the first three levels of dependency for launching and sustaining a viable branded product. The diagram becomes an expanding web, with each item depending on the items

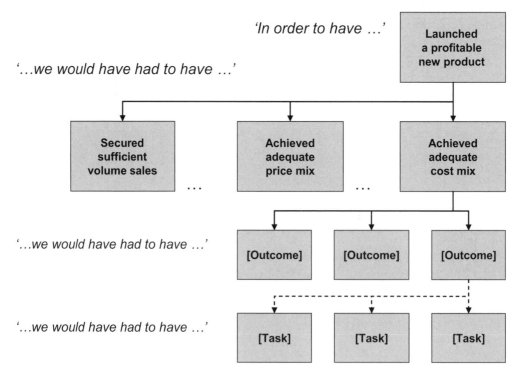

**Figure 6.11    'Sticky Steps'**

*Source: After Obeng (1996)*

---

‡        Microsoft® and Excel® are registered trademarks of Microsoft Corporation.

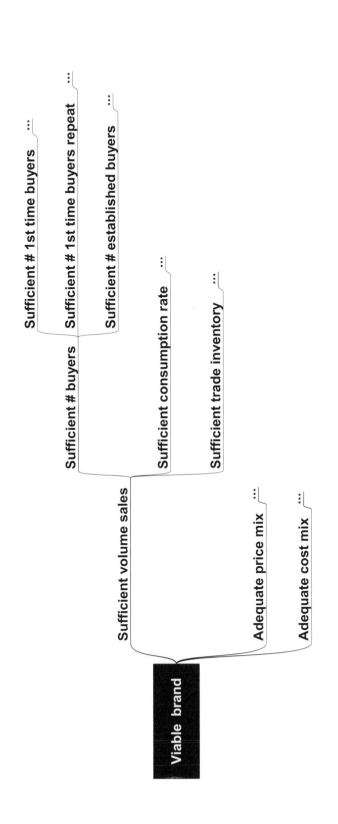

**Figure 6.12 Dependency model (illustrative)**

Mindjet MindManager Map

Viable brand

Sufficient volume sales
- Sufficient # buyers
  - Sufficient # 1st time buyers
  - Sufficient # 1st time buyers repeat
  - Sufficient # established buyers
- Sufficient consumption rate
- Sufficient trade inventory

Adequate price mix

Adequate cost mix

directly connected to its right. The continuation symbol, consisting of three dots, indicates that subsidiary detail would be available in a fully expanded view of the same model.

As you might expect, the conceptual model in Figure 6.12 shows that a new branded product depends on three overarching requirements for its viability: sufficient volume sales, an adequate price mix and an adequate cost mix. In this generic example, the achievement of sufficient volume sales is assumed to have its own set of dependencies: a sufficient number of buyers for the product, a sufficient average consumption rate amongst those buyers and a sufficient volume of goods held in inventory by distributors. Finally, we can see that the adequacy of buyer numbers is itself reliant upon there being a sufficient number of first-time buyers, a sufficient number of first-time buyers who buy again ('repeaters') and a sufficient number of established buyers who become regular purchasers over the longer term. Even this simplified example demonstrates how a dependency model can help to explain the interaction between the key contributors to commercial success.

For illustrative purposes we have chosen purely descriptive definitions for the goal of brand viability and its dependencies. In real application of the technique, you might want to be more concrete, so that the resulting web of dependencies would be more specific. For example, you might choose to express the central objective in time and money ('To achieve 25 per cent profit from operations on revenue of $10 000 000 by end 2010'). Bear in mind that dependency models are not limited to creating insight into the conditions necessary for achievement of minimum acceptable objectives, such as a budget commitment or a threshold rate of financial return. A dependency model can also adopt an aspirational objective as its starting point. In that case, attention is focused on maximization of opportunity rather than an avoidance of out-and-out failure. A comparison of two models that respectively identify the conditions necessary for achievement of the minimum acceptable result, on the one hand, and the upside or aspirational outcome, on the other, can add another useful layer of insight.

The distinct benefit of quantitative dependency modelling lies in its ability to describe and consolidate (1) the risk of individual component failure, (2) the extent of reliance between neighbouring components and (3) the existence of fallbacks.

By way of illustration, Figure 6.13(A) shows another extract from our 'viable brand' model. This subset of a larger model deals with the conditions necessary to induce trial purchase of a new product, assuming that adequate brand awareness – considered elsewhere in the model – has already been achieved or will be achieved by the trial purchase itself. Figure 6.13(B) adds a 'failure rate' for each dependency, expressed in percentage terms.

You will notice that the dependency between elements has now been characterized in one of two ways, using the so-called logical operators AND and OR. The outermost dependencies on each branch of the structure have a thundercloud or an umbrella symbol attached to them.

To consider each of these in turn:

- *Logical AND*. Where AND relationships exist, it means that all of the subordinate AND conditions must be satisfied, in order for the higher-level dependent event to occur. On the far right of Figure 6.13(A), you will see that the distribution channel for our new product is required to have both an appropriate service environment and an appropriate image. Assuming that the model is identifying the route towards a desirable end objective (a 'positively phrased' dependency model), it becomes apparent that AND dependencies signify points of weakness in a system. This is because the greater the number of AND relationships attached to a single dependent event, the more things have to go right in combination (sometimes simultaneously) for the event to occur.

(A)

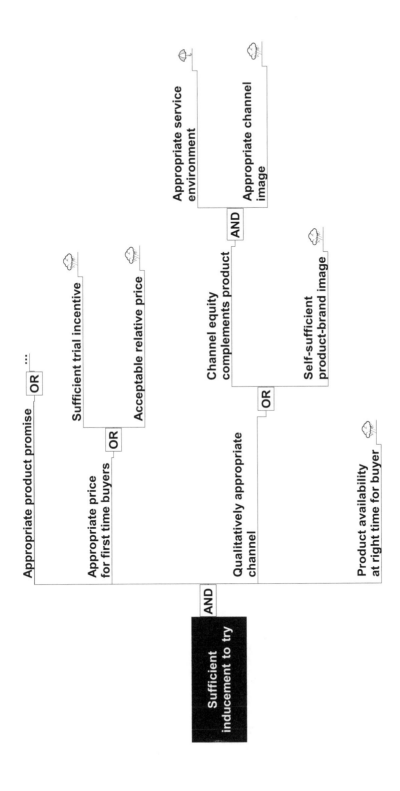

MindJet MindManager Map

**Figure 6.13    Dependency model – sufficient inducement to try**

**(B)**

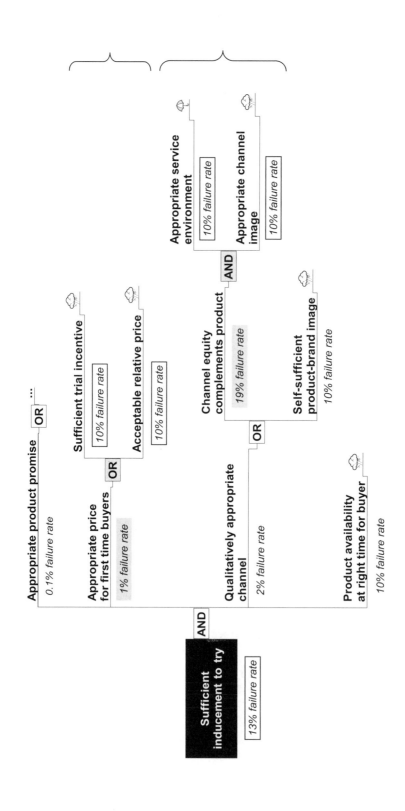

Appropriate product promise [OR] ...
*0.1% failure rate*

Sufficient trial incentive
*10% failure rate*

Acceptable relative price
*10% failure rate*

Appropriate price for first time buyers
*1% failure rate*

[OR]

Appropriate service environment
*10% failure rate*

Appropriate channel image
*10% failure rate*

Channel equity complements product
*19% failure rate*

[AND]

Self-sufficient product-brand image
*10% failure rate*

Qualitatively appropriate channel
*2% failure rate*

[OR]

Product availability at right time for buyer
*10% failure rate*

Sufficient inducement to try [AND]
*13% failure rate*

Mindjet MindManager Map

**Figure 6.13    *Concluded***

- *Logical OR*. Where OR relationships apply, it means that fulfilment of any single condition amongst alternatives would permit the higher-level dependent event to occur. Points of relative strength in a system have OR dependencies, because there is more than one route to their achievement. If one dependency fails, there is at least one fallback, and sometimes more than one. For example, our illustrative model in Figure 6.13 assumes that an appropriate price for first-time buyers is achievable in one of two ways: by means of normal pricing that is acceptable or by means of an alternative pricing incentive. All other things being equal, the more OR dependencies that exist – or that you can add to your plan – the more resistant to failure the outcome will be. The corresponding principle should encourage you to consider how to minimize the number of AND dependencies.

  As a point of interest, there is another logical OR, referred to as 'exclusive OR', represented by the letters XOR. This logical relationship applies if the simultaneous occurrence of two or more alternatives is impossible. For example, there cannot be two exclusive licensees for the same product in the same territory. From a risk management standpoint, however, the existence of alternative candidates would still be a good thing.

- *Thundercloud and umbrella symbols*. A thundercloud symbol appears on the lowest-level dependencies that either cannot be modelled further or have not been modelled further by choice, for reasons of practicality or relevance. For example, we may have put a mitigation measure in place, making us less sensitive to how the associated dependency might evolve. We can signal the existence of such a mitigation measure with the umbrella symbol shown in Figure 6.13. A thundercloud symbol may also indicate that the element in question has dependencies that cannot be controlled by us. Sometimes these uncontrollables can be regarded as beyond anyone's direct influence – such as average national household income. Other dependencies may be out of our own control, but remain under the control of others. For instance, in our example, the acceptability of our product's relative price is to some extent dependent on competitors' pricing reactions to our launch.

- *Failure rate*. A failure rate is the probability that the associated dependency might not occur precisely as defined. In developing and using a dependency model, you are only required to provide failure rates for the lowest-level dependencies situated on the far right-hand side of the model. All the other failure rates are calculated.

  In common with other expected value techniques, the failure rate for each dependency needs to be supplemented with an estimate of the gross impact of failure on project outcome, ignoring any mitigating effects suggested by fallbacks or other structural characteristics of the model. Impact can be expressed in a variety of ways, for example as an absolute value ('Would reduce profits by $5 000 000') or as a proportion of the project's targeted outcome ('Would decrease net profit by 2 per cent'). A typical dependency model allows you to enter both the impact and likelihood values into a table generated automatically from the tree diagram already created. This makes adjustments easier later on, especially if the same dependency appears in more than one location in the model.

Based on the AND-OR structure of the model and the input values for lowest-level dependencies, the model will calculate an overall probability of project failure and an expected variance from the central objective. It will also provide a sensitivity chart that ranks all of the dependencies in the model according to the extent of their impact on the calculated result.

To assist in interpretation of these outputs, the tree diagram can label every dependency with its own calculated failure rate. In our illustrative example at Figure 6.13(B), there is an overall 13 per cent probability that we will fail to induce consumer trial. This is a calculation based not only on the known or assumed risks of failure for each of the lowest-level dependencies; it is also determined by the *interdependence* of all events represented by the structure of the model. The example has been designed to demonstrate this. It shows a uniform 10 per cent failure rate for each of the far-right dependencies. The resulting failure rates elsewhere make it easy to see the influence of the model's structure on the final outcome. As we have seen, our model assumes that an appropriate channel must have both an appropriate service environment and an appropriate image. Since both dependencies have a 10 per cent failure rate and both need to be satisfied, the model shows an aggregate 19 per cent chance that the channel will not turn out to be appropriate. Conversely, we have made the hypothetical assumption that the product can also rely on its own brand strength to overcome any weakness in the 'fit' between the product and the channel of distribution. In this case, the existence of a fallback results in a sharply reduced likelihood of failure, at only 2 per cent. In this illustrative example, applying uniform failure rates, it turns out that the most critical point of dependency is product availability at the right time for the buyer – in other words, catching the buyers when they are open to buy, perhaps for reasons of seasonality.

## STRUCTURE AND VALIDATION

It is advisable to construct a reasonably comprehensive model initially and then trim it back, otherwise omissions may go unnoticed. It will emerge later where it would be sensible to cut superfluous detail. If one branch of the emerging structure has far fewer components than the others, this should prompt you at least to question whether you have forgotten a number of important dependencies. Conversely, you may find that a high-level component of the model has no subordinate dependencies. This may suggest a heightened risk of 'single-point failure': the likelihood of missing the central objective whenever this single component fails.

It is difficult to overemphasize the importance of checking and challenging the structure of a model, including its underlying assumptions.[19] It is not uncommon for simple deterministic models of customer behaviour to contain errors arising from wrongly assumed hierarchies of effect (for example, think of product sampling: trial does not always require prior brand awareness). Generally speaking, the technique of dependency modelling makes it easier to trace these errors. A fundamental purpose of dependency modelling is to make hierarchical relationships as transparent as possible – and convenient to adjust in a 'drag-and-drop' software environment.

In practice, you will probably find it easier to gauge what is *not* right, than what is right with a provisional model. This does not mean that the model will reveal the unknowable. However, it does mean that you should expect to work through a number of iterations of the model before it feels reasonably representative of the real world.

As we have seen, running the provisional model with a uniform failure rate is a useful way of testing its logic, before the effects of structure are obscured by the introduction of realistically different failure rates for individual dependencies. If a sense check based on uniform failure rates suggests that the model is producing illogical results, it probably means that the model structure is not yet a satisfactory representation of reality. Ask yourself how such a counter-intuitive result might have come about. Adjust the model accordingly and try again. Higher predicted failure rates often arise in parts of the model that have been worked on in greatest detail, typically those where we have greatest knowledge. This imbalance can create misleading distortions in the model.

In refining a model, there are three ways to adjust the influence of a dependency, without altering its failure rate or estimated gross impact:

- relocate it within the model

- change its logical relationships (ANDs and ORs) in one or more of its occurrences
- disable a dependency (temporarily or permanently), so that its influence is neutralized wherever it appears in the model, without having to remove it.

Bear in mind that the number of times a particular factor appears in the model usually increases sensitivity to that factor (the 'dependency count'). In addition, the higher upstream a failure is (closer to the project objective), the bigger its adverse effect is likely to be. This is also true of mitigation effects: the ultimate offset for a failed product introduction is another product.

## KEY APPLICATIONS

A good dependency model is much more than a financial management tool, although it is often the case that outcomes are most usefully expressed in financial terms. Dependency modelling is particularly well suited to carrying out sensitivity studies, to reveal sources of risk and to suggest a prioritization of risk management efforts. It can also be a powerful device for capturing and applying knowledge in structured decision-making.

### Sensitivity studies

By observing the results of increasing or decreasing component failure rates in the context of a particular project, individual dependencies can be better prioritized for management attention or mitigation expenditure. The logic of the model will quickly reveal the absence of fallback or contingency, on particular points of failure. Such insights are not always obvious until revealed in a dependency model. The model provides an environment within which both to set risk reduction targets for key dependencies and to evaluate the cost-benefit of particular mitigation efforts. In a given situation, some dependencies will prove to be more important than others.

Although the probability and magnitude of an individual failure may be well understood, a project's exposure to this failure may not be equal to its expected value in isolation. The net impact of a particular dependency's failure is determined by the interaction of its position, recurrence and redundancy within the system represented by the model. This interaction may alter either the probability or the severity of the individual failure. It may also create a cumulative risk that is greater than the sum of its parts.[20] Project outcome can be unexpectedly sensitive to certain failures, even if they have a relatively low probability of occurrence. A small change in the failure rate of a single component can also have a disproportionate overall effect, positive or negative.

Dependency modelling provides indications of sensitivity from limited information. If data are lacking or are difficult to estimate for a particular dependency, you can use the model experimentally to identify the 'tipping point' for gradual increases in its failure values. The tipping point is the minimum failure value for a dependency at which it has a material influence on the model's outcome. All other things being equal, this tipping-point value provides a benchmark against which to judge whether the actual performance of the real-life component is threatening to impede achievement of the overall objective. It follows that dependency models can also test for sensitivity to different combinations of component failure: two or more components failing simultaneously or the failure of one component making the failure of another more likely.

Importantly, dependency modelling encourages consideration of practical constraints and the causes of variability in performance, as well as sensitivity to one-off and remote risk events.

Consider how this might be useful in new product planning. If the values you entered for the downstream (i.e. ultimate) dependencies represent the typical failure rates and the financial impacts for these events, the model will have calculated the average expected shortfall for such a project and the likelihood of its occurrence. Even good plans will have a measurable chance of failure. All being well, the calculated shortfall will not exceed your appetite for risk. The generic brand viability model, from which our illustrative examples in this chapter are drawn, calculates a 66 per cent probability of overall target shortfall, assuming a uniform 10 per cent failure rate for each ultimate dependency. Compare this to received wisdom, which holds that up to 80 per cent of brand extensions into new categories fail to meet their objectives.[21] Whether or not you choose to accept this pessimistic assessment, the implications are obvious enough: in order to cheat the odds, we need to understand and manage the things that have an influence on the failure rate of each ultimate dependency. In Chapter 5 we reviewed the approach to 'marketing due diligence' proposed by McDonald, Smith and Ward (2006).[22] Figure 6.14 illustrates how this framework might be applied in sensitivity studies using a dependency model. By attaching the relevant due diligence criteria to each downstream dependency, it is possible to adjust its 'normal' failure rate according to the criteria for riskiness proposed by McDonald, Smith and Ward. The same due diligence criterion may affect a number of dependencies. A comparison of the best, worst and most likely outcomes suggested by the model will help to define and justify an appropriate contingency budget or profit cushion within the launch plan.

The riskiness revealed in a project may justify further work to review the range of possible project outcomes, using probability-based – or stochastic – forecasting. A powerful technique for stochastic forecasting is Monte Carlo simulation (see below). The key sensitivities identified through dependency modelling are usually the most appropriate stochastic (i.e. randomly determined) variables to choose in any subsequent Monte Carlo simulations.

### Distillation of knowledge

As illustrated by the examples in this chapter, dependency models can also be efficient representations of an accepted process by which a particular objective is expected to be achieved. They can be adapted to the circumstances of a new project or issue, whilst retaining agreed 'best practice' as their standard features. Such models can become a distillation of knowledge and marketplace experience. By reflecting the lessons of success or failure in a model, in the form of additional or adjusted dependencies, new thinking is less easily overlooked and the benefits of experience are more immediately available to colleagues. The modelling process can help both to capture a colleague's specialist insights and to secure their acceptance of the marketing plan and its rationale. Knowledge management professionals have shown that a dependency model can convert information into 'chunks' of learning that make them easy to absorb and recall.

# Stochastic models

As elsewhere, spreadsheet models of one kind or another are used universally in marketing. Whether these models support routine decision-making, annual budgeting or major investment plans, they are most often purely *deterministic*. As we saw in Chapter 4, this means that when the spreadsheet calculates, it assumes that all of the data inputs in the model are true or 'certain' as entered. The program takes no account of the fact that some value inputs might represent a frequency distribution of possible values – in other words, risk. Of course,

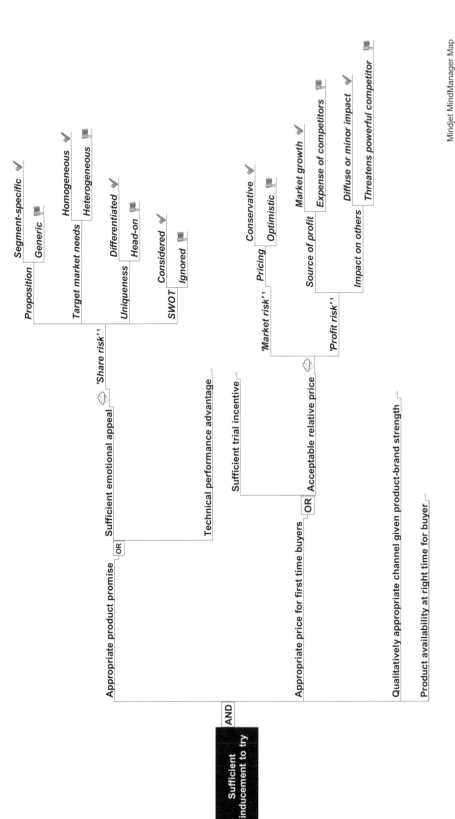

**Figure 6.14   Dependency model – application of 'Marketing Due Diligence'**

*Source:* [1]*McDonald, Smith and Ward (2006)*

MindJet MindManager Map

one can easily run separate scenarios, with individual variables taking different specific values. The good spreadsheet programs automate this process of scenario generation. Even so, the set of outputs cannot fully reflect the risk dynamics of the case and cannot help a decision-maker to draw statistical conclusions about the likelihood of achieving a particular outcome. As we have emphasized throughout this book, a base-case forecast calculated with single-point inputs is not the best foundation for decision-making where there is any material degree of risk or uncertainty.

Where a modelled outcome is sensitive to a number of risk variables simultaneously, it can be important to understand their compound effect. When we make such expected value calculations using decision trees and joint probabilities, we are usually limited to using discrete (i.e. stepwise) distributions to represent continuous distributions. Similarly, where there are a large number of risk variables, we are forced to make a selection for our decision tree if it is not to become unwieldy. A *stochastic* model addresses these practical issues: it allows us to supplement any number of single-point value inputs with their appropriate probability distribution. In return, the model calculates a probability distribution for any risky outcome that is of ultimate interest, such as profit contribution or the click-through rate of an online advertising campaign.

Palisade Corporation's @RISK[§] and Oracle Corporation's Crystal Ball[¶] are examples of stochastic (or probabilistic) modelling tools, available as an add-in to Microsoft Excel.[23] Readily accessed from the Excel toolbar once installed, these products allow one to convert any deterministic model into a stochastic one, supported by a suite of analytical features and graphing options. These are sophisticated tools, capable of responding to the demands of professional statisticians. Many marketers might prefer initially to work on a stochastic model with the support of a specialist colleague. Nevertheless, the tools are intuitive and easy to use once the basic principles and feature have been understood. As such they create an ideal environment in which to explore and experiment with probability distributions in decision-making. A well-constructed stochastic model is a very effective way of recording, refining and reporting on the risk parameters of any matter that is capable of being represented in a conventional spreadsheet. A marketing and financial model for a new product would be a typical case in point, with its numerous risk assumptions about segmentation, demand, prices, costs and distribution.

## MONTE CARLO SIMULATION

Originally made popular by John von Neumann (1903–1957), one of the most familiar forms of stochastic modelling is known as *Monte Carlo simulation*. A spreadsheet-based Monte Carlo simulation reruns a stochastic model many thousands of times 'behind the scenes', applying and analysing the consequences of the risk inputs provided by the decision-maker. Each rerun of a stochastic simulation is known as a 'trial'. Each trial generates a single plausible outcome for the model, picking random values for any risk variables consistent with their probability distribution functions. One of the practical problems of random sampling is its very randomness: a true Monte Carlo sample may fail to represent the required distribution function adequately. The solution is to instruct the application to use an alternative sampling method, known to statisticians as Latin Hypercube. This method effectively divides the probability distribution into segments and ensures a truly random sampling within each of them. The user decides how many trials to run for a particular simulation, typically (though not always) between 1000 and 5000. Models with a great many risk variables can require many more trials, perhaps even 10 000. All but the most complex models are calculated quickly. What is important is to allow the

§     RISK™ is a trademark of Parker Brothers, Division of Tonka Corporation and is used by Palisade Corporation under licence.

¶     Crystal Ball® is a registered trademark of Oracle Corporation.

model to generate enough possible alternative scenarios that the distribution characteristics of each uncertain variable can be fully reflected in the aggregate simulation outcome. As we have already touched on, if you run an insufficient number of trials in a simulation, the most likely combinations of value may not have a chance to arise. One might start with 1000 trials, with the aim of steadily increasing their number, until there is no longer any significant change in results arising from the increase. Changes are considered no longer to be significant when they amount to less than 0.5 per cent of the mean. The user can enter this (or any other) parameter into the simulation spreadsheet as a 'stopping rule', so that the whole process becomes automatic.

Once the simulation is finished, the original spreadsheet will display the calculated mean or expected value (EV) for any nominated outcome cell in the model, such as net profit. Switching to the stochastic results window in the specialist application provides a forecast distribution for each of these items of interest. These should be wisely interpreted like any other expected value indication (see 'Expected value and volatility' in Chapter 4). Figure 6.15 illustrates a probability distribution for likely profits based on a 500-trial run of a sales and profit forecasting model containing stochastic variables. The results window in the proprietary application used in this case provides 'certainty indications' in three lower boxes, here showing a 69.4 per cent chance that profits will fall somewhere between $0 and $20 million. By typing into these boxes or dragging the small triangular 'grabbers' along the x-axis of the graph, one can review and present graphically the confidence interval for any range of outcomes. Figure 6.16 illustrates equivalent output in the form of a cumulative distribution.

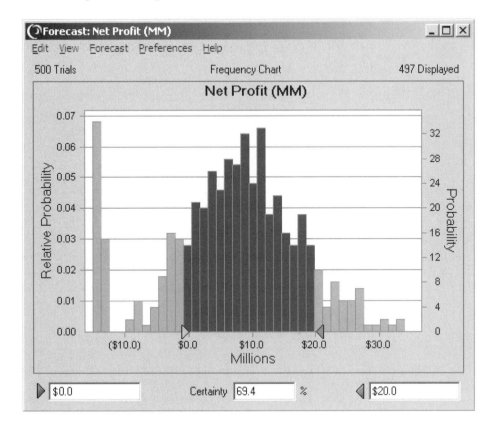

**Figure 6.15    Monte Carlo simulation output – frequency distribution**

Source: Reproduced by permission of Oracle Corporation

Monte Carlo simulation can be regarded as an advanced kind of sensitivity study in itself.[24] Experience suggests that two to five variables typically account for over 90 per cent of the uncertainty in a final outcome value.[25] One important output of a stochastic simulation is an analysis of sensitivities presented in the form of a *tornado diagram* (Figure 6.17). As illustrated, this automated feature is able to present graphically the ranking of variables in the model according to the magnitude of their influence on the target outcome, positively or negatively. The tornado diagram helps focus attention on the most critical variables, where risk management might bring the greatest benefits. It also provides a means of reviewing the sensitivity of the model's outcomes to the *choice* of probability distribution for a given input.

## Identifying risk variables

It is always important to check the extent to which a course of action suggested by any model is sensitive to changes in the model's variables or its structure. In preparation for stochastic modelling, a preliminary sensitivity analysis will suggest which value inputs might usefully be supplemented by probability distribution functions in the subsequent Monte Carlo simulation. These are the two simple steps to take if you have not already determined key sensitivities with a more comprehensive dependency model such as we reviewed earlier in this chapter:

1. *Develop the base case.* Assuming that you have developed a viable deterministic model, create a base case by running the model with 'most likely' or expected values for every variable in the model. Note the outcome as a reference point.

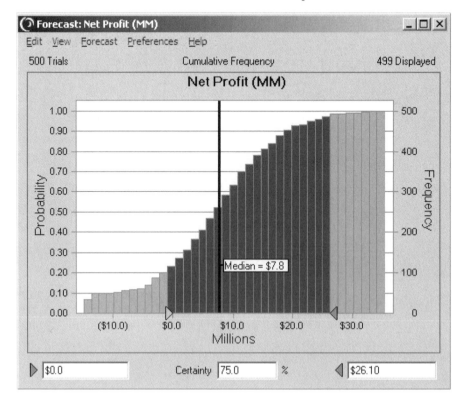

**Figure 6.16    Monte Carlo simulation output – cumulative frequency distribution**

*Source: Reproduced by permission of Oracle Corporation*

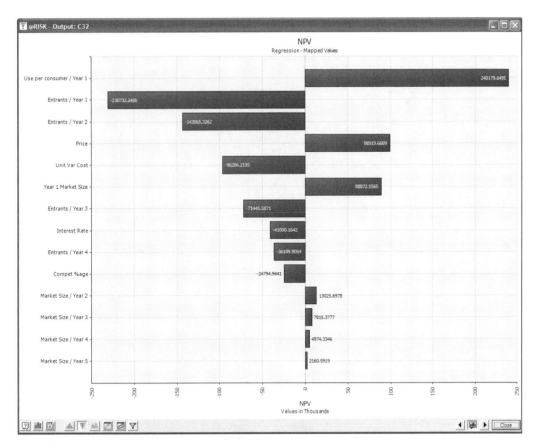

**Figure 6.17    Monte Carlo simulation output – tornado diagram**

*Source: Reproduced by permission of Palisade Corporation*

2.  *Test for sensitivity*. Run the base case model twice for each input variable: once at its lowest and once at its highest probable value, whilst leaving all the other variables at their 'most likely'. If the model's outcome is materially different under either of these two scenarios (i.e. the outcome, if certain to occur, would change your current course of action), you should consider replacing the single variable with an appropriate probability function in the simulation. Conversely, if final outcomes are not materially altered by extreme changes to a particular input variable, there will be little practical value in developing a probability distribution for the input variable in question.

## Probability distribution functions

We defined distribution functions in general terms in Chapter 4. Given the ready availability of simulation software, the mechanics of creating a stochastic model are straightforward. Where understanding and experience count for a great deal is in the selection of appropriate distribution functions and the interpretation of output. Figure 6.18 illustrates the selection palette for distribution functions in Palisade Corporation's @RISK,[26] and Figure 6.19 shows an example of the related specification window for a triangular distribution. Adjustable values for each parameter are normally suggested automatically by the application, if there is a value already entered into the underlying cell of the model.

As reflected in Figure 6.18, there are a large number of classic frequency distributions, each best suited to (or most representative of) particular variables. Where sufficient prior and valid data exist, proprietary risk modelling applications can perform the analysis and suggest distribution functions that appear to fit the data well. Otherwise, it remains a matter of combining theoretical suitability with practical experience to select the most appropriate function for the variable in question. Among the 30 or so commonly offered distribution functions, here is a short description of those most often encountered in the application of Monte Carlo simulation to marketing and commercial problems:

- *Binary* (not illustrated in Figure 6.18). This is the simplest form of discrete distribution. A single event is defined as having only two possible outcomes with complementary probabilities: occurrence or non-occurrence.

- *Poisson.* Used to express the frequency distribution of independent and random events occurring over a fixed period of time (per minute, per month, per annum), given a known average. Whilst the average must remain constant, there is assumed to be no limit on the actual number of occurrences possible in any single period.

- *Gamma.* Used to characterize the distribution of events over a fixed period of time where their occurrence is not entirely random: for example, purchasing frequency within a population of consumers.

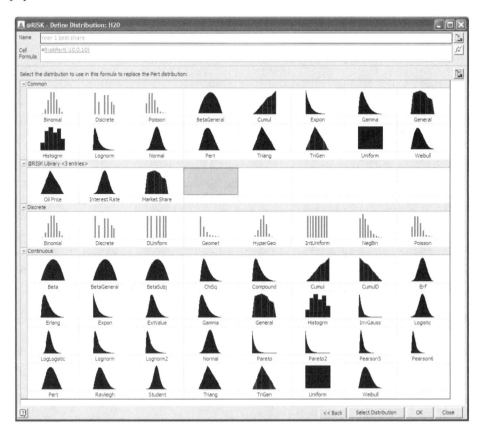

**Figure 6.18    Monte Carlo simulation input – frequency distribution palette**

*Source: Reproduced by permission of Palisade Corporation*

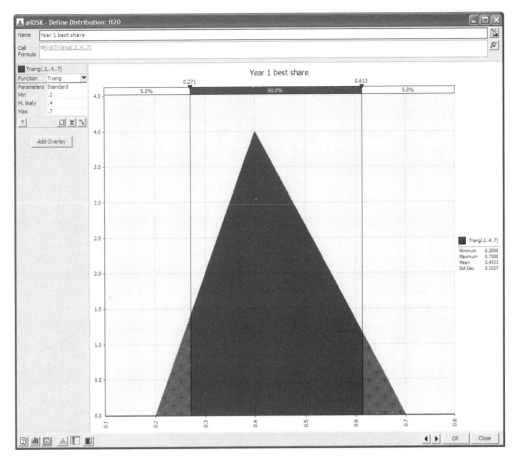

**Figure 6.19    Monte Carlo simulation input – triangular distribution window**

*Source: Reproduced by permission of Palisade Corporation*

- *Binomial.* Describes the distribution of positive outcomes, given the known average 'success rate' and a fixed number of independent 'attempts' at succeeding: for example, the probability of identifying good prospects from a random sample of sales calls.
- *Negative binomial.* Used to describe the distribution of independent 'attempts' necessary to achieve a defined accumulative outcome within a population, given the known probability of a single event: for example, the advertising frequency necessary to achieve a desired reach amongst target customers, given the likelihood of anyone seeing the advertisement.
- *Hypergeometric.* Similar to the binomial distribution (above), but alters the 'success rate' in each subsequent simulation trial after the first one, on the assumption that outcomes are not independent of each other. For example, as the assumed potential for new business is absorbed by new customers making initial purchases, the chance of the next random prospect becoming a new customer would be adjusted within the simulation.
- *Uniform.* As its name suggests, this distribution indicates that there is an equal chance that any of the values in a given range will occur. Within a range assumed to represent all the possibilities, the uniform distribution is therefore an expression of the greatest uncertainty in the mind of a decision-maker. In reality, it is unusual for there to be no convergence of values around the central part of the range.

- *Normal.* This bell-shaped distribution is an important representation of how a large number of independent, continuous chance events might distribute. It has particular characteristics that we reviewed in Chapter 4. The normal distribution is also used to qualify a confidently expressed 'most likely' value for an uncertain input: for example, retail price inflation. In such cases, the normal distribution expresses a belief that the actual value could be either higher or lower with equal probability, but will nonetheless remain closer to the expected value than further from it, according to the standard parameters for the function.

- *Triangular.* As we have already seen in Chapter 4, this is an easy distribution to define with its three values: maximum, minimum and most likely. This distribution allows any three-level estimate to be converted into a continuous distribution for the purposes of Monte Carlo simulation, if the decision-maker feels that the three discrete levels of probability do not fully represent the range of possible outcomes.

- *Trigen.* The triangular distribution (above) is easy for non-experts to specify, but it assumes that actual values could never fall outside its specified range. The trigen is a more conservative version of the triangular distribution, being truncated at either extreme – in effect, opened up – by a chosen percentile of the function (say, 2.5 per cent at either end). In Monte Carlo simulation, this is a way of dealing with any overconfidence that the range expressed in a triangular distribution has really captured every possibility.

## Other considerations

To complete our introductory review of stochastic modelling, there are five other considerations worth keeping in mind:

- model structure
- correlations
- strategic risk
- 'double risking'
- stochastic variance.

*Model structure.* Although detailed advice on model design is beyond the scope of this book, you should be aware that simple sequential models attempting to describe market demand may overlook important subtleties. The influence of structure on a model's outcome can be much more significant than the weighting you may choose to give to the variables within it. In consumer markets, for example, Ehrenberg (1974) questions the classic assumption that consumer recall, understanding and acceptance of advertising must always precede purchase. In particular, he argues that this logic cannot apply to the advertising of established brands.[27] Unmeasured variables may also be responsible for effects in prior data applied in the model, such as cultural influences on trends in market demand.

In preparing the underlying deterministic model for a subsequent stochastic simulation, it is advisable to check that the calculations in the model will remain valid when value inputs are run across their full range and in every possible combination.[28] Experimental adjustments to either the deterministic model or the distribution functions of key variables will also help to test the robustness of a decision and the need for further validation of critical assumptions, whether through desk research or fieldwork. Extreme or entirely unexpected results, in particular, may indicate anomalies in the model's structure, so it is always worth examining these trials to see how such 'outliers' might have come about.[29]

*Correlations.* In many situations we may want to take account of the correlation between variables, whereby one chance variable is assumed to have a greater or lesser dependence on another ('The uncertainty of X, given the uncertainty of Y'). Such joint probabilities may increase the overall risk and uncertainty of achieving a desired outcome. For example, the uncertain average market price of products may alter in some relation to an uncertain exchange rate. Stochastic modelling software makes these correlations easy to add as parameters of a simulation. However, you should exercise caution in using this feature unless the correlations have been well substantiated. It is an axiom of statistics that 'correlation does not imply causation'. A scatter diagram plotting paired data may exhibit a pattern to suggest correlation, but false conclusions about cause-and-effect relationships are easily drawn. Subjective assumptions about correlation can introduce substantial errors into results. One approach to reducing the risk of a misleading outcome is to apply sensitivity analysis, so that the effects of possible over- and underestimation of assumed correlations can be observed.

*Strategic risk.* Most of the risk inherent in a marketing plan lies in its attempt to shift established patterns of demand, whether in favour of a single brand or a new category. This means that the greatest risk in a plan may not to be found in a comparison between our base case ('most likely') and the expected outcome generated by a Monte Carlo simulation ('the mathematically expected'). Assuming the validity of our probability distributions for the key stochastic variables, a further important perspective on risk may be provided by comparing the Monte Carlo outcome with a forecast based on current market demand 'as is'.

*'Double risking'.* If you or your colleagues are using the output of your stochastic decision model to make return on investment (ROI) calculations, make sure that the discount rate applied does not inadvertently double-charge the project for risks that have already been accounted for in the probability distributions contained in the model. Schuyler (2001) considers this to be the most important single insight that he gained in 25 years of project evaluation experience.[30] Resolving this issue may pose technical, not to say political, challenges in a corporate environment, where a standard discount rate may be applied and decomposition of the rate may be resisted. Nevertheless, if you are truly confident that your model has fully discounted all identifiable project risks, it may be worth at least making ROI comparisons using both the established corporate rate and the opportunity cost of capital without further risk premium.

*Stochastic variance.* Do not necessarily expect to secure the expected value (EV) for a targeted outcome suggested by a Monte Carlo simulation, if you ultimately manage to achieve your model's calculated EV for every risk variable. This is because the achievement of these individual EVs will merely represent a single scenario and its deterministic outcome. By contrast, a simulation's EV outcome reflects a weighted mix of uncertain outcomes, including combinations at the more optimistic and pessimistic ends of the scale. Stochastic variance can mislead you into increasing or reducing base case expectations. It most commonly arises where a model incorporates contingent changes to one or more values that contribute to the net outcome. A simple example suffices to explain this important phenomenon. Let us assume that the cost of a product is dependent on volume, so that the more we sell, the lower the cost. For commercial reasons, this reduction is a 'step function': average cost for the entire volume will fall by 20 per cent once we hit 8000 units. We are certain that the actual sales volume will be somewhere between 5000 and 10 000 units, but have entered a distribution function for volume into the model to express our beliefs about the risks of selling more or less within this range. If the resulting probability distribution for volume has a mean (its expected value or EV) of 8000, this indicates that some simulation trials will have sampled lower volumes than 8000 and some will have sampled higher ones, at frequencies consistent with their probability function. This means that some scenarios will have qualified for the lower average cost and others will not. The stochastic EV for cost will therefore reflect the probability-weighted average for volume and will fall somewhere between 100 per cent and 80 per cent of base case cost. However, if we were to take the simulated EV for volume (8000 units) and run it through a deterministic model, the *entire* volume would qualify for the cost reduction. Average cost is then bound to be 0.8 of base case. The difference between the two cost results can be explained as stochastic variance: in our example, the cost consequences of volume risk. The overall extent of stochastic variance arising in any Monte Carlo simulation can be clearly seen by copying its EV outcomes as single-point values into a purely deterministic version of the same model.

Notwithstanding these cautionary considerations and the significance of stochastic variance on occasion, the EV output from a Monte Carlo simulation remains the best available risk-adjusted version of a base case, useful for comparative purposes and for testing the robustness of particular courses of action.

## Summary

We have reviewed a number of the most powerful tools and techniques in risk modelling:

- We have demonstrated how decision trees work with probabilities and expected values to identify the best course of action when faced with a number of risky alternatives.

- We have applied the same decision tree technique to suggest a maximum value for market research when attempting to improve predictions of outcome, taking into account the extent to which the research information is expected to be reliable.

- We have introduced dependency modelling as a way of creating constructive and highly relevant risk management frameworks, useful in analysis, practical project management and the transfer of knowledge.

- We have described the principles of stochastic modelling and Monte Carlo simulation as an efficient means of fully representing complex interactions of risk and uncertainty in spreadsheet models and forecasts.

In the next and final chapter we will take general stock and consider how to establish risk thinking within a work group or an organization.

## References

1   Mittelstaedt, R.E. (2005), *Will Your Next Mistake Be Fatal? Avoiding the Chain of Mistakes that Can Destroy Your Organization*, Wharton School Publishing.
2   von Winterfeldt, D. and Edwards, W. (1986), *Decision Analysis and Behavioural Research*, Cambridge University Press.
3   Hillson, D. and Murray-Webster, R. (2005), *Understanding and Managing Risk Attitude*, Gower Publishing Ltd.
4   Goodwin, P. and Wright, G. (2004), *Decision Analysis for Management Judgment – Third Edition*, John Wiley & Sons Ltd.

5   East, R. (1997), *Consumer Behaviour – Advances and Applications in Marketing*, FT Prentice Hall.

6   Ambler, T. (2003), *Marketing and the Bottom Line*, FT Prentice Hall.

7   Ehrenberg, A.S.C. and Uncles, M.D. (1996), *Dirichlet-type Markets: A Review*, South Bank University Working Paper.

8   Palisade Corporation, http://www.palisade-europe.com/precisiontree/default.asp; TreeAge Software, Inc., http://www.treeage.com/products/overviewPro.html.

9   TreeAge Software, Inc., op.cit.

10   Goodwin and Wright (2004), op.cit.

11   Keeney, R.L. and Raiffa, H. (1993), *Decisions with Multiple Objectives: Preferences and Value Tradeoffs*, Cambridge University Press.

12   Brownlie, D.T. (1991), 'A Case Analysis of the Cost and Value of Marketing Information', *Marketing Intelligence and Planning*, Volume 9 (Number 1), pp. 11–18.

13   Lacava, G. and Tull, D. (1982), 'Determining the Expected Value of Information for New Product Introduction', *Omega – The International Journal of Management Science*, Volume 10 (Number 4), pp. 383–389.

14   Arium Ltd (2003), *Making Sense of an Uncertain World*, http://www.arium.co.uk/products/dependency.htm.

15   Arium Ltd (2003), op.cit.

16   Arium Ltd (2003), op.cit.

17   Microsoft Corporation, http://office.microsoft.com/en-us/excel/FX100487621033.aspx.

18   Obeng, E. (1996), *All Change! The Project Leader's Secret Handbook*, FT Prentice Hall.

19   Schuyler, J. (2001), *Risk and Decision Analysis in Projects*, Project Management Institute.

20   Zeger, D. and Nicholson, N. (2004), *Risk: How to make Decisions in an Uncertain World*, Format Publishing.

21   Haxthausen, O. (2007), 'Risk Jockey', *Marketing Management*, March/April, pp. 35–38.

22   McDonald, M., Smith B. and Ward, K. (2006), *Marketing Due Diligence: Reconnecting Strategy to Share Price*, Butterworth-Heinemann.

23   Palisade Corporation, http://www.palisade-europe.com/risk/default.asp; Oracle Corporation, http://www.crystalball.com/products.html; Microsoft Corporation, op.cit.

24   Hertz, D.B. and Thomas, H. (1983), *Risk Analysis and its Applications*, John Wiley and Sons, Inc.

25   Schuyler (2001), op.cit.

26   Palisade Corporation, http://www.palisade-europe.com/downloads/pdf/Palisade_RISK_0306.pdf.

27   Ehrenberg, A.S.C. (1974), 'Repetitive Advertising and the Consumer', *Journal of Advertising Research*, Volume 14 (Number 2), pp. 25–33.

28   Schuyler (2001), op.cit.

29   Schuyler (2001), op.cit.

30   Schuyler (2001), op.cit.

# 7 *Making Progress*

As we approach the end of this book, we need to take general stock of the tools and techniques we have reviewed and consider some of the issues that arise when applying risk thinking in practice. In this final chapter we will:

- reaffirm the reasons for becoming a 'risk-literate' marketer
- suggest alternative ways in which the body of knowledge presented in this book can be viewed and usefully deployed
- consider the relevance of corporate culture to the introduction of brand risk thinking.

## Reaffirming the goals

The importance of 'brand protection' is now largely appreciated beyond the marketing function, even though there may not be universal agreement as to what a brand is or what protection amounts to. This realization has come about for two reasons: firstly, because firms rely increasingly on intangible assets, including brands, for success and sustainability; secondly, because there is considerable external interest in the adequacy of companies' risk management as an indicator of operational maturity. Against this background, we have argued that there are good reasons for marketers to become 'risk-literate', as a conscious competence alongside strategic insight and financial understanding. We defined risk literacy, in essence, as the acquisition and application of a body of knowledge about risk. This includes a familiarity with the nature of risk and risk-taking, an ability to specify and use suitable risk assessment approaches and an ability to deal appropriately (i.e. systematically) with risk issues that have been identified. We have suggested a threefold benefit for marketers:

1. *A currency of communication.* The recognized techniques of risk assessment amount to a currency of cross-functional communication within organizations. They offer an additional means by which marketers can present analysis of marketing matters to non-specialist colleagues, take best advantage of the corporate risk management frameworks already in place and support the company's external reporting as appropriate.

2. *Value contribution.* We saw that the perceived value and resulting influence of a function within an organization are generally proportionate to its effectiveness in dealing with critical uncertainties.[1] A risk-literate interpretation of brand opportunities and issues not only demonstrates a proper due diligence in the development of marketing plans, to oneself and to others, but also helps to *reveal* the extent to which the marketing function is, in effect, 'absorbing uncertainty' to the benefit of the organization.

3. *Performance management.* Above all else, risk literacy helps marketers to become better qualified as 'professional risk-takers', more fully equipped to identify, articulate and address the inevitable risks and uncertainties that arise in pursuit of brand performance.

## Body of knowledge

Figure 7.1 summarizes the body of knowledge that we have assembled and described in the preceding chapters. By way of aide-mémoire, the various topics, tools and techniques are grouped according to their principal function in contributing a risk perspective to marketing operations and decision-making. The logic of this classification is slightly different to the order in which it was appropriate to present the material earlier in technical terms.

- *Introducing.* These are the preliminary themes and introductory topics. Their purpose is to provide factual and theoretical insight into the role and nature of risk and risk-taking. In practice, these topics should also serve to win over 'hearts and minds', helping to engender a conviction that risk literacy is worth acquiring or at least prompting a curiosity to find out more. People are usually interested in learning about the psychology of decision-making under uncertainty, especially when it might reveal something they do not know about themselves. As such, a short introduction to heuristics and risk attitude can either stimulate useful discussion or supplement briefing material before people undertake work that calls for risk thinking, whether ahead or in hindsight.

- *Recognizing.* As the practical foundation of any risk thinking programme, it is important that there should be some universal preliminary mechanism for recognizing and ranking risks. Risk mapping is the conventional methodology. An existing company-wide protocol for risk assessment may already meet this requirement and may even be a mandatory feature of business plans. For some marketing teams, a complementary methodology more directly associated with day-to-day decision-making, such as Six Thinking Hats*[2] or 'Sticky Steps',[3] may establish a further 'bridgehead' into systematic risk thinking. In their different ways, each of the risk recognition methods identified here will help to capture and give some initial order to risk issues, although they do not deliver a complete presentation of their consequences, nor do they necessarily define the best course of action to address them. However, all three of the techniques are intuitive, broadly applicable and do not require substantial experience of risk thinking to be effective. The three other items in this branch of the diagram in Figure 7.1 ('Notable causes ...', 'Warning signs ...' and 'Four fields ...') are frameworks that are helpful as prompts in preliminary risk identification, suitable for marketing and non-marketing people alike.

- *Expressing.* These are the technical foundations for many of the classical approaches to risk modelling and assessment, whether the inputs are subjective or objective. The simplest explanation of risk thresholds and expected value ('Impact × frequency') will usually suffice in briefing participants for a risk-mapping exercise. Meanwhile, there are perhaps three positive reflexes associated with a reasonable technical understanding of risk expression. The first is dissatisfaction with single-point estimates of risky outcomes and a preference for the better perspective that even a triangular distribution provides. The second is a 'sense of system', in which outcomes are instinctively evaluated or planned in terms of their key dependencies or likely combination of causes. The third is an appreciation that risk is generally best understood in relative terms made explicit, for example in relation to strategy or objective ('Is this risk legitimate?'), in relation to reward or consequences ('Is this risk proportionate?') or in relation to capacity or experience ('Is this risk manageable?').

- *Evaluating.* These are the various frameworks reviewed which can be useful in the detailed assessment of brand risk, whether strategic, tactical or operational. Their combined scope

---

*     Six Thinking Hats® is a registered trademark.

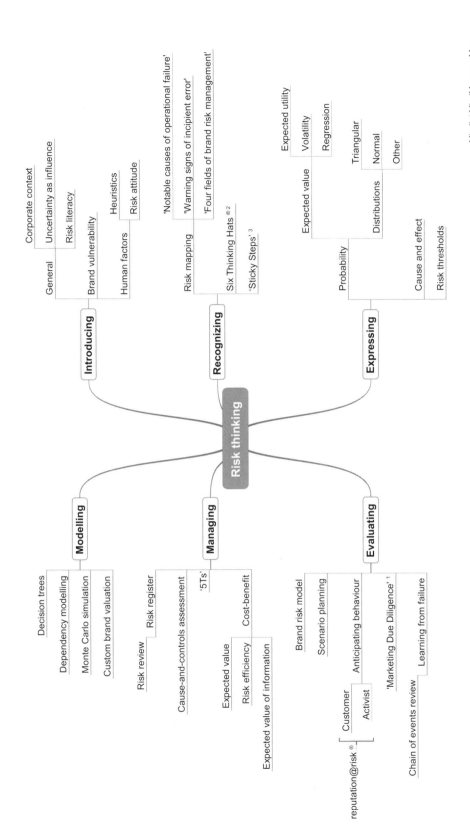

MindjetMindManager Map

**Figure 7.1    The body of knowledge**

*Source:* [1]*McDonald, Smith and Ward (2006);* [2]*de Bono (1999);* [3]*Obeng (1996)*

is broad: there are suggested approaches to thinking about the past, the present and the future. What they share is an emphasis on understanding context and (once again) 'systems' as the sources of risk and opportunity.

- *Managing.* These tools and techniques focus on the practical and efficient management of risk issues. They encourage evaluation and selection of the most appropriate management approach or help to establish the business case for proceeding to the next stage of resource commitment.

- *Modelling.* Without ever seeking to automate decision-making or to fall under the spell of spurious quantification, these high-powered techniques of assessment support judicious risk-adjusted modelling of the real-world environment, so that the implications of risk and uncertainty can be explored and alternative courses of action considered. They also consolidate and conserve risk thinking for future reference. The techniques which we have proposed amount to variants of sensitivity analysis, each having a different format, feel and function. What they have in common is that they test the robustness of decisions in the light of current assumptions about 'known unknowns'. Custom brand valuation finds it place here because it operates as a model for strategic decision-making, whilst the very process of valuation will have required the recognition and assessment of some key risk issues.

## COMBINING TECHNIQUES

Another way of consolidating our review of risk thinking is to identify specific marketing tasks and to see how the tools and techniques which we have reviewed can work usefully in combination. We shall look briefly at nine illustrative examples across three general areas of activity:

- recurrent exercises (such as budgeting)
- start-up situations (such as a new project undertaking)
- ad hoc review (such as activist issue analysis).

In each case you will see how the two chosen components of risk thinking are complementary. One component helps to create insight or understanding; the other component supports decision-making.

### Recurrent exercises (see Figure 7.2)

*Brand risk management.* For any given brand risk issue, the simple '5Ts' framework prompts strategic and creative thinking about the range of options available for its management. With these alternatives identified, a comparison of costs and benefits in terms of risk efficiency will relate the range of possible expenditure on risk controls to the likely changes in the volatility of outcome. (See Chapter 5.)

*Brand strategy development.* The brand risk model assists in articulating the brand's overall state of health. It helps to identify aspects of advantage or exposure, perhaps highlighting areas where objective performance measurement or fact-based market insight might be lacking. 'Marketing Due Diligence'[4] then supports refinement of the associated marketing plan, with an emphasis on assuring its viability and realistic adjustment for risk. (See Chapters 2 and 5.)

Mindjet MindManager Map

**Figure 7.2     Risk thinking in recurrent exercises**
*Source: [1]McDonald, Smith and Ward (2006)*

*Brand finances.* In situations where preliminary assessment demonstrates a material sensitivity of outcome to one or more risk issues, stochastic modelling offers an advance in budgeting technique. First comes a reconsideration of all key inputs in probabilistic terms (whether objective or subjective). The subsequent Monte Carlo simulation allows for a sophisticated interpretation of risk for the purposes of planning and budget building. (See Chapters 4 and 6.)

## Start-up situations (see Figure 7.3)

*New processes.* It makes good sense to consider operational risks that may arise when there is a significant change in an important process (for example, in reorganization of a customer-facing service function).[5] Reference to 'Notable causes of operational failure' will help in the recognition of common pitfalls, whilst prompting identification of other challenges particular to the situation. The subsequent cause-and-controls assessment is designed to encourage systematic management of the acknowledged issues. (See Chapters 3 and 5.)

*New projects.* Six Thinking Hats[6] facilitates an efficient 360-degree identification of a project's ambitions, its principal activities and key success factors. A subsequent dependency model helps to validate the critical relationships between project steps for practical purposes, simultaneously drawing out the further dependencies to which the project's desired outcome may prove to be sensitive. (See Chapters 5 and 6.)

*New relationships (joint ventures).* An early discussion of risk appetite can be a useful test of compatibility between potential parties to a joint venture or co-marketing project. The risk-mapping exercise which follows will encourage timely recognition of other key issues, their significance and the development of plans to address them. (See Chapters 4 and 5.)

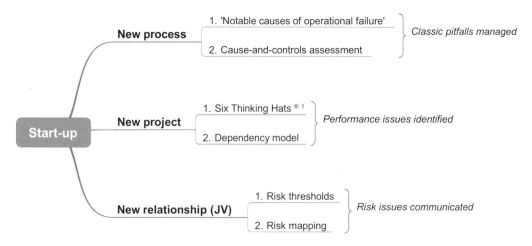

Mindjet MindManager Map

**Figure 7.3     Risk thinking in start-up situations**
*Source: [1]de Bono (1999)*

## Ad hoc review (see Figure 7.4)

*Major misadventure.* The need to recognize the enduring lessons of hindsight following a major misadventure (or a near miss) can be supported by the simple technique for chain of events analysis ('Learning from failure'). The insights generated in this way can be transposed into a 'standard' dependency model. Such a model can act as a repository of knowledge and experience important to success in a particular activity, such as the execution of a marketing plan or the licensing of brands in new markets. (See Chapters 3 and 6.)

*Activist issue.* Assessment of an organization's exposure to attack by an activist group should involve a review of known conditions that increase vulnerability ('Anticipating activist behaviour').[7] The controllable and uncontrollable risk factors relevant to decision-making can be modelled in a decision tree. (See Chapters 5 and 6.)

*Strategic review.* A scenario development exercise establishes the coherent set of narratives that describe alternative futures relevant to current decision-making. The cause-and-effect framework helps to extend the application of these scenarios to specific situations, where their further consequences need to be articulated and addressed. (See Chapter 5.)

## Organizational context

Boldly restated, the goals of risk literacy in brand management are to make the brands and their managers more successful and the organization itself more understanding of the judgements made by its marketing people. To gain fullest acceptance within the marketing team and the organization as a whole, an approach to brand risk thinking should not only complement strategy, but should also take careful account of the prevailing culture. This is self-evident, but needs to be reinforced: perfecting the administrative introduction of risk management

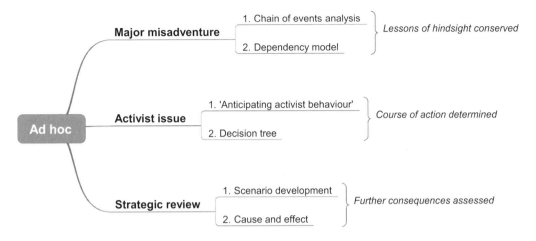

Mindjet MindManager Map

**Figure 7.4    Risk thinking in an ad hoc review**

does not guarantee behavioural change. A plan to 'embed' brand risk thinking should involve conscious consideration of what is culturally desirable and likely to be achievable in practice.

## DEFINING A CULTURE

Unless we have some way of deciphering an organization's culture, to say nothing of its needs, we may not set the right course or give ourselves the best chance of sustaining early progress. Even when an organization is seemingly familiar, a more deliberate assessment of its culture can prompt new and valuable insight. For example, it can useful to explore the actual evidence for the organization's risk attitude, the beliefs held by functions in the organization with greatest influence, the common behaviours requiring greatest attention from a risk management perspective, as well as the style of current management methods. The 'cultural web' (see Figure 7.5) provides one approach to structuring this assessment. As the evaluation proceeds, its findings are captured in concise bullet-points within each overlapping circle of the web. Johnson, Scholes and Whittington (2006) describe in detail how the key features of an organization's culture can be revealed through assessment of the web's seven interacting components.[8] These are characterized as follows, with our risk-thinking purpose in mind.

## Stories

The stories that circulate at various levels of an organization identify important events or individuals in its past and present. Stories are important because they are a means by which people coming into the organization are inspired or guided. Whether directly or indirectly, stories and their themes can reveal the extent of an organization's cohesion, it priorities, its definitions of success and failure, the behaviours that it values and (even if by implication alone) its appetite for risk. The marketing function may even feature as 'hero' or 'villain'.[9] Prevalent stories will reflect beliefs that may need to be accommodated in the advocacy for risk thinking, with possible differences in emphasis by function or level in the hierarchy of the organization.

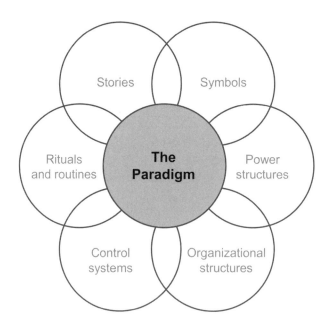

**Figure 7.5    The 'cultural web'**

*Source: Johnson, Scholes and Whittington (2006). Reproduced with permission of Pearson Education Ltd*

From a risk perspective, stories may indicate a culture so strong that it discourages questioning[10] or suggest 'groupthink' tendencies in decision-making generally (see Chapter 3).

## Symbols

The essential character of an organization is often reflected in its symbols, such as job titles and privileges, forms of address, workspace design, terminology and its graphic identity. For example, symbols evidently intended to reinforce both a firm's historic roots and a deference to seniority may suggest a conservative response to recommendations for change or new thinking.

The customary use of language in an organization can also be symbolic of its culture, giving insight into beliefs and behaviour. The institutionalized use of a disparaging term to describe dissatisfied customers in one particular organization ('complainers') suggested to Johnson, Scholes and Whittington (2006) that difficult complaints were likely to be handled unsympathetically.[11] The corporate vocabulary may or may not already include the word 'risk'.

In principle, the most effective 'anchoring device' for risk thinking across an organization will tend to be the one whose symbolic value is most closely aligned with the current culture. By way of illustration, the frankness encouraged by the Six Thinking Hats approach to problem solving[12] might not be the most appropriate way to initiate a habit of brand risk thinking in the type of conservative and strictly hierarchical culture which we have just described. A more formal approach might work better. On the other hand, Six Thinking Hats might readily overcome resistance to systematic risk thinking ('negative thinking') in a more entrepreneurial organization. Although a concession to the current culture may sometimes involve a degree of technical compromise, it is likely to be the best place to start, unless special circumstances or a particular issue demand a more trenchant or specific remedy.

## Power structures

It is often said of organizations that they are dominated by the influence of one or more functions. For example, firms may be 'sales-led', 'technology-led', 'finance-led' or 'marketing-led'. The distribution or fragmentation of power in an organization may determine which particular beliefs and assumptions about risk and opportunity are most likely to predominate, how priorities may be set and how resources may be allocated. There is usually an informal network of individual relationships that also influences decision-making. Power is not often surrendered voluntarily. This naturally suggests that the function(s) with decisive influence must be successfully co-opted if a new approach to risk thinking is to survive.

From a risk management perspective, a concentration of power may create an out-of-balance condition sufficient to cause concern in its own right. For example, some creatively-led companies pay insufficient attention to financial risk, while other production-led companies pay insufficient attention to marketing investment.

## Organizational structures

The structures of organizations vary in a number of their characteristics. Degrees of hierarchy and formality are important variables, perhaps evidenced by the symbols discussed earlier. Different formal structures support different power structures, though some power structures exist independently of the formal arrangements (such as a close network of former colleagues).[13]

Importantly, organizational design affects the extent of collaboration and knowledge sharing, both vertically (up and down the hierarchy) and horizontally (between divisions or functions). Lawrence and Lorsch (1967) found that less formal organizations were best able to deal with uncertain environments, especially if influence was evenly spread and any conflicts that arose between departments were adequately confronted.[14]

## Control systems

Reporting systems and incentive schemes are an important influence on behaviour and are an expression of a company's management priorities. All other things being equal, risk thinking that expressly supports achievement of these priorities is more likely to find management favour.

Current control systems should be considered in terms of their effect on attitudes to risk and risk-taking. Understanding how control systems are employed by management provides additional evidence. The same set of measures can be used to give people freedom of action or to constrain them. Unsurprisingly, there is evidence that creativity in individuals is discouraged if managers' feedback is expected by those individuals to be 'controlling' rather than 'informational' or supportive in nature.[15] This is one reason why it is important for marketers to understand risk thinking as a positive contributor to professional success, rather than as a pessimists' charter or a mechanism for negative scrutiny.

## Rituals and routines

Routine behaviours by the people in an organization can provide further evidence of its cultural beliefs, including how risk and uncertainty are acknowledged and addressed. Examples of such routines might be the way in which new products are brought to market or how unsolicited approaches from external inventors or patent owners are handled. Although routines promote consistency and efficiency, they are not always easy to change.

Similarly, organizations engage in 'ritual' activities that reinforce 'the way we do things around here'.[16] Among the common rituals are company conferences, employee consultation exercises or individual assessment procedures. Training courses can be important rituals too, their subject matter and key messages giving useful insight into the organization's values and priorities. Other occasional rituals might invoke or celebrate significant moments of change in the life of an organization. For example, a chief executive's roadshow to announce an impending restructuring is likely to have two objectives: firstly, to explain the change; secondly to use the ritual of a large gathering to give the announcement some 'emotional momentum'. There will almost invariably be a symbolic use of language, often a slogan, and sometimes new terminology.

## Paradigm

The 'paradigm' is the essence of an organization's culture that sits at the centre of the 'web'.[17] It is a concise statement of the prime assumptions and beliefs that underpin all the other components of the culture and operating manner noted elsewhere in the model. Examples of this essence might be an organization's 'social mission', its 'professional ethic' or its overriding commitment to 'quality not quantity'.

Evaluation of an organization's culture will suggest the right *style* of brand risk thinking to adopt, whilst at the same time helping to validate its initial scope (the right *substance*).

# Conclusions

We can now draw two general conclusions:

- As normal in business, it is important to be clear about the needs and objectives for the introduction of risk thinking in any context. This will help to ensure that it is appropriately specified, accurately positioned and usefully employed.

- There is a difference between risk thinking in organizations and risk literacy in individuals. Organizations usually require a degree of standardization or simplification of method. Meanwhile, motivated individuals (in particular marketers) will seek out opportunities to apply their creative and strategic imaginations and to challenge the status quo. In principle, the available techniques of risk management offer solutions to satisfy and reconcile both constituencies.

  The promise of risk literacy can be described. Its value needs to be experienced.

# References

1   Piercy, N. (1985), *Marketing Organisation: An Analysis of Information Processing, Power and Politics*, George Allen & Unwin.
2   de Bono, E. (1999), *Six Thinking Hats®*, Penguin Books.
3   Obeng, E. (1996), *All Change! The Project Leader's Secret Handbook*, FT Prentice Hall.
4   McDonald, M., Smith B. and Ward, K. (2006), *Marketing Due Diligence: Reconnecting Strategy to Share Price*, Butterworth-Heinemann.
5   Hoad, T. (2006), 'Extending Ansoff', unpublished paper.
6   de Bono (1999), op.cit.
7   Winter, M. and Steger, U. (1998*), Managing Outside Pressure: Strategies for Preventing Corporate Disasters*, John Wiley & Sons.
8   Johnson, G., Scholes, K. and Whittington, R. (2006), *Exploring Corporate Strategy: 7th edition*, FT Prentice Hall.
9   Johnson et al. (2006), op.cit.
10   Barsoux, J-L. and Bottger, P. (2006), 'Can we Really "Master" Uncertainty?', *FT Mastering Uncertainty Part 1*, supplement to *Financial Times*, 17 March, p. 11.
11   Johnson et al. (2006), op.cit.
12   de Bono (1999), op.cit.
13   Johnson et al. (2006), op.cit.
14   Lawrence, P.R. and Lorsch, J.W. (1967), *Organization and Environment: Managing Differentiation and Integration*, Harvard University Press.
15   Shalley, C.E. and Perry-Smith, J.E. (2001), 'Effects of Social-Psychological Factors on Creative Performance: The Role of Informational and Controlling Expected Evaluation and Modeling Experience', *Organizational Behavior & Human Decision Processes*, Volume 84 (Issue 1), pp. 1–22.
16   Johnson et al. (2006), op.cit.
17   Johnson et al. (2006), op.cit.

# *Chapter Maps*

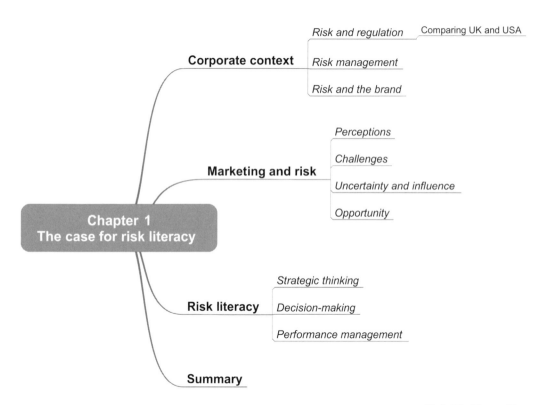

Chapter 1
The case for risk literacy

Corporate context
- Risk and regulation — Comparing UK and USA
- Risk management
- Risk and the brand

Marketing and risk
- Perceptions
- Challenges
- Uncertainty and influence
- Opportunity

Risk literacy
- Strategic thinking
- Decision-making
- Performance management

Summary

Mindjet MindManager Map

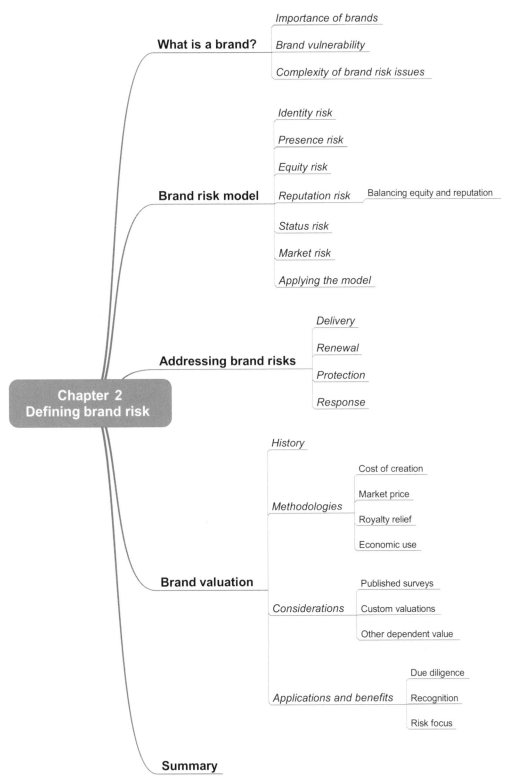

What is a brand?
- Importance of brands
- Brand vulnerability
- Complexity of brand risk issues

Brand risk model
- Identity risk
- Presence risk
- Equity risk
- Reputation risk — Balancing equity and reputation
- Status risk
- Market risk
- Applying the model

Addressing brand risks
- Delivery
- Renewal
- Protection
- Response

Chapter 2
Defining brand risk

Brand valuation
- History
- Methodologies
  - Cost of creation
  - Market price
  - Royalty relief
  - Economic use
- Considerations
  - Published surveys
  - Custom valuations
  - Other dependent value
- Applications and benefits
  - Due diligence
  - Recognition
  - Risk focus

Summary

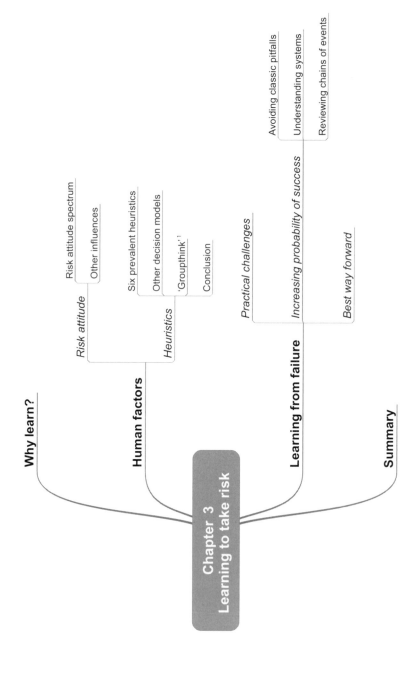

Source: [1] Janis (1982)

MindJet MindManager Map

**Why learn?**

**Human factors**

*Risk attitude*
  Risk attitude spectrum
  Other influences

*Heuristics*
  Six prevalent heuristics
  Other decision models
  'Groupthink'[1]
  Conclusion

**Learning from failure**

*Practical challenges*

*Increasing probability of success*
  Avoiding classic pitfalls
  Understanding systems
  Reviewing chains of events

*Best way forward*

**Summary**

Chapter 3
Learning to take risk

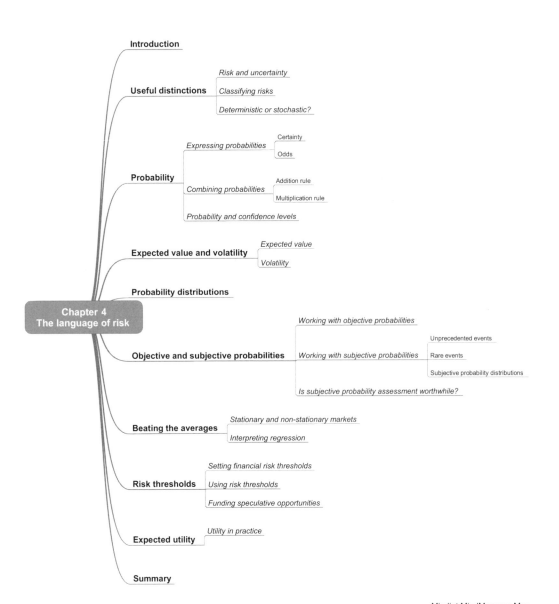

Introduction

Useful distinctions
- Risk and uncertainty
- Classifying risks
- Deterministic or stochastic?

Probability
- Expressing probabilities
  - Certainty
  - Odds
- Combining probabilities
  - Addition rule
  - Multiplication rule
- Probability and confidence levels

Expected value and volatility
- Expected value
- Volatility

Probability distributions

Chapter 4
The language of risk

Objective and subjective probabilities
- Working with objective probabilities
- Working with subjective probabilities
  - Unprecedented events
  - Rare events
  - Subjective probability distributions
- Is subjective probability assessment worthwhile?

Beating the averages
- Stationary and non-stationary markets
- Interpreting regression

Risk thresholds
- Setting financial risk thresholds
- Using risk thresholds
- Funding speculative opportunities

Expected utility
- Utility in practice

Summary

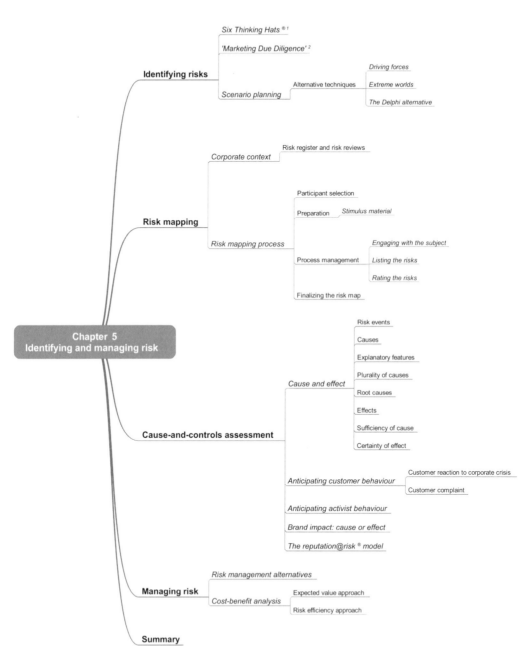

Mindjet MindManager Map

Source: [1]de Bono (1999); [2]McDonald, Smith and Ward (2006)

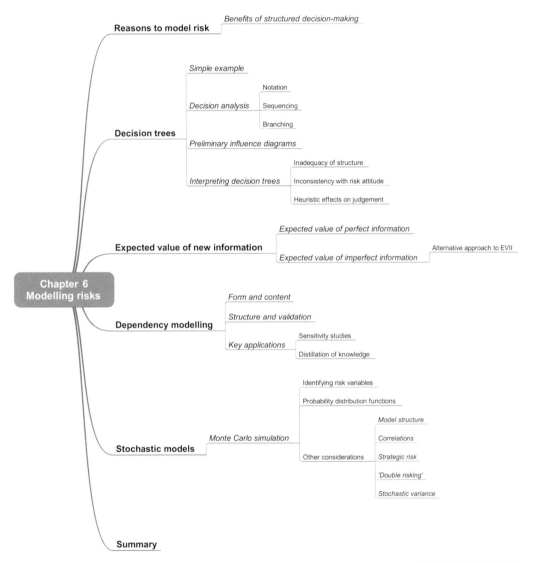

Reasons to model risk — *Benefits of structured decision-making*

Decision trees
- *Simple example*
- *Decision analysis*
  - Notation
  - Sequencing
  - Branching
- *Preliminary influence diagrams*
- *Interpreting decision trees*
  - Inadequacy of structure
  - Inconsistency with risk attitude
  - Heuristic effects on judgement

Expected value of new information
- *Expected value of perfect information*
- *Expected value of imperfect information* — Alternative approach to EVII

Chapter 6
Modelling risks

Dependency modelling
- *Form and content*
- *Structure and validation*
- *Key applications*
  - Sensitivity studies
  - Distillation of knowledge

Stochastic models — *Monte Carlo simulation*
- Identifying risk variables
- Probability distribution functions
- Other considerations
  - *Model structure*
  - *Correlations*
  - *Strategic risk*
  - *'Double risking'*
  - *Stochastic variance*

Summary

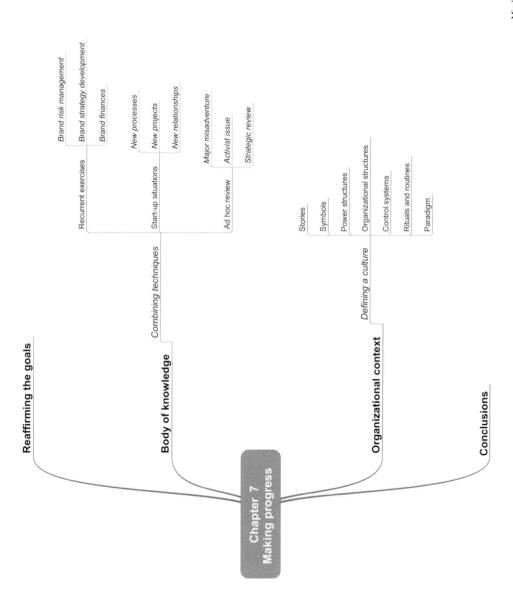

Reaffirming the goals

Body of knowledge

Combining techniques

Recurrent exercises

Brand risk management
Brand strategy development
Brand finances

Start-up situations

New processes
New projects
New relationships

Ad hoc review

Major misadventure
Activist issue
Strategic review

Organizational context

Defining a culture

Stories
Symbols
Power structures
Organizational structures
Control systems
Rituals and routines
Paradigm

Conclusions

Chapter 7
Making progress

# Bibliography

Aaker, David A. (1991), *Managing Brand Equity. Capitalizing on the Value of a Brand Name*, The Free Press.

Aaker, David A. (2002), *Building Strong Brands*, Free Press Business.

Abrahams, D.J. (2001), 'Social and Ethical Risk', *The Marsh Topic Letter*, Number V, Marsh Ltd.

Abrahams, D.J. (2002), 'Brand Risk', *The Marsh Topic Letter*, Number IX, Marsh Ltd.

Abrahams, D.J., Hinton, P., Jurkowich, G. (2000), 'Valuing and Protecting Brands', *ACT Manual of Corporate Finance and Treasury Management*, Issue 2 (August), Gee Publishing.

Ajzen, I. (1985), 'From Intentions to Action: A Theory of Planned Behavior', in J. Kuhl and J. Beckmann (eds), *Action-Control: From Cognition to Behavior*, Springer.

Ajzen, I. (1988), *Attitudes, Personality and Behavior*, Dorsey Press.

Ajzen, I. (1991), 'The Theory of Planned Behavior', in E.A. Locke (ed.), *Organizational Behavior and Human Decision Processes*, Volume 50, Elsevier, pp. 179–211.

Ajzen, I. and Fishbein, M. (1980), *Understanding Attitudes and Predicting Social Behavior*, Prentice Hall.

Ambler, T. (2003), *Marketing and the Bottom Line*, FT Prentice Hall.

Arium Ltd (2003), *Making Sense of an Uncertain World*, http://www.arium.co.uk/products/dependency. htm.

Barsoux, J-L. and Bottger, P. (2006), 'Can We Really "Master" Uncertainty?', *FT Mastering Uncertainty Part 1*, supplement to *Financial Times*, 17 March.

Bernstein, P.L. (1996), *Against the Gods: The Remarkable Story of Risk*, John Wiley & Sons, Inc.

Bertalanffy L. von (1950), 'An Outline of General System Theory', *British Journal for the Philosophy of Science*, Volume 1, pp. 139–165.

Blau, P.M. (1964), *Exchange and Power in Social Life*, Transaction.

Brand Finance (2005), *The Brand Finance Report* (May), Brand Finance (Australia) Pty Limited.

Brand Finance (2006), *Global 100 Banking Brands Index* (November), Brand Finance plc.

Brownlie, D.T. (1991), 'A Case Analysis of the Cost and Value of Marketing Information', *Marketing Intelligence and Planning*, Volume 9 (Number 1), pp. 11–18.

Bunn, D.W. and Thomas, H. (1975), 'Assessing Subjective Probability in Decision Analysis', in D.J. White and K.C. Bowen (eds), *The Role and Effectiveness of Theories of Decision in Practice*, Hodder and Stoughton.

Cacioppo, J.T. and Petty, R.E. (1985), 'Central and Peripheral Routes to Persuasions: the Role of Message Repetition', in A.A. Mitchell and L.F. Alwitt (eds), *Psychological Processes and Advertising Effects: Theory, Research, and Applications*, Lawrence Erlbaum Associates.

Campbell, I. and Kennedy, S. (1971), 'Routinisation in Marketing', *European Journal of Marketing*, Volume 5 (Number 3), pp. 83–92.

Clemons, E.K. (2006), 'Past Experience Points the Way to the Future', *FT Mastering Uncertainty Part 1*, supplement to *Financial Times*, 17 March, pp. 6–8.

Clifton, R. and Maughan, E. (2000), 'Introduction', in R. Clifton and E. Maughan (eds), *The Future of Brands: Twenty-Five Visions*, Interbrand and Macmillan Business.

Condorcet, Marquis de (1785), *Essai sur l'application de l'analyse à la probabilité des décisions rendues à la pluralité des voix*.

De Bondt, W. and Thaler, R. (1986), 'Does the Stock Market Overreact?', *Journal of Finance*, Volume 40 (Issue 3), pp. 793–805.

de Bono, E. (1967), *The Use of Lateral Thinking*, Jonathan Cape.

de Bono, E. (1994), *Parallel Thinking*, Viking Press.

de Bono, E. (1999), *Six Thinking Hats®*, Penguin Books.

Dorffer, C. (2007), 'Brand-Driven Shareholder Value Creation', *European CEO*, May–June, pp. 47–49.

Dubé, L, Schmitt, B.H. and Leclerc, F. (1991), 'Consumers' Affective Response to Delays at Different Phases of a Service Delivery', *Journal of Applied Social Psychology*, Volume 21 (Issue 10), pp. 810–820.

East, R. (1993), 'Investment Decisions and the Theory of Planned Behaviour' *Journal of Economic Psychology*, Volume 14 (Issue 2), pp. 337–375.

East, R. (1997), *Consumer Behaviour – Advances and Applications in Marketing*, FT Prentice Hall.

East, R., Hammond, K. and Wright, M. (2007), 'The Relative Incidence of Positive and Negative Word of Mouth: A Multi-Category Study', *International Journal of Research in Marketing*, Volume 24 (Issue 2), pp. 175–184.

Edwards, W. (1954), 'The Theory of Decision Making', *Psychological Bulletin*, Volume 51 (Issue 4), pp. 380–417.

Ehrenberg, A.S.C. (1974), 'Repetitive Advertising and the Consumer', *Journal of Advertising Research*, Volume 14 (Number 2), pp. 25–33.

Ehrenberg, A.S.C. and Uncles, M.D. (1996), *Dirichlet-type Markets: A Review*, South Bank University Working Paper.

Elster, J. (1989), *The Cement of Society: A Study of Social Order*, Cambridge University Press.

Farquahar, P.H. (1984), 'Utility Assessment Methods', *Management Science*, Volume 30 (Issue 11), pp. 1283–1300.

Fishbein, M. (1963), 'An Investigation of the Relationships between Beliefs about an Object and Attitude toward that Object', *Human Relations*, Volume 16 (Number 3), pp. 233–240.

Fischoff, B. (1975), 'Hindsight is not Equal to Foresight: The Effect of Outcome Knowledge on Judgment under Uncertainty', *Journal of Experimental Psychology: Human Perception and Performance*, Volume 1, pp. 288–299.

Fombrun, C.J. (1996), *Reputation: Realizing Value from The Corporate Image*, Harvard Business School Press.

Gigerenzer, G. (1994), 'Why the Distinction between Single Event Probabilities and Frequencies is Relevant for Psychology and Vice Versa', in G. Wright and P. Ayton (eds), *Subjective Probability*, John Wiley & Sons.

Gigerenzer, G., Todd, P.M. and the ABC Research Group (1999), *Simple Heuristics that Make Us Smart*, Oxford University Press.

Gladwell, M. (2001), *The Tipping Point: How Little Things Can Make a Big Difference*, Abacus.

Goodwin, P. and Wright, G. (2004), *Decision Analysis for Management Judgment – Third Edition*, John Wiley & Sons Ltd.

Green, P. (2005), 'Risk Management in the Balance', *StrategicRISK*, October, pp. 10–12.

Griffiths, T.L. and Tenenbaum, J.B. (2006), 'Optimal Predictions in Everyday Cognition', *Psychological Science*, Volume 17 (Issue 9), pp. 767–773.

Haig, M. (2003), *Brand Failures: The Truth About the 100 Biggest Branding Mistakes of all Time*, Kogan Page Ltd.

Halstead, D. (1993), 'Five Common Myths about Consumer Satisfaction Programs', *Journal of Services Marketing*, Volume 7 (Issue 3), pp. 4–12.

Haxthausen, O. (2007), 'Risk Jockey', *Marketing Management*, March–April, pp. 35–38.

Hertz, D.B. and Thomas, H. (1983), *Risk Analysis and its Applications*, John Wiley and Sons, Inc.

Hillson, D. and Murray-Webster, R. (2005), *Understanding and Managing Risk Attitude*, Gower Publishing Ltd.

Hoad, T. (2006), 'Extending Ansoff', unpublished paper.

Hope, J. and Fraser, R. (2003), *Beyond Budgeting – How Managers Can Break Free from the Annual Performance Trap*, Harvard Business School Press.

Interbrand (2007), *All Brands Are Not Created Equal: Best Global Brands 2007*, Interbrand in association with BusinessWeek.

Interbrand (1997), *Brand Valuation,* 3rd edition, R. Perrier (ed.), Premier Books.

Internal Control Working Party of the Institute of Chartered Accountants in England and Wales (1999), *Internal Control: Guidance for Directors on the Combined Code*, Institute of Chartered Accountants in England and Wales.

Janis, I.R. (1982), *Groupthink: Psychological Studies of Policy Decisions and Fiascos*, Houghton Mifflin.

Johnson, G., Scholes, K. and Whittington, R. (2006), *Exploring Corporate Strategy: 7th edition*, FT Prentice Hall.

Kahneman, D. and Tversky, A. (1979), 'Prospect Theory: An Analysis of Decision under Risk', *Econometrica*, Volume 47 (Issue 2), pp. 263–292.

Kay, J. (2007), 'The Same Old Folly starts a New Spiral of Risk', *Financial Times*, 14 August.

Keen, P.G.W. (1981), 'Information Systems and Organizational Change', *Communications of the ACM*, Volume 24 (Number 1), pp. 24–33.

Keeney, R.L. and Raiffa, H. (1993), *Decisions with Multiple Objectives: Preferences and Value Tradeoffs*, Cambridge University Press.

Kelly, E. (2006), 'The Tall Order of Taming Change', *FT Mastering Uncertainty Part 1*, supplement to *Financial Times*, 17 March.

Knight, F.H. (1921), *Risk, Uncertainty, and Profit*, Houghton Mifflin.

KPMG (2006), *The Directors' Report and the Business Review*, KPMG LLP (UK).

Lacava, G. and Tull, D. (1982), 'Determining the Expected Value of Information for New Product Introduction', *Omega – The International Journal of Management Science*, Volume 10 (No. 4), pp. 383–389.

Lawrence, P.R. and Lorsch, J.W. (1967), *Organization and Environment: Managing Differentiation and Integration*, Harvard University Press.

Lehmann, D.R. (2003), Foreword, in T. Ambler (2003), *Marketing and the Bottom Line*, FT Prentice Hall.

Levitt, B. and March, J.G. (1988), 'Organizational Learning', *Annual Review of Sociology*, Volume 14, pp. 319–340.

Lindemann, J. (2007), *Brand Valuation: The Economy of Brands*, Interbrand.

Lloyds in association with the Economist Intelligence Unit (2005), *Taking Risk on Board: How Global Leaders View Risk*, Society of Lloyds.

Lowe, E.J. (2005), 'Contingent and Necessary Statements', in T. Honderich (ed.), *The Oxford Companion to Philosophy – New Edition*, Oxford University Press.

McDonald, M. and Dunbar, I. (2004), *Market Segmentation: How to Do It, How to Profit from It*, Butterworth-Heinemann.

McDonald, M., Smith B. and Ward, K. (2006), *Marketing Due Diligence: Reconnecting Strategy to Share Price*, Butterworth-Heinemann.

Mackie, P.J. (2005), 'Causality', in T. Honderich (ed.), *The Oxford Companion to Philosophy – New Edition*, Oxford University Press.

Macleod, H. (2004), *Thoughts on 'Smarter Conversations'*, www.gapingvoid.com, http://www.gapingvoid.com/Moveable_Type/archives/000939.html.

Madden, T.J. and Ajzen, I. (1991), 'Affective Cues in Persuasion: An Assessment of Causal Mediation', *Marketing Letters*, Volume 2 (Number 4), pp. 359–366.

Madden, T.J., Ellen, P.S. and Ajzen, I. (1992), 'A Comparison of the Theory of Planned Behavior and the Theory of Reasoned Action', *Personality and Social Psychology Bulletin*, Volume 18 (Issue 1), pp. 3–9.

Madden, T.J., Fehle, F. and Fournier, S.M. (2002), 'Brands Matter: An Empirical Investigation of Brand-building Activities and the Creation of Shareholder Value', working paper, Harvard Business School.

March, J.G. and Simon, H.A. (1958), *Organizations*, John Wiley and Sons, Inc.

Markowitz, H. (1952), 'Portfolio Selection', *The Journal of Finance*, Volume 7 (Issue 1), pp. 77–91.

Marsden, P., Samson, A. and Upton, N. (2005), *Advocacy Drives Growth: Customer Advocacy Drives UK Business Growth*, London School of Economics and The Listening Company.

Marsh, A. and Matheson, J. (1983), *Smoking Attitudes and Behaviour: An Enquiry Carried Out on Behalf of the Department of Health and Social Security*, HMSO.

Marsh Risk Consulting (2007), 'Divisional Risk Tolerances', unpublished paper, Marsh Ltd.

Matthews, R. (2007), 'How to Work a Rumour Mill', *Financial Times*, 28 June.

Microsoft Corporation, http://office.microsoft.com/en-us/excel/HP052092771033.aspx?pid=CH062528 311033.

Millward Brown Optimor, http://www.millwardbrown.com/Sites/Optimor/Content/KnowledgeCenter/ BrandzRanking2007.aspx.

Mindjet, LLC, http://www.mindjet.com/us/products/mindmanager_pro7.

Mintzberg, H., Ahlstrand, B. and Lampel, J. (1998), *Strategy Safari: The Complete Guide Through the Wilds of Strategic Management*. FT Prentice Hall.

Mittelstaedt, R.E. (2005), *Will Your Next Mistake Be Fatal? Avoiding the Chain of Mistakes That Can Destroy Your Organization*, Wharton School Publishing.

Nielsen BuzzMetrics (2007), 'BlogPulse™ Stats', 5 July, www.blogpulse.com.

Obeng, E. (1996), *All Change! The Project Leader's Secret Handbook*, FT Prentice Hall.

Option Technologies Interactive, LLC, http://www.optiontechnologies.com/audience/response/option finder.asp.

Oracle Corporation, http://www.crystalball.com.

Palisade Corporation, http://www.palisade-europe.com/precisiontree/default.asp.

Palisade Corporation, http://www.palisade-europe.com/risk/default.asp.

Petts, J., Wheeley, S., Homan, J., Niemeyer, S. (2003), *Risk Literacy and the Public – MMR, Air Pollution and Mobile Phones, Final Report For the Department of Health*, January, Centre for Environmental Research & Training, University of Birmingham.

Petty, R.E. and Cacioppo, J.T. (1986), 'The Elaboration Likelihood Model of Persuasion', in L. Berkowitz (ed.), *Advances in Experimental Social Psychology*, Volume 19, Academic Press, pp. 123–205.

Petty, R.E., Cacioppo, J.T. and Schumann, D. (1983), 'Central and Peripheral Routes to Advertising Effectiveness: The Moderating Role of Involvement, *Journal of Consumer Research*, Volume 10, pp. 135–146.

Piercy, N. (1985), *Marketing Organisation: An Analysis of Information Processing, Power and Politics*, George Allen & Unwin.

Podolny, J.M. (2005), *Status Signals: A Sociological Study of Market Competition*, Princeton University Press.

Porter, M.E. (2004), *Competitive Advantage: Creating and Sustaining Superior Performance*, new edition. Free Press.

Pringle, H. and Gordon, W. (2001), *Brand Manners*, Wiley.

Quattrone, G.A, Lawrence, C.P., Finkel, S.E. and Andrus, D.C., 'Explorations in Anchoring The Effects of Prior Range, Anchor Extremity and Suggestive Hints', unpublished manuscript, Stanford University.

Rayner, J. (2003), *Managing Reputational Risk – Leveraging Opportunities Curbing Threats*, John Wiley and Sons Ltd.

Reputation Institute, 'Rankings Across Seven Categories', http://www.reputationinstitute.com-press-Rankings_Across_Seven_CategoriesFORBES21may2007.pdf.url.

Ringland, G. (1998), *Scenario Planning: Managing for the Future*, John Wiley & Sons Ltd.

Rosenberg, M.J. (1956), 'Cognitive Structure and Attitudinal Affect', *Journal of Abnormal and Social Psychology*, Volume 53 (Issue 3), pp. 367–372.

Ross A. (2005), *The Evolving Role of the CIO*, G. Lofthouse (ed.), Economist Intelligence Unit.

Ruff, P. and Aziz, K. (2003), *Managing Communications in a Crisis*, Gower Publishing Ltd.

Schuyler, J. (2001), *Risk and Decision Analysis in Projects*, Project Management Institute.

Schwartz, P. (1998), *The Art of the Long View: Planning for the Future in an Uncertain World*, Doubleday.

Shafir, E. (1993), 'Choosing versus Rejecting: Why Some Options are Both Better and Worse than Others', *Memory and Cognition*, Volume 21 (Issue 4), pp. 546–556.

Shalley, C.E. and Perry-Smith, J.E. (2001), 'Effects of Social-Psychological Factors on Creative Performance: The Role of Informational and Controlling Expected Evaluation and Modeling Experience, *Organizational Behavior & Human Decision Processes*, Volume 84 (Issue 1), pp. 1–22.

Shaw, R. and Merrick, D. (2005), *Marketing Payback – Is Your Marketing Profitable?*, FT Prentice Hall.

Smith, A.K., Bolton, R.N. and Wagner, J. (1998), *A Model of Customer Satisfaction with Service Encounters Involving Failure and Recovery*, Report No. 98-100, Marketing Science Institute.

Stael von Holstein, C-A.S. and Matheson, J. (1979), *A Manual for Encoding Probability Distributions,* SRI International.

Sull, D. (2006), 'Difficult Decisions for an Uncertain World', *FT Mastering Uncertainty Part 1,* supplement to *Financial Times*, 17 March, pp. 2–3.

Tasgal, A. (2003), 'Marketing: Art, Science or Alchemy?', *Market Leader*, Issue Number 21, pp. 43–49.

Thaler, R. (1987), 'The Psychology of Choice and the Assumptions of Economics', in A.E. Roth (ed.), *Laboratory Experiments in Economics: Six Points of View*, Cambridge University Press.

*The Economist* (2005), 'Runner-Up, Up and Away', *The Economist*, 14 December, p. 12.

*The Economist* Intelligence Unit (2005), *Reputation – Risk of Risks*, *The Economist* Intelligence Unit.

Toft, B. and Reynolds, S. (1997), *Learning from Disasters – A Management Approach: Second edition*, Perpetuity Press.

TreeAge Software Inc., http://www.treeage.com/products/overviewPro.html.

Tricks, H. (2005), 'Predicting Change: Future Gazing is on the Cards', *Financial Times*, 24 October.

Tripas, M. and Gavetti, G. (2000), 'Capabilities, Cognition and Inertia: Evidence from Digital Imaging', *Strategic Management Journal*, Volume 21, October–November, pp. 1147–1161.

Turnbull Report (1999), *Internal Control for Directors on the Combined Code*, Institute of Chartered Accountants in England and Wales.

Tversky, A. (1969), 'Intransivity of Preferences', *Psychological Review*, Volume 76, pp. 31–48.

Tversky, A. (1972), 'Elimination by Aspects: A Theory of Choice', *Psychological Review*, Volume 79, pp. 281–299.

von Winterfeldt, D. and Edwards, W. (1986), *Decision Analysis and Behavioural Research*, Cambridge University Press.

Wason. P.C. (1960), 'On the Failure to Eliminate Hypothesis in a Conceptual Task', *The Quarterly Journal of Experimental Psychology*, Volume 12, pp. 129–140.

Weinstein, A. (2004), *Handbook of Market Segmentation – Strategic Targeting for Business and Technology Firms*, Haworth Press, Inc.

Westbrook, R.A. and Oliver, R.L. (1991), 'The Dimensionality of Consumption Emotion Patterns and Consumer Satisfaction', *Journal of Consumer Research*, Volume 18, pp. 84–91.

Willman, J. (2006), 'Valued Measure of Success', *Financial Times Special Report - Global Brands*, 3 April, Financial Times, p. 1.

Wind, J. and Crook, C. (2006), 'Changing Mental Models in an Uncontrollable World', *FT Mastering Uncertainty Part 1*, supplement to *Financial Times*, 17 March, pp. 10–11.

Winter, M. and Steger, U. (1998), *Managing Outside Pressure: Strategies for Preventing Corporate Disasters*, John Wiley & Sons.

Wisniewski, M. (2006), *Quantitative Methods for Decision Makers – Fourth Edition*, FT Prentice Hall.

Zaman, A. (2004), *Reputational Risk – How to Manage for Value Creation*, FT Prentice Hall.

Zeger, D. and Nicholson, N. (2004), *Risk: How to Make Decisions in an Uncertain World*, Format Publishing.

# Index

**If you have found this book useful you may
be interested in other titles from Gower**

**Commercial Due Diligence:
The Key to Understanding Value in an Acquisition**
Peter Howson
978-0-566-08651-9

**Commoditization and the Strategic Response**
Andrew Holmes
978-0-566-08743-1

**Competitive Intelligence:
Gathering, Analysing and Putting it to Work**
Christopher Murphy
978-0-566-08537-6

**Complete Guide to Business Risk Management
Second Edition**
Kit Sadgrove
978-0-566-08661-8

**Deception at Work:
Investigating and Countering Lies and Fraud Strategies**
Michael J. Comer and Timothy E. Stephens
978-0-566-08636-6

**Due Diligence:
The Critical Stage in Mergers and Acquisitions**
Peter Howson
978-0-566-08524-6

# GOWER

**Estimating Risk:**
**A Management Approach**
Andy Garlic
978-0-566-08776-9


**How to Measure and Manage Your Corporate Reputation**
Terry Hannington
978-0-566-08552-9


**Information Risk and Security:**
**Preventing and Investigating Workplace Computer Crime**
Edward Wilding
978-0-566-08685-4


**New Business Models for the Knowledge Economy**
Wendy Jansen, Wilchard Steenbakkers and Hans Jägers
978-0-566-08788-2


**Understanding and Managing Risk Attitude**
**Second Edition**
David Hillson and Ruth Murray-Webster
978-0-566-08798-1


For further information on these and all
our titles visit our website –
**www.gowerpub.com**

All online orders receive a discount

Join our e-mail new titles newsletter at:
**www.gowerpub.com/mail.htm**


# GOWER